MW00650935

Ahead *of* the Curve

Written by:
John C. Hughes & Bob Young
Research by:
Lori Larson

First Edition

ISBN 978-1-889320-42-7

Front cover photo credits, top to bottom:
Linea Laird, *Washington State Department of Transportation*
Chris Gregoire and Ana Mari Cauce, *Dan Schlatter/University of Washington*
Elsie Parrish, *Associated Press*
Stephanie Coontz, *Karissa Carlson/The Evergreen State College*
Josephine Corliss Preston, *Library of Congress*
Mary-Claire King, *University of Washington*
Fawn Sharp, *Northwest Indian Fisheries Commission*
Mabel Seagrave, *University of Washington Libraries*
Trish Millines Dziko, *Redstone Pictures Inc.*

Title page:
Suffragist figurine is from the collection
of Jeffrey Coppersmith, *Bettina Hansen/The Seattle Times*

Book Design by Lori Larson
Cover Design by Amber Raney

Printed in the United States of America
by Gorham Printing, Centralia, Washington

Office of the Secretary of State
Legacy Washington

To the Washington suffragists who led the way.

Washington Equal Suffrage Association posting signs to promote woman suffrage, Seattle, 1910. *Asahel Curtis/Washington State Archives*

Contents

INTRODUCTION

Washington Women
Lead the Way

With the ratification of the 19th Amendment on August 18, 1920, the women of America—most of them at least—finally won the vote. But as the late, great Cokie Roberts put it so eloquently: "We had the right to vote as American citizens. We didn't have to be granted it by some bunch of guys."

Washington women won back that fundamental right—the cornerstone of participatory democracy—a decade earlier. This remarkable book celebrates the fact that the suffrage victory in our state on November 8, 1910, energized the national movement and created role models for generations to come.

Fittingly, the book opens with a biography of Josephine Corliss Preston, the Walla Walla suffragist who in 1912 became our first female statewide elected official. Our nationally prominent Superintendent of Public Instruction was also a charter member of the League of Women Voters.

Fast forward to 2020 for a chapter spotlighting another trailblazing educator, Ana Mari Cauce, the first female president of the University of Washington.

Ahead of the Curve also features Dr. Mabel Seagrave, the pioneering Seattle physician who volunteered to serve in France during World War I, as well as Mary-Claire King, the brilliant scientist who discovered the first gene linked to hereditary breast cancer.

Another chapter reminds us that extraordinary "ordinary" women can change history. Elsie Parrish, a Wenatchee hotel chambermaid, was shortchanged by her employer. She took her case to the U.S. Supreme

Court and won a landmark victory in 1937. Her triumph cleared the legal path not only for minimum wages, but also for Social Security.

Still, it took a long, hard struggle to achieve the $500 million settlement for underpaid female state workers that future governor Chris Gregoire spearheaded in 1986.

Thanks to women's votes and women's voices, 127 women—a record number—now serve in the United States Congress. Among them, we can proudly boast, are seven from Washington. A chapter on the extraordinary Chief Justice Mary Fairhurst documents the rise of female judges in our state. In addition to full-length profiles of Washington women who led the way, this book features panels from the *Ahead of the Curve* exhibit that spotlight other "sheroes."

In 1954, Julia Butler Hansen of Cathlamet came within a few votes of becoming the first female Speaker of the Washington State House of Representatives. The men closed ranks at the last minute to deny her the honor and privilege she had earned and deserved. Julia went on to become one of the most powerful and admired women in the history of the United States Congress. How proud she would be to know that in 2020 a woman finally wields the gavel in the House of Representatives at Olympia.

In the hundred years since ratification of the 19th Amendment, the cause of gender equality has made remarkable gains. Yet in the ramp-up to the celebration of the Suffrage Centennial, the National Women's History Museum has discovered that only 178 female historic figures are included in national K-12 social studies guidelines—or as *Smithsonian* magazine calculates, "one woman for every three men."

Washington women have always been ahead of the curve. Clearly, however, there's a lot more work to do.

Kim Wyman

Washington Secretary of State

19TH AMENDMENT:

DEMOCRACY FOR SOME, NOT ALL

As originally written, the U.S. Constitution did not address voting rights. In early U.S. history, states allowed only white male property owners to vote. Women were largely prohibited from voting, or disenfranchised, as were non-white men.

The property-owning requirement faded by the Civil War. In 1870, the 15th Amendment said states couldn't deny voting rights to citizens because of race or color—although some states erected barriers such as poll taxes and literacy tests. But it was silent on women, who were still disenfranchised.

In 1920, the 19th Amendment cleared the way for most white and black women to vote. But there were exceptions. Until 1922, an American-born woman couldn't vote if she was married to an immigrant (foreign-born and not yet naturalized, or a citizen). And even after 1922, she couldn't vote if she had married an Asian immigrant.

suffrage [suf·frage]

noun

1. the right to vote, especially in a political election.
2. a vote given in favor of a proposed measure, candidate, or the like.

In 1924, Native American men and women were granted voting rights, although, again, some states created obstacles to exercising those rights.

But it would be several decades before prohibitions on Asian immigrants becoming citizens were removed. A 1943 law sponsored by Congressman Warren G. Magnuson of Washington allowed Chinese immigrants already residing in the U.S to become naturalized citizens with voting rights. Federal law three years later extended the opportunity for citizenship and voting rights to Filipino and Indian immigrants. And the federal McCarran-Walter Act did the same for Korean and Japanese immigrants in 1952.

WASHINGTON

1883: Washington territory grants women voting rights, making it the third territory with women's suffrage, after Wyoming and Utah.

Emma Smith Devoe, leading suffragist. *Tacoma Public Library*

1888: All-male territorial Supreme Court revokes women's voting rights, saying they conflict with federal law.

Nena Jolidon Croake, minimum wage advocate. *Washington State Archives*

1910: Washington becomes the fifth state in the nation to enact women's suffrage.

1911: An eight-hour workday for Washington women (except in fruit and fish canneries) is adopted; federal law for men and women is not phased in until 1940.

HATS OFF TO THIS WAITRESS

MISS ALICE LORD.

Alice Lord, lobbied for eight-hour day. *The Spokane Press*

1913: Minimum wage established for women; national law follows in 1938.

LEADS THE WAY

1943: Equal pay for equal work becomes law; federal version passed in 1963.

1986: Washington state workers, mostly women, receive more than $500 million in the largest comparable worth settlement in the U.S.

Women rally for pay equity in 1985. *AFSCME Council 28*

1993: Washington leads the nation in percentage of women in the state Legislature from 1993-2004, including 40.8 percent in 1999, then a record. (Washington ranks 4th in 2019 with 40.1%.)

In 2003 women achieved a majority on the Washington Supreme Court.

2003: Women account for a majority of Washington Supreme Court justices. Only Minnesota had a majority of female justices sooner.

Maria Cantwell, Chris Gregoire, Patty Murray. *U.S. Senate*

2005: First state with a woman governor (Chris Gregoire) and two women U.S. Senators (Maria Cantwell and Patty Murray) at the same time.

JOSEPHINE CORLISS PRESTON

EDUCATOR, SUFFRAGIST, POLITICIAN

1: THE TEENAGE TEACHER

Two little girls snuggled together in front of the fireplace, books on their laps. It was the winter of 1880—and well below zero outside the farmhouse on the prairie not far from Fargo. Josephine "Josie" Corliss, who was 7, loved to read even more than did her big sister, Myrtia. Both liked to play school. Josephine said she always knew what she wanted to be when she grew up: A teacher.

By the time she was 14 the tall, precocious girl was helping first graders learn their ABCs. In 1891, having taught full time for nearly two years, she was a fully certified, 18-year-old teacher in Otter Tail County, Minnesota, with high marks from the superintendent's examiners. A pot-belly stove took the edge off bitterly cold days outside the rough-hewn schoolhouses north of Fergus Falls, the county seat. Locals still quip that the only thing that stopped the cold north wind back then was a barbed-wire fence. Boarding with farm families, Josie Corliss slept in more than one attic. She was "so lonesome" that she resolved to improve the lives of rural teachers if she ever got a chance.

She got her chance in Walla Walla, Washington, an influential agricultural city that practically doubled in size to 20,000 in the first decade of the 20th century. And she made the most of it.

In 1912, two years after Washington women won the right to vote, 39-year-old Josephine Corliss Preston was elected State Superintendent of Public Instruction, the direct beneficiary of a suffrage movement propelled by thousands of resourceful female campaigners. She prevailed in a tricky four-way race by out-campaigning her opponents, including two other women. Support from women's clubs was decisive in her victory.

Washington's first female statewide elected official was idealistic, disarmingly bright and politically nimble—simultaneously puritanical and progressive; a proto-feminist divorcee who sang in the church choir. In 16 years as state school superintendent she effected 55 new laws "with alacrity, clarity and confidence," as one historian puts it, creating a modern school system. Early on she emerged as

one of America's most influential educators. There was speculation she might become the first female member of a presidential cabinet as Secretary of Education.

In 1919 Preston was elected president of the 52,000-member National Education Association, which then included principals and superintendents as well as teachers. Six-thousand delegates attended the national convention in Milwaukee. She also led the Council of State Superintendents and Commissioners of Education and was elected a vice chairman of the new Women's Division of the Republican National Committee.

During the 1919-1920 votes-for-women campaign that saw Washington emerge as the penultimate state to ratify the 19th Amendment, Preston and national suffrage leader Carrie Chapman Catt became close friends. Unsurprising, for they had much in common. Catt had been a 14-year-old teacher in Iowa, and both belonged to the Women's Christian Temperance Union. Preston arranged the 1919 luncheon in Olympia where Catt rallied Washington women to round up pledges of support from male lawmakers when Governor Louis F. Hart balked at calling a special session to ratify the suffrage amendment. Catt ended her address by calling for the formation of a league of women voters.

The governor ended up signing into law the cornerstone of Preston's legislative agenda that year: "An act to prevent discrimination in the payment of salaries between male and female teachers in the public schools of this state."

On Preston's watch, state per-pupil funding increased, kindergartens were established and vocational education classes incorporated in the secondary school curriculum. She improved teacher pay and retirement benefits—though not nearly as much as she had hoped—and promoted higher standards for teacher certification.

Remembering the cold nights when she graded papers in a barn, Preston helped rural communities build cottages for teachers, emphasizing that better housing would also attract competent men to a female-dominated profession. The superintendent preached the importance of school attendance, lengthened the school year, instituted hot-lunch programs, improved pupil transportation, consolidated districts to improve curriculum and promoted Parent-Teacher Associations. Preston was also an early proponent of junior high schools and two-year community colleges. In 1913, the year she took office in Olympia, 2,512 students graduated from high schools around the state. In 1928, the year she left office, 21,587 received diplomas.

It was Preston who mandated a Washington State History course for sixth graders.

Chin up, posture perfect, Josephine Corliss Preston exuded confidence. She wore frameless spectacles that amplified her striking eyes. Reporters covering a national NEA convention observed that when anyone asked which lady Mrs. Preston was, delegates advised them to just look for the woman in the jaunty wide-brimmed hat trimmed in red.

Preston was also an exacting workaholic. "People who offended her were quick to realize her wrath," Gary Gordon Rude wrote in a thoughtful 1985 doctoral thesis on Preston's educational leadership. Subordinates who saw her as high-handed called her "The Duchess," at least behind her back. When several resigned in two separate public huffs during her first term, the strong-willed superintendent calmly told reporters, Good riddance! They were readily replaceable. It took a manufactured mini-scandal to finally defeat her after she crossed Governor Roland H. Hartley, a mercurial conservative with retrograde ideas about school funding.

Preston's Laura Ingalls Wilder girlhood helps explain how she became the remarkable woman she was.

FERGUS FALLS IS A RIVERFRONT TOWN in west central Minnesota adjacent to the Dakotas. In 1873, when Josephine Corliss was born, it had around 1,500 citizens and was on the cusp of incorporation. Her father, John Wesley Corliss, uncles, aunts and grandparents had left Vermont in the 1850s, lured by the chance to acquire up to 160 acres of government-owned land for as little as $1.25 an acre. The 1862 Homestead Act encouraged even more Western migration.

Josephine was named in honor of her mother, Josephine Kinney, a member of another pioneer family in Otter Tail County. "Josie" to her family and childhood friends, the little girl who loved to read grew up hearing tales of covered wagon caravans, Indian uprisings and Civil War battles. The Corlisses ranked among Minnesota's leading citizens. They are well remembered there to this day.

Ebenezer E. Corliss, Josie's uncle, served with distinction in the Union army for three years during the Civil War, as did her father, who suffered a "terrible" leg wound that never fully healed. "Uncle Eb" survived a bullet to the back of his head, convalesced and re-enlisted. The Corliss men were "big in stature" and "possessed great resolution and force of will." While serving in the Minnesota Legislature, E.E. Corliss engineered a bill that designated Fergus Falls as the county seat and served on the Republican State Central Committee. Elected county attorney, E.E. cultivated 320 acres of farmland on the side. A third Corliss brother, Josie's Uncle William, was Otter Tail County's superintendent of schools and clerk of the district court before his untimely death at 28 in 1871.

Josie and Myrtia Corliss were home-schooled in early childhood while their father managed his farms in and around Otter Tail County and studied law. Following his brothers "into town" in 1880, John W. Corliss purchased 80 acres

Josephine, second from left, with her parents and siblings in 1887, the year she became a teenage teacher in rural Minnesota. *Otter Tail County Historical Society.*

of real estate, built a handsome house, joined his brother's law practice and was initiated into the Masonic Lodge. John Jr. was born in 1881. The Corliss brothers, their wives and children were mainstays of the Congregational Church. The family's "home training" prized patriotism, "self-reliance, truthfulness and the inculcation of a helpful spirit."

Josie completed high school by 16. She was teaching in a rural school on the plains north of Fergus Falls in the fall of 1889 when her world turned upside down.

John W. Corliss spent a long day visiting one of his farms 30 miles north of town. Too tired to head home, he checked into a hotel. The next morning, he was discovered dead in his bed at 52. Vexed with "heart disease" and relentless pain from his Civil War wound, he had ignored his doctor's warnings to "shun all excitement" and "keep away from his business and other cares." The funeral procession "was one of the longest that has ever been seen in this city, a silent and suggestive testimony of the esteem and respect in which Mr. Corliss was held by this community," Otter Tail County newspapers reported.

JOSIE'S GRIEVING MOTHER, only 37, decided to head farther west, perhaps because her nephew, Charles W. Corliss, was making a name for himself as a lawyer in Seattle. With Myrtia and 8-year-old John Jr. in tow, the widowed Mrs. Corliss became a matron at the Umatilla Indian Boarding School near Pendleton, Oregon. Josie, 16, stayed behind and enrolled at Carleton College's Academy, a prep school at Northfield, Minnesota, near the Twin Cities of Minneapolis-Saint Paul. Founded in 1866 by the Congregational Church, Carleton College was theologically conservative and academically rigorous. She studied Greek and Latin for a year and departed as "Josephine," a more grown-up name.

In the summer of 1891 she was teaching alongside her aunt at another rural school on the plains when her mother returned to Fergus Falls for a visit, regaling old friends with the beauty and mild climate of the Northwest. "She wishes her daughter to return with her," the *Fergus Falls Daily Journal* noted.

That fall, Josephine boarded a train for her new life. She secured a $30-per-month teaching position in Waitsburg, a picturesque farm town nestled in the rolling hills of Walla Walla County. The railroad had arrived 10 years earlier, connecting wheat farmers and the local flour mill to far-flung markets. Miss Corliss was a popular, "conscientious" elementary school teacher who organized spelling bees and often met with parents. She attended teacher's institutes and enrolled in correspondence courses in pursuit of the four-year degree she coveted throughout her career.

2: ON HER OWN

Josephine met a handsome young man soon after arriving in Waitsburg. And not just any young man. Herbert P. "Bert" Preston was the oldest son of W.G. Preston, co-owner of the town's landmark five-story flour mill. "If he will but follow in the footsteps of his father, he will be one of the best men the country affords," the *Waitsburg Times* wrote when the pair were married in 1893, hailing the bride as "a lovely and lovable young lady of good accomplishments." Josephine had just turned 20; Bert was still 19. The new Mrs. Preston—judging from comments in Walla Walla County's newspapers—was readily granted a waiver from the era's widespread belief that married women should be housewives. Her admiring father-in-law was also the leading benefactor of Waitsburg's public schools.

Unfortunately, it appears the young couple's marriage was in trouble by the time they moved to Walla Walla around 1897. Bert was overseeing the Preston Grocery Company. Josephine was teaching at the city's Baker School. In 1899, Bert

The faculty of Walla Walla's Baker School—including the janitor—around the turn of the century, with Josephine Corliss Preston third from right. *Whitman College Archives*

filed for divorce, charging that Josephine had "disregarded the solemnity of their vows" and "abandoned him willfully and without cause" to live "separately and apart." The Preston family's stature may have been the reason the news was not reported by the county's newspapers. Other divorce filings certainly were, especially ones featuring titillating allegations.

The divorce was quietly granted in 1901 in Walla Walla Superior Court. Bert and Josephine had no children. Did he object to her insistence on advancing her teaching career, believing a woman's place was in the home? By taking the dramatic step of moving out, Josephine obviously objected to their home life. Bert Preston would marry again—the very next year; Josephine remained single. She would be "Mrs. Josephine Corliss Preston" for the remainder of her very public life, with no scandal accruing to her name in an era when divorce was the subject of tongue-clucking, especially when a wife was the defendant. Josephine appears in all written accounts as a virtuous, church-going woman, rapidly advancing in her career.[*]

ON FEBRUARY 1, 1904, Josephine Corliss Preston, now 30, was appointed deputy county superintendent of schools by the Walla Walla County commissioners at a salary of $75 per month. Newspaper accounts made it clear the "prominent teacher" with "many friends" was being groomed by the Republican Party to succeed the two-term incumbent, who endorsed her appointment. "It is said that no such opportunity to honor fair womanhood had ever been given here," newspapers reported.

Her new job and growing interest in Republican politics added to a daunting schedule. While taking evening and Saturday-morning classes in English, philosophy and history at Whitman College, she earned a "life diploma" Washington state teaching credential and began writing articles about educational practices. She was active in the Order of the Eastern Star, a Masonic group, the Women's Christian Temperance Union and the Walla Walla Art Club. She taught Sunday School, wrote children's songs and was interested in birds. She also enlisted in the campaign to secure for Washington women the right to vote.

It was a long time coming.

SEATTLE PIONEER ARTHUR A. DENNY, who abhorred liquor and respected women, was the grandfather of the suffrage movement in Washington state. At the first meeting of the Territorial Assembly in 1854, Delegate Denny proposed that "all white females over the age of 18" be allowed to vote. The amendment was defeated by one vote. Fits and starts would follow over the next 56 years:

In 1857 women in Washington Territory apparently gained a voice in granting liquor licenses, according to suffrage historian Shanna Stevenson. Saloon

[*] In 1916, when Josephine's former father-in-law died, he left her $1,000, the equivalent of $24,500 in inflation-adjusted dollars. Her annual salary that year as superintendent of public instruction was $2,500. A house cost $3,500; a car $500.

Abigail Scott Duniway, *Library of Congress*

and gambling parlor interests were a powerful lobby against suffrage, warning that women were out to outlaw alcohol. Thousands certainly were.

In 1867, a territorial voting law declared that "all white American citizens twenty-one years of age" had the right to vote—a claim bolstered over the next three years by the 14th and 15th Amendments to the U.S. Constitution. Washington women who tested the law at polling places over the next few years met with mixed results. When the Legislature enacted a progressive community property law, naysayers warned that women would next argue for liberalized divorce laws.

In 1871, famed suffragists Susan B. Anthony and Abigail Scott Duniway toured the Northwest, rallying women to the national campaign for equal rights. By then Washington women had secured the right to vote in local school district elections.

In 1878, two suffrage proposals failed at a territorial constitutional convention in Walla Walla, despite an impassioned address by Duniway. Speaking for the "silenced and unrepresented" women of the territory, she urged the delegates to be "the first in the grand galaxy of States to wheel majestically into her proper orbit in harmony with the Declaration of Independence."

Northwest suffragists—led by church-based ladies aid societies and the Women's Christian Temperance Union—redoubled their efforts to secure the vote. Opponents sneered that suffrage advocates were "an odd looking lot" of "short-haired women and long-haired men." However, one rural editor wrote, "If they can reform politics …then in God's name let them vote."

Victory—short-lived—came in 1883 when the Territorial Assembly accorded women the vote in all elections as well as the right to serve on juries. The lawmakers reiterated their intent three years later, clarifying that when they said "his" in the earlier statute they meant "her" as well. In the 1885 and 1886 elections, women "voted intelligently and well," a suffrage historian wrote, adding:

> In fact, it is on record that gamblers and thugs were driven out of the territory…as long as women held the power of the ballot in their hands. During that time they served on juries, filled certain suitable political positions and withal preserved their homes, gave parties, entertained their friends, got dinners for their husbands' chums; in fact, exploded the pet theories of old-line conservatives who hold that when women vote the domestic fabric is rent and the home goes to pieces.

When the Territorial Supreme Court revoked suffrage in 1887, the Legislature promptly re-enacted the law. Then things went to pieces. Male-privilege judicial activism was on full display a year later when the high court ruled that the federal government had intended to put "male" before "citizenship" in the Washington Territory Organic Act when establishing voter qualifications. In the typewritten decision signed by the judges, "male" is hand-written above the applicable text and marked with an insertion symbol. Olympia historian Gerry Alexander, a former chief justice of the Washington Supreme Court, shakes his head and smiles as he renders his verdict: "Judicial jujitsu."

"The disqualification of women from voting weakened the cause of suffrage at the 1889 Washington State Constitutional Convention since women could not vote for electors to the conclave," Shanna Stevenson notes. Edward Eldridge of Whatcom County, who had championed suffrage for decades, made an "eloquent and exhaustive" speech urging the delegates to remove "male" from the proposed section on voting rights. Citing the Declaration of Independence and the platforms of both political parties, Eldridge declared, "Give woman the right to vote and it opens the avenues to her of self support and independence. The more we exercise the mind the more intelligent we become, and participation in the government is one of the greatest means of exercising the mind." The delegates listened intently "for one hour and 15 minutes," then exercised their right to reject his motion.

The constitution was ratified at the polls a month before Washington joined the union as the 42nd state. A separate suffrage proposal was backed by only 31.5 percent of the voters, while 62 percent of the electorate rejected prohibition—saloon license fees being a major source of revenue for many counties and cities, including staid old Walla Walla. The editor of the *Walla Walla Union*, who had backed female suffrage, opposed prohibition, writing, "To attempt to absolutely and completely stop the manufacture and sale of whisky is as impossible as it would be to attempt to stop the Columbia flowing over the falls at the Cascades."

On March 27, 1890, Governor Elisha P. Ferry signed into law a School Suffrage Act that once again granted women the right to vote in local school district elections, but not for county or state superintendents.

In 1897, the Washington State Legislature overwhelmingly approved a suffrage amendment that was signed by the governor and placed before the voters in the 1898 General Election. The proposed Article VI of the State Constitution was rejected by nearly 60 percent of the electorate. Women seeking the franchise fared far better with lawmakers than judges or the electorate—and not just in Washington. "Had state constitutions allowed legislatures to amend [constitutions] without a vote of the people, woman suffrage would have advanced far more rapidly than it did," Richard J. Ellis wrote in his 2002 book on the initiative process in America, *Democratic Delusions*. "Between 1870 and 1900 ten suffrage amendments were passed by state legislatures and referred to the voters for approval. In only two cases (Colorado in 1893 and Idaho in 1896) did the voters accept the amendment."

3: VOTE-BY-MALE ELECTIONS

When Josephine Corliss Preston declared her candidacy for county school superintendent in the summer of 1908, she and her sizable group of female supporters around Walla Walla County chafed at the reality they would have no say in the election. Nevertheless, Preston handily defeated R.E. Stafford, a Walla Walla grade-school principal who ran as a Democrat. Preston was the choice of nearly 57 percent of the male voters. Granted, it was a Republican county, but it was clear that the ladies were gaining momentum all across the state. *The Colfax Gazette,* noting that 17 of the 37 school superintendents elected that year were women, observed, "As Uncle Jasper would say, 'The world do move.' "

U.S. Senator Moses E. Clapp, a former Fergus Falls lawyer who had been a close friend of Preston's father, was emerging as one of the most outspoken suffragists in Congress. Preston saved a newspaper clipping that told of his activism. "The time is inevitable," the Minnesota Republican predicted, "when the American people will confer upon American womanhood the only peaceable weapon known to free government for her own protection, for the protection of her property and the protection of her children, and that is the ballot."

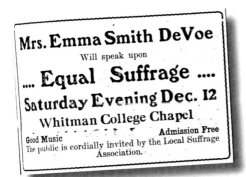

On Dec. 12, 1908, Preston heard the indefatigable, yet ladylike Tacoma suffragist Emma Smith DeVoe speak at the Whitman College Chapel. The *Walla Walla Evening Statesman's* front-page write-up said the large crowd was "more than pleased" with DeVoe's ability "to handle the subject in an intelligent and interesting manner," adding:

> Mrs. DeVoe, who is president of the Washington Equal Suffrage Association, is a woman who appeals to people, her simple, unassuming manner, free from that "mannishness" which many imagine to be inherent in all workers for equal suffrage, makes for her hosts of friends wherever she goes as a public speaker. Mrs. DeVoe is in the foremost ranks of women oratory, and the manner in which she handles her subject, producing statistics to support

her arguments, is most pleasing. She is strong in her statements regarding the present system of government, by which the men have absolute control. … "There is nothing new in our campaign for equal suffrage," said Mrs. DeVoe. "Not a thing; it is simply a revival of the spirit which stirred our forefathers in precipitating the revolutionary war—taxation without representation."

Those words resonated for Walla Walla County's first female school superintendent. The Corlisses were proud of their patriot ancestors. Preston became an enthusiastic "Votes for Women" campaigner.

Reflecting on the suffragists' gumption nearly a century later, political commentator Cokie Roberts said, "We had the right to vote as American citizens. We didn't have to be granted it by some bunch of guys."

In the summer of 1909, Preston attended the National American Woman Suffrage Association Convention in Seattle during the Alaska-Yukon-Pacific Exposition, the state's first world's fair. It appears that Preston, busy with school activities, shrewdly steered clear of a nasty leadership feud that erupted between Emma Smith DeVoe and May Arkwright Hutton, a wealthy, flamboyant suffragist from Spokane.

The next year saw the equivalent of a political full-court press by Washington suffragists and their allies in the growing women's club movement as white, middle-class women in social and literary clubs seized the reform zeitgeist of the Progressive era. The support of a populist-progressive-farmer-labor coalition, notably the Grange and the Washington State Federation of Labor, would prove decisive in the campaign for an amendment to the Washington State Constitution. The Women's Christian Temperance Union was an unshakeable ally from the beginning. African Americans accounted for only 0.53 percent of the state's population in 1910 (6,000 residents, mostly men) but Tacoma boasted a remarkable black suffragist and NAACP activist in Nettie J. Asberry, a piano teacher with a doctorate in music. In 1878, she was the 13-year-old secretary of the Susan B. Anthony Club in Leavenworth, Kansas, having met the famed suffragist.

Emma Smith DeVoe also sought support from the state's substantial bloc of progressive women of Scandinavian descent. Posters, handbills, ribbons,

campaign buttons, get-out-the-vote rallies and countless club meetings and teas boosted enthusiasm for ratification of the amendment. DeVoe attended Woman's Days at county fairs in Walla Walla, Puyallup and Yakima "while her foot soldiers canvassed their voting precincts."

On November 8, 1910, the women of Washington won the right to vote—permanently. Nearly 64 percent of the electorate approved the amendment, with all 39 counties favoring ratification. "The stunningly decisive victory…is widely credited with reinvigorating the national movement," Shanna Stevenson wrote. "When Washington joined her western sisters in 1910, it had been 14 years since a state had enacted irrevocable women's suffrage." *

On December 3, 1910, Mrs. Mary Wilson of Renton became the first woman in the state to cast a vote under the newly ratified amendment, according to *The Seattle Daily Times*, which accorded her a two-column photo and double-deck headline. She was "the first of more than 50 of the maids and matrons of Renton to appear to vote on the question of forming Renton Waterway District No. 2."

National suffrage would take another 10 years.

JOSEPHINE CORLISS PRESTON was re-elected county superintendent without opposition, as well as a state delegate to the 1910 convention of the National Federation of Women's Clubs. She enlisted in the National Council of Women Voters, a nonpartisan coalition organized by Emma Smith DeVoe.

Preston's statewide stature grew in 1911 when Governor Marion Hay, a former Eastern Washington businessman who styled himself as "a reformer on the right," appointed her to the State Board of Education.

The late Zola Burnap Irwin, an eastern Washington historian who taught at a reasonably well-equipped one-room school in Walla Walla County in the 1930s, was the beneficiary of Preston's lifelong concern for rural schools. Irwin wrote that Preston "was keenly interested in the quality of education in the rural areas of the county, aware that the city schools of Walla Walla drew the outstanding teachers, while the isolated county schools sometimes had to hire beginners or those who were inadequately prepared or teachers who were at best unprofessional."

Some male politicians harrumphed that the lady county superintendent was

---

* Some Washington women remained disenfranchised, including those who had lost their citizenship by marrying foreigners. That law was changed in 1922. Two years later, Congress finally granted citizenship to all Native Americans, though some states suppressed their ability to vote for decades more. A 1943 act sponsored by then-Congressman Warren G. Magnuson of Washington allowed naturalized citizenship to Chinese immigrants already residing in the U.S.—a nod to our World War II ally. But immigrant West Coast Japanese—sent to concentration camps during the war, together with their U.S.-born children—were denied voting rights until the federal McCarran-Walter Act of 1952.

Cassandra Messegee, a teacher in Walla Walla County, lived in this portable cookhouse until the community could provide better housing. *Teachers' Cottages in Washington*, 1915

headstrong. "It takes trouble to get things started sometimes," Preston said. "We were in a rut, and nothing short of a good jolting would lift us out. ...I believe in working and fighting for that which appears to us to be the greatest good for the greatest number. I fight fairly, however, and I have never held a 'grouch.' " Preston admired Emma Smith DeVoe's advice that civility invariably carried the day: "Always be good natured and cheerful." Sometimes, however, her temper got the best of her.

Preston always stopped at rural schools as she traveled through neighboring counties on her way to teacher institutes in Spokane and Pullman. The lonely young female teachers she met kindled memories of those sub-zero schooldays and bleak nights on the Minnesota prairie. Preston became the foremost advocate of a campaign to construct teachers' cottages. Parsonages helped recruit good preachers; teachers needed "teacherages," Preston said.

"As early as 1904, school administrators, women's club members and other progressive reformers" around Washington had championed the idea, which sprang from Nebraska. Preston embraced it. Recruiting and retaining qualified teachers while ensuring their comfort—and the moral propriety of young female teachers— also was "of particular concern because of the large numbers of single men working nearby in the logging, mining, agricultural, or fishing industries. ... "

A fledgling teacher named Cassandra Messegee visited Preston's office at the Walla Walla Courthouse one day to lament she could find no place to stay within miles of her rural school. The school board member who formerly offered board and room to teachers, "had moved his family to the city so his children could attend high school." He was embarrassed, "and the teacher humiliated and discouraged."

As they weighed options, Miss Messegee mentioned to the superintendent that there was "a crude little cook house" across the road from the school.

> It had been used during harvest and brought in from the wheat fields at the end of summer. Would it be possible to move it to a site near the school house and use it? Mrs. Preston thought it could be done. …
>
> The canvas roof was left intact but the canvas sides were boarded up inside. Miss Messegee moved her furniture into the stopgap home and when school started she was ready, with her 12-year-old brother to keep her company. All went well until the first rain. All their belongings, clothing and beds were drenched. Not to be defeated, they dried their possessions and the teacher bought and applied some water-proof roofing, which solved the problem. The following September a new cottage was ready. … Miss Messegee stayed for three years, longer than many rural teachers remained in a district. She left to continue her education.

Superintendent Preston's innovations caught the attention of Spokane's influential *Spokesman-Review* newspaper. It covered a "Know Your City Congress" that featured a children's day attended by some 1,200 Walla Walla pupils. A local historian related the city's history, and two ladies spoke on "What the city does for the children." The children, "represented by Master Chauncey Minard and Misses Mazie Penrose and Ruth Martin," outlined what the children believed they could do for their city. Miss Penrose's father was Stephen B.L. Penrose, the activist president of Whitman College. The Yale Divinity School graduate, who would head the college for 40 years, spent a long afternoon chatting with the superintendent. He soon concluded that Josephine Corliss Preston was an educator with limitless possibilities.

Preston was delighted when the faculty at Whitman College granted her 48 hours of credits toward a bachelor's degree, based on her studies at Carleton College, other course work, professional achievements and demonstrated skill in public speaking. Whitman would award her an honorary master's degree in 1914 in recognition of her "distinguished work in the field of education."

Preston became active in the Inland Empire Teachers' Organization and the Good Roads movement. She visited Puget Sound several times a year. Her influential cousins, Charles and John Corliss—also Carleton College alumni—bolstered a growing network of admirers around the state. By 1912, Charles W. Corliss was a well-established Seattle attorney, a member of the Arctic Club and the Municipal League. He served as foreman of a King County grand jury that handed down 27 indictments for vice and graft in Seattle's controversial "restricted district," where prostitution and gambling had free reign. John H. Corliss, a physician, joined his brother in Seattle in the 1890s before purchasing a 160-acre ranch in the Puyallup Valley. He became a beloved doctor—the Puyallup Indians paid for his services in fish—and in 1900 helped organize the Western Washington Fair. Dr. Corliss headed the House Education Committee in the Washington Legislature during 1902 while also serving on the Sumner School Board. "An ardent supporter of public education," he helped boost Josephine's political career.

4: "Woman against woman"

Henry B. Dewey, the state superintendent of public instruction, announced in the fall of 1911 that he would not seek re-election in 1912, opting instead to run for Congress. Preston immediately announced her candidacy for the $2,500-a-year job. Stephen Penrose, a prominent early endorser, declared she had the experience, character and tact to serve the state with "wisdom, integrity and efficiency." Well-connected male contenders for the job scoffed that she didn't even have a college degree.

Albert S. Burrows, King County's superintendent of schools, was elected president of the Washington Education Association at a lively convention in North Yakima at year's end. Burrows' victory was hailed in the press as a political boost for one of his friends: James M. Layhue, a steadfast Republican with a Fuller Brush mustache. Layhue was Superintendent Dewey's assistant.

Preston appeared unfazed. She told reporters covering the convention that she had the support of 15 leading educators, including Frank Cooper, the Seattle school superintendent. Layhue retorted that 30 of the state's 39 county superintendents were in his corner, along with 113 city superintendents and principals, as well as 21 college professors. Among them was the bright, yet judgmental Dr. Noah D. Showalter, the new president of the Washington State Normal School at Cheney.* Showalter sniffed at Preston's skimpy academic credentials, never mind her years of practical experience. (Dr. Penrose would later note that she knew "vastly more about education than anybody on the faculty" at Whitman College.) Showalter would become Preston's nemesis.

Preston rounded up more support when she headed a delegation of 16 Walla Walla women to the first meeting of the Women's Good Roads Congress in Tacoma in January of 1912. The meeting drew club women and other activists from around the state, including Emma Smith DeVoe, as well as the State Grange master, the secretary of the Seattle Chamber of Commerce and the engineer for the State Highway Commission. Preston was the keynoter, emphasizing that good roads were crucial to good schools, especially in rural areas. She was staking out a leave-no-child-behind theme for her campaign for state superintendent. To keep moving forward

---

* Opened in 1890, the teacher-training school at Cheney was the forerunner of Eastern Washington University. Bellingham and Ellensburg were also granted Normal schools after statehood. "Cheney won the prize for Eastern Washington because its boosters had fought hard for it after losing the county seat to nearby Spokane in 1886," according to Spokane historian Jim Kershner.

Mrs. Josephine Corliss Preston.

America needed "the best teachers," Preston said, adding that "it was far more important to select competent teachers for rural schools, where there necessarily can be but slight supervision, than in the city schools, where there is close supervision."

THE RACE FOR THE REPUBLICAN NOMINATION for state superintendent of public instruction took a new twist in February of 1912. Men being men, politics appears to have trumped friendship because James Layhue dropped out of the race "in interest of harmony," having discovered that his candidacy had generated "some antagonism" in "a certain part of the state" (transparently Seattle/King County) among supporters of a certain other candidate. Albert Burrows immediately announced his candidacy.

The fight between the King County school superintendent and the lady Republican from Eastern Washington "promises to be a pretty one," *The Tacoma Daily Ledger* predicted, especially since Preston was asserting that "the head of the schools is one office which rightfully should be held by a woman." Burrows' supporters asserted she lacked the experience to oversee the state's school system. Fast-growing King County, population already 300,000, coveted political dominance.

Two well-known Democrats entered the race: Mary A. Monroe of Spokane and Eldridge Wheeler of Montesano, the party's 1908 nominee. Monroe for 20 years had been principal of Spokane's Lincoln School, the largest elementary school in the Northwest. It had a thousand students and 23 teachers. She was active in the National Education Association and an avid supporter of the Democrats' presidential nominee, New Jersey Governor Woodrow Wilson. Monroe shared Josephine Corliss Preston's commitment to promoting parent-teacher relations and boosting rural schools. Professor Wheeler, Montesano's popular school superintendent, was a delegate to the 1912 Democratic National Convention and a future regent of the University of Washington.

The resurgent Socialists nominated Frances Cora Sylvester for Superintendent of Public Instruction. She was the niece of Olympia's founding father, Edmund Sylvester. The ardent 38-year-old Socialist had taught in Olympia schools for eight years. She was the party's nominee for state superintendent in 1904 and ran an impressive race for mayor of Olympia in 1911. Rallying their comrades to "fall in" and help "make short work of bloody capitalism," Sylvester and Anna A. Maley of Everett, the first woman to run for governor of Washington, waged an aggressive campaign of well-attended rallies for a ticket headed by the Socialists' charismatic presidential candidate, Eugene V. Debs. It was said that Sylvester, vowing to be "a workman for the people," held her own sharing a platform with Maley, a spellbinding lecturer. The Socialists and the more radical Industrial Workers of the World exemplified everything Josephine Corliss Preston and fellow conservatives viewed as inimical to "American values."

Some saw the race for state superintendent of public instruction as an historic "woman against woman" battle between Preston and Mary Monroe, "owing to the popularity of both women and their well-known accomplishments in the field of education." That was how *The Town Crier*, an influential Seattle magazine, put it. "This contest, it is safe to say, has done more than any one thing to bring out the feminine vote. So far, be it said to the credit of the women, the campaign has been carried out in a thoroughly clean and honorable manner. At both headquarters, the women speak in high terms of the rival candidate and say she is undoubtedly qualified—but on the other hand they can give you reasons why their own candidate has the advantage in experience."

Preston and Monroe were intent on ensuring they were perceived as not just Eastern Washington candidates. The Mary Monroe Club worked closely with the Women's Wilson-Marshall League while the Women's Republican Club of Washington, featuring "numerous well-known society and club women," enthusiastically backed Preston. The Socialists said Preston and Monroe were capitalist peas in a pod.

Everyone underestimated the strength of former president Theodore Roosevelt's new Progressive Party.

5: MIXED BLESSINGS

The impact of women's votes and women's voices was the wild card in the 1912 presidential election and on races up and down the ballot in Washington. There were 1.3 million women of voting age in the six states where women had won the right to vote—notably California, which enfranchised women in 1911, the year after Washington.

Theodore Roosevelt, hugely popular in Washington state, loomed larger than life in one of the most tumultuous national elections in U.S. history. In the midterm elections two years earlier, Democrats won 58 seats to gain control of the U.S. House for the first time since 1894. Roosevelt excoriated his erstwhile friend, President William Howard Taft, as a backsliding "fathead" with "the brains of a guinea pig." Roosevelt was deeply aggrieved that Taft "had all but abandoned" his environmental policies, having dismissed his friend Gifford Pinchot as the nation's chief forester. When Roosevelt declared his hat was "in the ring" Republicans began choosing up sides. The Democrats nominated New Jersey Governor Woodrow Wilson, the former president of Princeton University.

Let's reimagine 1992 to put 1912 in a contemporary perspective: Suppose Ronald Reagan, outraged that George H.W. Bush had broken his no-new-taxes pledge, had formed a third party (à la H. Ross Perot) and ended up electing the Democrat, Bill Clinton?* In 1912, there was also a consequential fourth-party candidate, the Socialists' Eugene V. Debs.

James Chace, author of *1912, Wilson, Roosevelt, Taft & Debs, the Election That Changed the Country*, wrote: "Above all, the contest …over reform at home and later over American involvement abroad—recalls the great days of Jefferson and Hamilton, as the 1912 presidential campaign tackled the central question of America's exceptional destiny."

---

* Nitpickers will note that the 22nd Amendment, ratified in 1951, would have barred Reagan from seeking a third term.

When stand-pat Republicans denied Roosevelt the 1912 GOP nomination, the former president bolted the convention and became the standard bearer of the new Progressive Party. Thumping his broad chest, Roosevelt boasted he felt as fit "as a bull moose." The party now had its mascot. It already had considerable momentum in The Evergreen State. An eight-hour day for female workers had been passed by the Legislature in 1911, despite "vociferous protests" by laundry, hotel and retail store proprietors. "If girls were horses, you'd be more careful of their health," said the activist wife of a University of Washington professor. The average factory girl was being paid $1.57 for a nine-hour day.

Teddy Roosevelt on the cover of *Harper's Weekly* during the 1912 campaign.

The Progressive Party platform declared that votes for women were "a matter of natural right alone." Jane Addams, the renowned social worker from Chicago and "arguably the most famous woman in America," entered their convention "waving a great banner inscribed with 'Votes for Women' ...a Bull Moose badge on her breast." A reporter for *The New York Times* was shocked by the delegates' reaction when Roosevelt promised he would lead the fight for suffrage. "In most cases where men applaud the mention of woman suffrage, they do it with a grin," the newsman observed. But at this convention "old men and young men alike got up on their chairs, yelled like wild Indians and waved anything available and portable." When Roosevelt declared, "We stand at Armageddon, and we battle for the Lord!" the delegates broke into *The Battle Hymn of the Republic*.

Some suffragists blanched at the theatrics, maintaining that Addams had betrayed the movement's nonpartisan stance and presented a false impression that Roosevelt was their new champion. As for "natural rights," he had excluded African Americans from the Progressive platform, worried that a civil rights plank would cost him votes in the South.

ROOSEVELT CHOSE AS HIS RUNNING MATE California Governor Hiram Johnson. With California and Washington in play—11 and 7 electoral votes,

respectively—the electoral college vote women could effect more than doubled, suffrage historian Jo Freeman notes.*

Washington's population also had more than doubled—to 1.14 million—since 1900. Women accounted for approximately 43 percent of the state's population. Approximately 200,000 were now of voting age. And at least 85 percent—170,000—were expected to vote in the 1912 elections. From right to left on the political spectrum, they were highly motivated. That made many men nervous.

Some, however, were dedicated "suffragents." In New York City that November more than 500 men marched in a torchlight parade alongside 20,000 suffragists. National suffrage leader Carrie Chapman Catt described the Men's League for Women's Suffrage as "the thinking men of our country—the brains of our colleges, of commerce and literature." All things considered, "a blessing to us."

AS ROOSEVELT WHISTLE-STOPPED the West, wooing female voters to the delight of editorial cartoonists, Woodrow Wilson asserted suffrage was a state issue "not within the purview of a presidential candidate." President Taft, a suffrage proponent during his college years, now worried that women were "too emotional." When he addressed the national convention of the American Woman Suffrage Association in 1910 the portly president said, "If I could be sure that women as a class would exercise the franchise, I would be in favor of it. At present time there exists in my mind considerable doubt."

Washington Governor Marion Hay, a Taft adherent, earlier had equivocated on suffrage. But

THE MILITANT RECRUIT
DRAWN BY E. W. KEMBLE

Teddy Roosevelt in *Harper's Weekly,* E.W. Kemble cartoon

---

* The four pioneer suffrage states were Wyoming (1869), Utah (1870/96), Colorado (1893) and Idaho (1896).

when the constitutional amendment was approved in 1910 Hay said the voters had "acted wisely." His ambivalence would cost him crucial votes in a tight election. Dedicated "suffs" in Washington state represented a potentially pivotal voting bloc.

Roosevelt campaigned in Spokane the day before the September 10 primary, jabbing the air with his fists and flashing his trademark toothy smile. He ended the day with an address to an audience of 2,000 women. Asked about the Republican platform, Roosevelt quipped that he never discussed "dead folks." He had a lot to say, however, about women voters. "The argument that participation in politics will take women from home is just as well grounded as it would be to say that men should not vote because it would take them from their business," the former president said, adding that he had learned "a great deal" from Jane Addams. Women in the progressive Western states had already proven to be a force for better government, Roosevelt said. "I think I have the right to ask the women of Washington to stand by the Progressive Party. We need your help!"

PRESTON WAS TROUBLED by Taft's lackluster campaign and conflicted about Roosevelt. During his presidency, she saw him as the embodiment of red-blooded American exceptionalism. She admired every tenet of his "Square Deal," including antitrust laws to rein in "the malefactors of great wealth," as Roosevelt put it. She favored the direct election of U.S. senators, the initiative and referendum and an end to child labor. She campaigned for equal pay and minimum wages—especially for women—and an 8-hour day. But she could not bring herself to follow Roosevelt out of the Republican Party. That appears to have been a good political decision, too.

She won the GOP nomination for superintendent of public instruction, nipping Albert Burrows by 2,365 votes. Preston's superior ground game in the state's rural counties—including a 1,600-vote margin in Walla Walla—offset the Seattleite's 5,300-vote plurality in King County. In populous Spokane County Preston ran nearly even with Mary Monroe, who handily defeated Eldridge Wheeler for the Democratic nomination. Frances Sylvester advanced to the finals with 8.4 percent of the votes cast.

Now there was a new hat in the ring for superintendent of public instruction. The Progressive Party nominated Chancey E. Beach, the superintendent of schools in Olympia. An early Roosevelt supporter, Beach was the state director of the National Education Association. His wife was president of the state PTA and his father a noted economics professor at the University of Washington.

The Oregonian's political correspondent, M.M. Mattison, reported that the "old-time prophets" were perplexed about the possible outcome of the elections in Washington state:

> Nobody knows, to begin with, what the women's vote, which will be cast in a state election for the first time this year,

will amount to; nobody knows how the women as a voting factor feel about National and state politics, and nobody knows whether there is any likelihood of a last-minute switch in the women's vote.

In other words, as the old saying went, it was a woman's prerogative to change her mind. The Socialists had been making "remarkable gains," Mattison wrote.

But Washington has been a "three-to-one" Republican state and the Republican Party is so strong here that it could stand a big defection and still win. …[T]he present unrest would not worry Republican politicians so much if men alone were voting, but the uncertain quantity of the women's vote upsets any calculation that is made.

That said, "it seems generally admitted that there is a strong undercurrent of sentiment among women voters in favor of Woodrow Wilson," the widely-read correspondent wrote, though with his prim Presbyterian face Wilson had all the charisma of a bill collector.

IN THE EIGHT-WEEK SPRINT to the general election, Preston benefited from the support of the Republican State Central Committee headed by Werner A. Rupp, editor and publisher of *The Aberdeen Daily World*, one of the state's leading Republican newspapers. Rupp was a protégé of Tacoma newspaperman Samuel A. Perkins, a GOP insider since the days of William McKinley. There was a Walla Walla connection, too: Rupp and his lawyer brother, Otto B. Rupp, were proud Whitman College graduates. The party chairman promised "a campaign of hustle" to defeat the Progressives. Privately, Rupp was worried about Hay. The governor received 48 percent of the vote in a crowded primary. He now faced a bumptious Bull Moose candidate, King County Sheriff Robert T. Hodge, and a well-known Tacoma Democrat, Ernest Lister.* Socialist Anna Maley received more votes in the primary than any of the seven Democrats. As elections go, this one was for the record books.

The Seattle Daily Times tweaked the Progressives for being "not especially gallant," finding it hard to square their profession of support for equal suffrage and equal rights with the fact that theirs was "the only party in the state to run a man for Superintendent of Public Instruction." *The Morning Olympian* wrote that Superintendent Beach was being subjected to a lot of "joshing" by his male friends for running "among a flock of the fair sex." However, the consensus was that "the female voters will have a chance to split their votes among three women, while the

---

* A former Populist, Lister received his party's nomination when the victor in the primary, Snohomish County Judge W.W. Black, was declared ineligible by the state Supreme Court because he was running for partisan office while on the bench.

lone man will have a clear field for those who insist upon voting for a man under any circumstances. The situation is one of the most unusual that has ever been brought about in political mix-ups of any state."

On election eve, Chairman Rupp predicted the Bull Moose movement had collapsed. President Taft would carry the state "by a plurality of not less than 20,000," he said, while Governor Hay and the entire Republican ticket would be elected by margins ranging from 30,000 to 40,000 votes.

It was a good thing Rupp was not a betting man.

ON NOVEMBER 5, 1912, Theodore Roosevelt was victorious in Washington, California and four other states. But he lost the presidency to Woodrow Wilson, who carried 40 states. President Taft collected only two. Together, Roosevelt and Taft received 1.3 million more votes than Wilson. So it's likely their feud cost the Republicans the White House—and the Governor's Mansion in Olympia. Democrat Ernest Lister defeated Governor Hay by 622 votes, with the Bull Moose candidate, Robert Hodge, the spoiler.[*]

Josephine Corliss Preston bucked the tide. In a tight four-way race, she was elected state superintendent of public instruction, defeating Chancey Beach, the Bull Moose candidate, by 10,360 votes. Democrat Mary Monroe finished third. Some 40,000 left-leaning voters (13.5 percent of the electorate) backed Socialist Frances Sylvester. Preston won 23 of the state's 39 counties, finishing a close second to Beach in King and Thurston counties. Her strong showing in Walla Walla County—nearly 60 percent of the vote—helped offset Monroe's sizable margin in Spokane.

"Women of all ages" packed the Walla Walla YMCA on election night, "cheering wildly whenever a report favorable to their candidate" was posted. One of their own was leading in a race to become the first female statewide elected official in Washington history. "The man who two years ago voted against woman suffrage, giving as his argument that most women really didn't care to vote, had occasion to hunt a hiding place," the *Walla Walla Union* observed. The county's long-suffering Democrats, meantime, hooted and hollered as national returns forecast Wilson's victory. "Many a staunch Republican who for years had walked in the paths of the righteous" despaired at Taft's ignominious third-place showing, while "bleeding bull-moosers had salt rubbed into their wounds," the newspaper said.

The consolation prize for the GOP in Washington state was substantial. Republicans easily maintained control of the Legislature and defeated Progressives to win six other statewide offices, though by margins far below their chairman's rosy predictions. Progressives won 30 seats in the Washington State House and eight in the State Senate. Roosevelt's insurgents also captured two at-large seats in Congress

---

[*] It was the closest gubernatorial election in Washington history until 2004 when Chris Gregoire defeated Dino Rossi by 133 votes. President Taft, meanwhile, finished a distant third in Washington state, barely 30,000 votes ahead of Eugene V. Debs, who received nearly a million votes nationwide.

and changed the face of Washington politics with two constitutional amendments. More than 70 percent of the electorate endorsed allowing voters to enact laws by initiative, reject legislative enactments by referendum and recall elected officials. The vote in Washington mirrored the nationwide enthusiasm for reform.

Women's votes clearly elected Josephine Corliss Preston and sent two women to the Legislature—Progressive Nena J. Croake of Tacoma, a physician who was vice president of the Washington Equal Suffrage Association, and Republican Frances C. Axtell, an energetic suffragist from Bellingham. Women's votes also likely elected Ernest Lister governor, "despite his lingering doubts" as to whether suffrage was a good thing.* The total vote for governor in 1912 was 318,359 compared to 176,141 four years earlier. The state's robust population growth alone would not account for the higher vote, former state archivist George W. Scott believes.

Tenacity, organization and her reputation as an innovative educator were the key ingredients in Josephine Corliss Preston's victory. She appealed to both male and female regular Republicans, with the enthusiastic backing of the Women's Republican Club, including society and club women from around the state who emphasized that women needed to make the most of their newly acquired franchise. Preston had appeared at hundreds of neighborhood and social club gatherings. Additionally, she was a stalwart of the Women's Christian Temperance Union, undeterred by the worries of some sister suffragists that the specter of shuttered saloons would create a male-voter backlash.

* Two years later, in 1914, 36 women were elected to public office in Washington state, including Annie Gaston, Thurston County's first female auditor. A staunch Republican, Gaston was a descendant of George Washington Bush, the mixed-race Tumwater pioneer who arrived in 1845.

6: More saloons—and Democrats

Preston, unsurprisingly, was underwhelmed by Olympia. When she took office on January 13, 1913, the capital city's population was 7,000—roughly a third the size of Walla Walla—at least when the Legislature wasn't in session. To the disgust of the WCTU, the city had "more saloons (17) than doctors and dentists put together." The sewers were primitive; rats everywhere. Preston's office was in what we today call the "Old Capitol"—the Richardson Romanesque former Thurston County Courthouse in downtown Olympia. (The building is now occupied entirely by the offices of the Superintendent of Public Instruction.) Work was underway on the stately new Temple of Justice, the first building on a splendid new Capitol Campus being developed by a special commission.

There was an air of excitement as nearly 2,000 guests, including Superintendent Preston, descended on the not-yet-finished Temple for Governor Lister's Inaugural Ball. "There were more Democrats than the capital city had ever seen," an Olympia historian reported.

The old State Capitol, which then, as now, housed the Office of the Superintendent of Public Instruction. Out front in Sylvester Park stands a statue of Governor John R. Rogers, architect of the landmark "Barefoot School Boy Law," the 1895 act to fund public schools. *State Library Collection, Washington State Archives*

Governor Lister, a hard worker, proved to be a progressive reformer "willing to spend money and innovate," George W. Scott notes in his 2012 book *Governors of Washington*. "His transparent sincerity often persuaded the Republican legislature." During the 1913 session it produced a minimum wage bill for women and children that he promptly signed into law. Preston was impressed, redoubling her efforts to seek additional state support for schools, especially the "poor and needy" rural districts.

As she settled in and began squinting at ledgers, Preston determined there were 238,663 school children in the state. The local school districts employed a total of 8,459 teachers at an average annual salary of $772.67. Total expenditures for state schools amounted to $9.1 million in 1913, for an average cost per pupil of $53.22. That's the equivalent of $1,344 per pupil in today's dollars.

Preston discovered that being superintendent of public instruction meant she was also president of the State Board of Education, CEO of the State Board for Vocational Education, chairman of both the State Library Commission and the Agricultural and Rural Life Commission, president of the State Teachers' Retirement Fund and a member of the Archives Commission. She was also a member of the Voting Machine Commission and the State Humane Bureau, which had "oversight" of

MRS. JOSEPHINE PRESTON
Superintendent of Public Instruction

Washington State Historical Society

"delinquent and deficient children" and of "insane and feeble-minded persons." Her staff in 1913 consisted of a secretary and a chief deputy. She added three more employees early on. When she left office in 1929, the Department of Education had grown to 23, though 11 of those employees were clerks or stenographers. The annual operating budget for the superintendent's office had grown from $13,357 in 1913 to $102,400.*

One of Preston's first acts was to step up her campaign to promote construction of cottages for rural teachers. Washington's attorney general had ruled in 1912 that school districts could not use public funds to build teacher cottages. Preston persuaded the 1913 Legislature to pass a law allowing the practice. *Sunset Magazine* took note of her success, writing that her goal was to give every teacher "a comfortable place to live, a clean bed to sleep in, wholesome food to eat, and a quiet, warm room where she may work undisturbed." The districts that furnished a cottage never go "a-begging" for the "A-number 1" teachers, the magazine reported.

By 1915, there were 108 teachers' cottages around the state, from Pend Oreille

---

* For the 2017-18 school year, Washington public school teachers on average earned $55,693, with beginning teachers earning $44,240. Defining "average" is inherently complicated. Teacher pay varies widely based on experience, advanced degrees, contracts for extra duties such as coaching, and size of the district. The cost per pupil in 2017-18 was $12,834.89, according to OSPI. The total statewide full-time equivalent student enrollment was 1,112,719.23. There were 65,619 certificated teachers and 73,046 total certificated instructional staff. For the 2020 state fiscal year, $11,090,000 is allocated for the operation and expenses of the Office of the Superintendent of Public Instruction, which has approximately 400 employees.

County along the Idaho border to Humptulips in north Grays Harbor County at the doorstep of the Olympic National Forest. Nine years later, there were more than 400 cottages. Some were still in use as late as the 1950s. Jane Sandberg, whose husband was in a tuberculosis hospital, moved into the teacher's cottage at Humptulips with her two children in 1938 when she was hired to teach in the community's two-room school. In 2019, her daughter, 92-year-old Vicki Fenton, was living in Hoquiam. "The cottage was a blessing for the whole family—even for my dad, who couldn't be there, to know we were safe and happy," she said.

Though Preston was deeply concerned for the comfort and security of young women teaching in the vicinity of logging camps and canneries, she also urged county superintendents to "give a man with a wife and children first chance" at newly built cottages. One man with 15 years of experience as a teacher and rural school principal wrote Preston a letter of appreciation. His wife had "often remarked that a cottage should be built for the teacher, the same as for a minister." As he contemplated a job offer from the Snoqualmie School District, "I nearly fainted with surprise when I was told that a cottage was built near the school for the use of the principal! My wife's prayers were answered, and here we are." A young woman who taught at a school near Mount Vernon wrote: "This is my fourth year here, and I must acknowledge that the cottage has been the greatest factor in my staying so long." A bulletin issued by Preston's office—she kept the state printer busy with publications—included architectural plans and cost estimates, together with tips on planting fruit trees, vegetable and decorative gardens.

Preston said that by building this cottage near Edwall in Lincoln County the school district was able to retain its male teacher, J. Frank Hall, shown with his family. *Teachers Cottages in Washington*

NATIONAL EDUCATOR STARTED TEACHER'S COTTAGE PLAN IDEA

Josephine Corliss Preston.

Miss Josephine Corliss Preston, president of the National Educational association, the third woman to occupy that position in the history of the organization, has been known nationally among educators for a number of years. She was the originator of the teacher's cottage plan and she has put the idea into actual practice in the state of Washington, where she is superintendent of education, and now beside many a district school building stands an attractive bungalow which is "teacher's house."

The cottages were part of Preston's plan to make wider use of school buildings as "community centers," also authorized by the 1913 Legislature. Why should a schoolhouse sit idle every evening and on weekends? It should be a continuing education and social center for families, including adults of all ages, she said. "A good evening lecture, a lively spelling bee, a community sing, a literary program or any other neighborhood event that may take place at the schoolhouse is materially educating." Her essays on wider use of school buildings attracted national attention.

When the National Education Association met in St. Paul in the summer of 1914, Preston was elected vice president. She renewed old Minnesota acquaintances and moderated a panel on her plans to introduce new vocational and industrial training programs to lower the alarming dropout rate. It was a bitter disappointment when 81 percent of Washington voters rejected a 1914 referendum on the creation of a better retirement fund for the state's educators. Preston regrouped, as usual.

IN HER ROLE AS STATE SUPERINTENDENT and increasing involvement with the NEA, Preston was an enthusiastic advocate for Parent-Teacher Associations. PTAs' power for good "is inestimable," she wrote. "Home and school are equal agencies in the education of the child. Neither can work effectively in ignorance of the other or at cross purposes with the other."

In Preston's era, teachers "generally served at the whim and mercy of local school boards," with no unions to defend their rights or arbitrate disputes. They often wrote directly to her to plead their cases. Constrained by statutes governing her office, she rarely intervened except to "cite laws and steps necessary for solution." There were occasions, however, when she came to the defense of competent teachers who had run afoul of meddlesome parents or arbitrary administrators. Preston counseled compassion when she felt discipline had been too harsh. Lord help the teacher, however, who arrived at work with alcohol on his breath or frequented bars. (Her scrapbook contains no reports on any female teacher tempted by alcohol.) In 1914, Preston advised the superintendent in Benton County: "It is your duty … to revoke the certificate of any teacher you know is using liquor." She was WCTU through and through.

That year, to Preston's enormous satisfaction, imbibers' worst fears came true: 52.6 percent of Washington voters approved an initiative mandating prohibition. The law took effect on January 1, 1916, four years before the 18th Amendment enacted prohibition nationwide. Washington was ahead of the curve once again, though the "noble experiment," fraught with hypocrisies, would prove short-lived. Preston mourned the day in 1933 when alcoholic beverages became legal again.

PRESTON, UNQUESTIONABLY, was a Protestant moralist and something of an enigma if we judge her by today's standards. In the suffrage movement—where the WCTU, Grangers and sophisticated university-educated club women found common cause—Preston forged friendships with liberal-minded women. What they all had in common was their passion for equal rights.

Most of her friends and associates were mothers. Preston's lifelong vocation was maternal. She could have invented the phrase "No child left behind." The inequities in public-school education could move her to tears. Her work with the State Humane Bureau often took her to the school for delinquent girls at Grand Mound near Centralia. "The 20th century is demanding a new ideal in education, which cries for an equal opportunity for every child," Preston said in a 1914 address to the National Education Association. She "endeared herself to multitudes of parents and children," one national report said, by sending hand-written letters of congratulations to every child in the state who completed the eighth grade—nearly 10,000 in 1920. "Each letter carries a direct appeal to the student to stay in school."

Her former grade-school pupils fondly remembered Preston as a kindly teacher who made learning fun with story times and spelling bees. High schoolers—footloose in any era—likely viewed her as strait-laced, though her attitudes on the management of adolescent behavior were not unusual for her era. She warned against allowing teen dances in school houses, acknowledging, "If to say that young people should not dance would mean that they would not dance, it would be different. … the only way for us to do something is to attempt to control it." Dancing and alcohol often went hand in hand, she cautioned.

7: "Officious advisers"

Library of Congress

Preston's penchant for "being very exacting in her demands on her employees" prompted headlines in the *Morning Olympian* in 1915. When Preston fired her deputy superintendent "on account of incompetency," his assistant demanded to be put in charge. Preston called for his resignation on the spot. Her secretary and another office worker quit, too. They had found themselves "out of sympathy" with the policies and methods of her administration, as one put it. Two replacements were named within a day. The "rumpus" quickly blew over. If anyone advised her to lighten up, it fell on deaf ears.

A walkout the following year sparked considerably more front-page fireworks, it being an election year. While Preston was out of town attending a meeting, Deputy Superintendent Mary A. Bryan resigned, together with a young stenographer. They charged Preston with "abuse of women subordinates and extravagance." Mrs. Bryan, a 15-year employee of the office, was the widow of former state superintendent R.B. Bryan. She declared that in all a dozen employees had quit since Preston took office three years earlier. Preston was "entirely unfit" for high office, Mrs. Bryan told the capital press corps, and her re-election would be "a public calamity and genuine disaster to the educational interests of the state."

The seven remaining staffers issued a blistering statement in defense of Preston, emphasizing they were doing so without her knowledge, as she had not yet returned from her trip. The staff had received "nothing but the most courteous and considerate treatment at all times," they wrote, and Preston's only expectation was that "a day's work be given in return for a day's pay." By making "malicious and willfully misleading" statements to the press, the disgruntled pair had "repaid kindness and courteous treatment by disloyalty and treachery," the seven said. "The self-elimination of this disloyal faction is a source of intense satisfaction to the present office force."

Preston issued a forceful three-page "Official Statement" that was reprinted widely. She had appointed Mrs. Bryan as her deputy a year earlier when she expressed regret and contrition over playing a role in the first "disloyal conspiracy," Preston said. "The fact that she was a widow making her way, and that she had a dependent father past eighty years old, made me willing to forgive [her] indiscretion." Preston said the affair reeked of politics. But her constitutional responsibilities were "too great to dwell long" on the petulance of "disgruntled former appointees" who lacked commitment to the cause. Preston said her candidacy for a second term was steeped in the conviction that "there has never been a time in the history of the development of public-school education when the wisdom of the expenditure of the state's school money is of so great importance."

Preston had learned early in her career that not only did men resent forceful female leadership, some women did too. The *North Yakima Republic* put it this way: "The main trouble with Mrs. Josephine Preston, state superintendent, is that although a woman, she has refused to be guided by any number of self-constituted officious advisers who have come forward to help her handle her job. As a result, she will have plenty of opposition in the primaries. She probably ought to be re-nominated."

After her first year in office, Preston told an admirer that "the best men" in education in the state had helped her win election. But "a few of the second grade of men in the state stated that if a woman was elected, a man could never again hope to hold this office."

Whenever Preston lost her temper—usually over errors regarded as egregious or perceived disrespect—the staff made itself scarce. Few, however, faulted her work ethic or concern for children. Loyalists remembered her kindnesses—summertime picnics on Puget Sound for employees and their families—and dry sense of humor. An Oregon educator heading to Olympia for a meeting joked that the brewery at Tumwater was conveniently nearby. "Try to forget" about that, she advised. And in a letter to a contemporary with a full plate, her opener was, "Knowing that you have very little to do…"

PRESTON HAD TOO MUCH TO DO and a burning desire to do it all. She was active in the WCTU and the Olympia Council of Women Voters, which was active in the push for national suffrage. In the middle of the 1916 campaign, Preston came down with pneumonia in Bellingham but refused to be hospitalized. In addition to her work with the National Education Association and travels around the state to host teachers' institutes and dedicate new schools, she was addressing club women and PTA groups and working with the Daughters of the American Revolution to promote the flag salute.

Preston was soon on the road again. She was one of seven division leaders of the first World Conference on Education. The National Thrift Association appointed her to its panel of judges to review school children's essay contest entries. (She was surprised and delighted to discover Henry Ford was a fellow judge.) She visited New York to attend a reception in honor of Charles Evans Hughes, the 1916 GOP nominee for president, and became a member of the Women's National Committee of the Hughes Alliance. The event was at the Long Island estate of socialite artist Gertrude Vanderbilt Whitney. Preston's relatives read all about it when Otter Tail County newspapers proudly printed the story. She also met and became an admirer of the brilliant new president of the University of Washington, Henry Suzzallo, whose forte was educational sociology. A national survey by the New York-based Russell Sage Foundation found that Washington ranked first in "efficiency" of public-school spending, as well as number one for per-capita spending on education, largely due to the number of new school buildings being erected to deal with escalating enrollment.[*]

THE PREDICTION THAT PRESTON would have plenty of opposition in 1916 came true in a hurry. Merritt E. Durham, King County's superintendent of schools, launched an aggressive statewide campaign for the Republican nomination. If elected, he promised to do three things that were already hallmarks of the Preston administration at OSPI: Improve rural schools, boost vocational training and promote better relations with county and local superintendents. Ruth C. Hoffman, a veteran teacher at the State Normal School in Ellensburg, also filed as a Republican. Her platform was that the office ought to be nonpartisan. The fourth Republican in the race had a wonderful Dickensian name: DeFore Cramblitt. He was the 26-year-old principal of a Centralia elementary school. The lone Democrat in the race was the last territorial superintendent of public instruction, John H. Morgan. He had headed the math department at the Ellensburg teachers' college for 23 years.

Preston prevailed in the hotly contested primary, collecting 30 percent of the vote. The elderly Professor Morgan, crippled in a stagecoach accident in 1888, was unopposed for the Democratic nomination, collecting only about 7 percent of the vote.

In November of 1916, Preston easily won a second term, with nearly 55 percent of the vote. Her detractors were temporarily flummoxed. She was newly energized.

THE 1917 LEGISLATURE gave Preston the first victory of her second term, authorizing state-funded kindergartens. The State Federation of Women's Clubs was a staunch ally as Preston pushed for hot lunches and expanded school bus routes.

---

[*] When Preston arrived in Cathlamet for the dedication of its new school building, she met an exceptional teacher, Maude Kimball Butler, Wahkiakum County's first female school superintendent. Maude Kimball Butler would become an assistant state superintendent on Preston's staff. Her precocious daughter, Julia, was destined to become Washington's second female member of Congress.

She intensified her efforts to elevate the state to the first rank of teacher certification standards. Beginning in 1917, candidates for a teaching certificate were required to have a high school diploma and at least nine weeks of training at a teacher college. A decade later, as she was leaving office, the minimum standard was two years of training at one of the teachers' colleges. "From 1913 to 1924, teachers with diplomas and certificates from the state's five institutions of higher learning increased from 563 to 5,000," an NEA study said.

In 1919, Josephine and her mother moved into a handsome Craftsman-style house in the South Capitol Neighborhood, an easy walk to downtown shops and the Capitol.

8: Mandatory allegiance

The U.S. entered World War I in the spring of 1917 after Germany escalated its U-boat attacks on shipping in war-zone waters. Preston, like most Americans, was outraged by the mounting casualties on American vessels but prayed that "Divine Providence" would intervene. When President Wilson asked for a declaration of war, famously telling Congress "the world must be made safe for democracy," Preston wrote that he had italicized "the fundamental issue" at stake: Halting Germany's designs on "feudalistic world-dominion."

While Wilson emphasized "we have no quarrel with the German people," home-front patriotic fervor rose to incendiary levels, with a government-funded propaganda bureau fanning the flames. One military enlistment poster depicted the enemy as a barbaric "Hun," another as a "mad brute" gorilla invading the U.S. after laying waste to Europe. Americans of German ancestry—2.3 million had immigrated between 1881 and 1910—tried to lay low or emphasize their loyalty amid growing public paranoia about sabotage and subversion. "100% Americanism" became the litmus test of patriotism. Sauerkraut became "liberty cabbage"; Berlin, Iowa, changed its name to Lincoln; libraries canceled their subscriptions to German-language newspapers.

Superintendent Preston, who was named to the NEA's wartime Emergency Educational Commission, compiled and issued "A Patriotic Bulletin" to inspire school boards, educators and schoolchildren to help "crush down the evil attempt at world-wide autocracy." From her earliest days as a teacher, Preston believed the public schools had to instill patriotism. The bulletin featured Governor Ernest Lister's proclamation exhorting every Washingtonian to do his or her part to promote victory, as well as the words to *The Battle Hymn of the Republic*; Lincoln's Gettysburg Address; a primer on flag etiquette and detailed instructions for an obligatory "School Flag Salute." Preston wrote:

> At a given hour in the morning, the pupils are assembled and in their places in the school. A signal is given by the teacher. Every pupil rises in his place, while the flag is being brought forward from the door to the stand [by] the teacher. Every pupil gives the flag the military salute. …
>
> While thus standing, all the pupils repeat together, slowly and distinctly, the following pledge: "I pledge allegiance to my flag

and to the republic for which it stands. One nation, indivisible, with liberty and justice for all."

At the words "to my flag," each one extends the right hand, palm to the front, toward the flag until the end of the pledge affirmation. Then all hands drop to the side. The pupils, still standing, may sing together in unison the song "America."*

Preston's office worked with the Washington State Council of Defense—headed by Dr. Suzzallo—and the Washington Federation of Women's Clubs to promote patriotism and rally the home front to help win the war. Preston happily enlisted the state's schoolchildren in campaigns to sell "Liberty Loan" bonds. Responding to a letter from a patriotic grade-school girl, Preston urged the child to save 25 cents and buy a war bond stamp to help her country during "this great war crisis."

The Woman's Work Committee of the State Council of Defense—dubbed the "Minute Women"—had Preston's enthusiastic support, especially when it targeted teachers with "pro-German inclinations" and the radical Industrial Workers of the World. Preston viewed the "Wobblies" as home-grown Bolsheviks intent on fomenting strikes to disrupt the war and, ultimately, destroy democracy. Preston passionately believed it was the duty of educators—from the teacher at the smallest rural school to the largest public university—to inculcate students with the meaning of "Americanism." Socialist teachers and slippery "infidels" were a threat to American values, Preston wrote. She was not anti-immigrant, however. Far from it. Where you were born didn't matter so long as you were committed to becoming an American in thought, word and deed. Likely drawing on her mother's experiences at the Umatilla Indian Boarding School, Preston also understood that ruthless forced assimilation did great harm to the self-esteem and cultural heritage of Native American children. When a county superintendent asked whether Indian children should be attending the regular public schools in his jurisdiction, Preston replied, "I feel it is your duty to provide a school for those children."

Preston's hard-nosed patriotism made headlines when the Thurston County Council of Defense accused an Olympia grade school teacher of making seditious remarks at school during a Liberty Bond event. Dismissed by the school board, Charles R. Carr asked Preston to intervene. She presided over a packed hearing in the State Senate chambers, an assistant attorney general at her side. Carr admitted

---

* The original Pledge of Allegiance, first published in 1892, was likely the handiwork of Frances Bellamy, a Baptist minister. Six years later, during the Spanish American War, New York became the first state to mandate that school children recite the pledge each morning. Encouraged by the DAR and other patriotic groups, many states adopted the practice. Placing one's hand over heart while reciting the pledge replaced the outstretched arm "Bellamy salute" in 1942 because the Nazis used a similar gesture to "Heil" Hitler. *The Pledge of Allegiance* was revised in 1923 to change "my flag" to "the flag of the United States of America." In 1954, during the Cold War, "under God" was added.

Bain News Service, Library of Congress

to being a pacifist, but said he had forgotten ever having said he would not lift a finger to help the government win an "unholy, unrighteous" war. "But if I did make such a statement …I must have meant that I would not raise a finger to help kill a man." Since then, however, he had changed his mind and now believed in killing Germans, "although I would not like to kill them myself." The defendant called 16 school children, ranging in age from 8 to 10, as character witnesses. Their testimony was not reported, but "after they were sworn in" they took turns sitting in the lieutenant governor's big chair and "grinned down on the proceedings the rest of the morning." It must have been the best field trip of the school year.

Preston weighed the testimony for several days before revoking Carr's teaching certificate for "unprofessional conduct … detrimental to the interests of the government." A few months later, she revoked the teaching certificate of an Island County teacher who expressed contempt for the Red Cross and refused to require his students to salute the flag or recite the Pledge of Allegiance.

Today, Preston's hyper-patriotism may sound as radical as the radicals' disdain for the "malignant capitalism oppressing working-class wage-slaves." Praised by editorial writers around the state, her views were mainstream. The Bolshevik Revolution, anarchist bombings and labor unrest fanned the flames of nationalism. Woodrow Wilson ordered his attorney general "not to let this country see Red." The administration conducted wholesale roundups of radical unionists, suspected anarchists and "seditionists." Eugene Debs, the Socialist who had won six percent of the presidential vote in 1912, was sent to prison for denouncing the war as the handiwork of the "master class."

9: Nagging became necessary

On February 14, 1919, Lieutenant Governor Louis F. Hart, a centrist Republican, signed into law House Bill No. 20, which made it unlawful for school boards to pay women teachers less than men. The female teachers at Seattle's high schools played a key role in the campaign for the bill, Preston's top legislative goal during her first six years as state superintendent. "If the task is performed as well by a woman as a man, the pay should be the same," she said.

Governor Hart, *Washington State Archives*

Governor Lister, a liberal Democrat, would have signed it too. Suffering from heart failure and kidney disease, he was a dying man, succumbing four months later on the day before his 49th birthday. Preston and the governor had had their political differences. She wanted him to be tougher on the Wobblies. Yet he was also a longtime member of the Good Templars, an international temperance society, and unquestionably earnest.

Preston's largely successful 1919 omnibus package of school legislation also promoted vocational education and school district consolidation. It liberalized bond issue rules, boosted the salaries of county school superintendents and strengthened the teaching of patriotism and "American ideals." A one-year course in American history and government became a high school graduation requirement.

THE DEATH OF THE GOVERNOR was followed by high drama in Olympia in the winter of 1919-1920. On November 5, 1919, when Maine ratified the proposed 19th Amendment to the U.S. Constitution, the measure granting women the right to vote was still 17 states short of victory. Suffragists were prodding the new governor to call a special session of the Legislature to ratify the amendment. Carrie Chapman Catt, the president of the National American Woman Suffrage Association, and her friend Josephine Corliss Preston visited the Governor's Office. "From all accounts," it was a cordial meeting, but neither the governor nor the ladies revealed its outcome. Catt counseled patience. "I am married and I know you can't reach a man by nagging," she told a luncheon arranged by Preston. It attracted more than 40 prominent Olympia women, including First Lady Ella Hart, who was seated next to Catt and Preston. "Get out and work, all of you women, and first create a demand for the special session so that it won't embarrass the governor to call it," Catt said, adding:

> For years we have quoted the west and pointed out what you people have done. It was our chief stock in trade. We expected all the western states to rise up in unison and call special sessions to ratify the national suffrage amendment. But this is the sad, cruel part of the story. The only state to have a special session in the west so far is Kansas.

Catt said the "wets"—mostly men opposed to prohibition—were mobilizing in Washington to halt the amendment's progress. She sounded a call to arms:

> What we want you women to do is to secure the pledges of all the legislators in this state that they will meet for one day and ratify the national suffrage amendment and then adjourn.
> The second message that I have to bring to you is the future that the suffrage women are now peeping into and which we want all women to join in. It is to set up a league of women voters which would call for such things as the abolition of illiteracy, to have a nation where everyone reads, speaks and writes the English language and has love and honor for the American flag. We want to put a new aim in politics and to install something there that has been sadly lacking. So, remember first, we want you to work for this national liberation of women and second to take part in our big national program.

Afterward, Catt was "gladsomely greeted" by a cluster of influential male legislators. The ladies believed they had the votes. Getting them cast was another story.

AS 1920 DAWNED, the conspiracy-sniffing *Morning Olympian* reported that there was a "secret compact" between Governor Hart and Secretary of State Ithamar M. Howell to stave off a special session. The state was "already carrying an overdraft of $888,000 in the general fund and the need for economy in the use of public funds is absolute," the governor told reporters after a meeting with the state treasurer.

Hart was preparing for a long train trip to Washington, D.C., to promote irrigation projects. Howell would be the acting governor. If Hart encountered Carrie Chapman Catt back East, sources told the paper he would say "the whole thing" was up to the secretary of state. And if Howell was nagged by Emma Smith DeVoe, he would say that a special session was beyond his "temporary executive capacity."

Catt was not amused. In an open letter to the people of Washington the suffrage leader intimated that some members of the Legislature were also making it difficult for the governor to call a special session, "their argument being that Washington ought to wait until ratification is publicly assured in 35 other states." Catt said The Evergreen State needed to lead the way once again: "Washington, the first of the coast states to give suffrage to its own women, surely will lead the way again this time for the women of the nation."

Stopping in Spokane on his way east, the governor held a news conference at the Davenport Hotel. Judging from a house-to-house survey of women "of all classes" by a friend in Tacoma, Hart said he believed the thinking women of the state opposed a special session. His amateur pollster chum found that only "one out of 100" backed the idea. And why should he place the state "in a position of blame" if national women's suffrage ultimately failed to secure enough states for ratification?

Preston helped Catt turn up the heat. "Washington is one of the leading states in progressive, forward-looking movements," Preston said. "Whatever Washington does is regarded by other states as of the greatest importance."

The governor surrendered, calling a special session to convene on March 22. Hart declared that the session should be limited to the "Susan B. Anthony Amendment" and emergency funds for the state's colleges, their enrollment capacities overwhelmed by discharged doughboys.

Since the Legislature normally convened only in odd-numbered years, Preston jumped at the chance to secure more funds for the common schools. She was presiding over a meeting of the National Education Association in New York when a telegram arrived with the news of the special session. She immediately issued a call to all of the state's superintendents and high school principals to assemble in Olympia on the first day of the session. "Horrified" at the prospect of public-school officials descending on Olympia to corral their legislators, Governor Hart "fired off" a plaintive telegram to Chicago," one stop on Preston's train trip home. He begged her to defer the conference by a week and help hold the work of the Legislature "within reasonable bounds." Nothing doing, Preston wired back. There was a crisis in education, "and I am sure you will join me in presenting the needs of our schools to the honorable body in their true light."

Hours after she arrived back in Olympia, Preston and the chairman of the teachers' committee met with the governor and legislative leaders. The governor said the public school situation wasn't an emergency. Nonsense, the superintendent said. The only difference between the college enrollment crisis and the plight of the underfunded public schools was that public school teachers hadn't threatened to join UW professors in a mass walkout. Furthermore, "teachers were leaving the classrooms in droves, unable to subsist on the average public-school teacher's pay of $900 a year… compared to the $3,000 to $5,000 sinecures of the university instructors."

WHEN THE LEGISLATURE CONVENED, State Representative Frances E. Haskell, a Republican from Pierce County who had lobbied the First Lady to lean on her husband, escorted Emma Smith DeVoe to the House dais. Haskell, one of only two women in the 139-member Legislature, proceeded to introduce the ratification resolution with a soaring admonition that the woman's hour was at hand. "The women of our grandmothers' time lived in a very small and narrow sphere," Haskell said, "but civilization has advanced by leaps and bounds in the last quarter of a century." Now the lawmakers could:

Suffragist Emma Smith Devoe, left, and State Representative Frances Haskell, right, lobbied First Lady Ella Hart to prod her husband to call a special session. *Library of Congress and Washington State Archives*

> …prove to the world the greatness of our Evergreen state, which is not determined by the number of acres that it contains, nor by the number of its population, but by the character of its men and women who today are extending to all the women of America the privilege of the ballot. …

The suffrage amendment was duly ratified by unanimous votes in both the House and Senate.

Preston was jubilant, but soon left the packed galleries to buttonhole legislators. Her school relief package was next on the agenda. A key funding bill had failed during the regular session. An old friend—Senator Oliver Cornwell of Walla Walla County—was an important ally as chairman of the Senate Committee on Education. Late that night, the Senate passed Preston's "20-10" law, which doubled state aid to local school districts to $20 per pupil but left the counties' contribution at $10 per pupil. The House concurred. Preston had "worked it through most cleverly," newspapers reported. The lawmakers were working overtime with no per diem, so a lot happened in a hurry. Funds were also appropriated to shore up the colleges for the rest of the biennium. A committee was appointed to study the common school crisis. Preston was pleased with the increase in state aid but believed "true equalization could never be achieved through a general distribution system." In a practical compromise, she would advocate an equalization fund aimed at rural grade schools.

Tennessee put the suffrage amendment over the top on August 18, 1920, after a young lawmaker who had been opposed to votes for women changed his vote at the urging of his mother.

PRESTON BECAME A CHARTER MEMBER of the National League of Women Voters when it was formally organized in Chicago on February 14, 1920. Carrie Chapman Catt summed up the league's goal:

> The League of Women Voters is not to dissolve any present organization but to unite all existing organizations of women who believe in its principles. It is not to lure women from partisanship but to combine them in an effort for legislation which will protect coming movements, which we cannot even foretell, from suffering the untoward conditions which have hindered for so long the coming of equal suffrage. Are the women of the United States big enough to see their opportunity?

In her bid for a third term in the fall of 1920 Preston faced opposition from three other women who saw an opportunity. They were: Elizabeth Jones of Everett, a fellow Republican who shared her disdain for radicals; Catherine Montgomery of Bellingham, a Democrat active in the suffrage movement, and Alfa S. Ventzke of the newly formidable Farmer-Labor Party. Ventzke, a former North Dakota teacher, was the wife of an Okanogan farmer. Governor Hart, still smarting over being outmaneuvered by Preston in the run-up to the special session, was said to be a backstage supporter of Jones, a former Snohomish County school superintendent.

Preston was a large, immaculately groomed woman. The capital press corps portrayed her as a blend of gumption and grace—always good for a good quote. The *Olympia Daily Recorder* observed that wise men steered clear of "woman warfare." It predicted "fireworks" during the campaign. "If anything or anybody stands in the way of what Mrs. Preston considers the best educational policy for the state, that object or individual is scheduled for a remarkably busy experience with all sorts of vicissitudes." The *Seattle Post-Intelligencer* said "no other Western woman" was better known in national educational circles.

After easily outpolling Jones for the GOP nomination, Preston won re-election with 58 percent of the vote. The Farmer-Labor lady was the runner-up.[*]

For Preston, winning a fourth term in 1924 was easier yet. Chancey E. Beach, the Bull Moose candidate from 1912, was back in the GOP fold, his apostasy

---

[*] The Farmer-Labor Party, backed by the Grange, the Federation of Labor and the Socialist Party, "appeared suddenly as a new political force" in Washington's 1920 elections. Its candidates outpolled Democrats in statewide races and in many other contests. It was the best showing by the party anywhere in America outside Minnesota, where Preston was born and raised.

apparently not forgotten. Preston trounced him in the primary, carrying 38 of the state's 39 counties. In November, she received 62.5 percent of the vote.

For the 1923-24 school year, the chief statistician of the U.S. Bureau of Education ranked Washington first in the nation based on a 10-point scale that graded states on school attendance, the length of the school year, high school graduation, teacher certification, educators' salaries and per-pupil expenditures.

Josephine Corliss Preston

CANDIDATE FOR RE-ELECTION

Superintendent of Public Instruction

Republican Primary, Sept. 9th, 1924

I have a deep and abiding interest in the children of this state, and in building a school system that makes our boys and girls worthy American Citizens.

(Over)

DURING MRS. PRESTON'S TERM OF OFFICE THE FOLLOWING HAVE BEEN ACHIEVED:

1. State support of common schools raised from $10 to $20 for each census child.
2. Teachers' qualifications increased from a low minimum to one of the highest west of the Mississippi River.
3. Teachers' average annual salaries increased from $773 to $1396.
4. Annual elementary school enrollment increased from 202,499 to 247,635.
5. Annual high school enrollment increased from 27,494 to 58,440, ranking Washington second in the United States in high school development.
6. Annual number of eighth grade graduates increased from 9,867 to 17,053.
7. Annual number of high school graduates increased from 2,675 to 7,738.
8. Vocational education established and 24,595 students given specific training in their respective wage earning occupations and chosen vocations.
9. Living conditions of teachers improved. 447 teachers' cottages built.
10. Reorganization of pioneer districts has steadily taken place through consolidation of school districts into natural neighborhood or community unit districts providing rural high school advantages near home.

CITIZENSHIP.

The following laws dealing with Citizenship and Patriotic Observance have been passed:

Requiring American History and Government as a prerequisite for high school graduation; requiring school directors and teachers to be American citizens; providing penalty for not teaching patriotism; requiring Flag Salute in all schools; providing penalty for failure of school boards to replace Flag when tattered, torn or faded; requiring the observance of Temperance and Good Citizenship Day and the observance of Armistice Day.

Vote to re-elect JOSEPHINE CORLISS PRESTON, Superintendent of Public Instruction, and continue the above progressive school program.

(Over)

Washington State Historical Society

10: A MARKED WOMAN

Preston's landslide victory in 1924 was no portent of her choppy final four years as superintendent of public instruction. She disliked the new governor. And the feeling was mutual. Roland H. Hartley, a squirrely conservative with "hard blue eyes," embraced antediluvian ideas about public education. It could not have helped that Preston was at least three inches taller and fast on her feet. She was on Hartley's enemies list from day one. It was a long list, too. The controversial former Everett mayor became Washington's 10th governor in his third try after narrowly outpolling nine other Republicans in the primary. It is the consensus of Northwest historians that by comparison the polarizing Dixy Lee Ray was a veritable Lincoln.

Refusing to name a representative to the 1925 National Child Welfare Conference, Governor Hartley maintained that the common schools of the early 1890s were superior to "modern" education, even though the state had contributed nothing to their support. He fumed that on Preston's watch the total state budget for teacher salaries was now $16.6 million.* The return on that investment was sadly lacking, Hartley said:

> Can we wonder why our children go wrong? Petted, pampered, educated at the expense of the state, robbed of self-reliance and independence, we send them forth as weaklings to take up the rugged path of life for themselves.

When he vetoed an old-age pension act approved by the Legislature, Hartley declared:

> The embryo citizen we start out…coddled and prepared for a life of ease in a playhouse (public school) maintained at public expense, and then we build an alms-house in which to receive him when he has failed.

Hartley railed against Preston's "extravagant" demands for higher pay for teachers and fairer funding for rural schools. Moreover, she was an admirer of Dr. Suzzallo, the visionary president of the University of Washington. In Hartley's eyes the cosmopolitan university was an incubator of socialism. The governor was egged on by Ernest Holland, the president of Washington State College, who resented

---

* In the 12 years since Preston took office, school enrollment was up 30 percent to 329,888. The state's 11,377 teachers, on average, were paid $1,459 per year.

that Suzzallo was being paid $18,000 a year, nearly double what he was earning. Further, State Representative Duncan Dunn of Yakima, who had managed the governor's 1924 campaign, was a WSC regent.

Hartley introduced a measure in 1925 that produced "audible gasps of amazement" from the Legislature, Northwest historian David M. Buerge wrote in a 1987 essay. Claiming his plan would increase efficiency and economy in the state's higher education system, Hartley proposed:

In 1926, *The Seattle Times* skewered Governor Hartley as a pint-size tyrant. *Tom Thurlbly/Seattle Daily Times*

…to abolish the boards of regents of the UW, Washington State College, and the Normal schools, to abolish the state Board of Education, and to pass a constitutional amendment abolishing the office of state superintendent of schools. He would replace these with a single superboard made up of his appointees, who would manage the budgets of all state educational institutions from kindergarten to graduate school. …

The proposal was met with outrage from educators as well as legislators. It was quickly tabled. It split the Republican Party, but its public support would not evaporate. In a revolt actively supported by the university, the legislature voted to increase funding for higher education. Hartley vetoed the bill; the veto was overridden. In this massive repudiation, Hartley believed he saw Suzzallo's fine hand.

A year later, Governor Hartley secured Suzzallo's dismissal after replacing two of the president's supporters on the university's Board of Regents. One was Werner A. Rupp of Aberdeen, who had helped Preston win election in 1912. Another friend, Ruth Karr McKee of Kelso, the university's first female regent and a prominent club woman, resigned on the spot when the new Hartley majority fired Suzzallo. That night, 3,000 students marched to Suzzallo's home on campus, chanting "Suzzallo for governor!" Mrs. Suzzallo and Mrs. McKee joined him on the porch. "I deeply appreciate your coming here tonight," he said. "I have devoted my life to the upbuilding of the university, and I want you to devote your lives to it. Don't do anything now that will reflect discredit on your alma mater."

A citizens committee, outraged over the "ruthless exercise of executive power," drafted a recall indictment charging the governor with malfeasance, misfeasance and violation of his oath of office. They alleged he had removed regents and trustees on baseless charges and was seeking to destroy the Legislature's independence by appointing his cronies to state jobs "carrying large salaries and emoluments." Hartley shrugged it all off. Education remained in his crosshairs. When he vetoed a 1927 bill designed to equalize state support to struggling rural districts, Preston issued a stinging rebuke. She reminded the governor that the state constitution stipulated it was "the paramount duty of the state to make ample provision for the education of all children residing within its borders. …" Noting that the bill had passed the Legislature by a vote of more than four to one, Preston said that with the stroke of a pen the governor had denied 40,000 children a better education. "The purpose of the bill was to give further state support to our poor and needy school districts, thus strengthening the principle of equal educational opportunity, as initiated by the Barefoot School Boy Law, to which our state has been committed for a third of a century," the superintendent said. The Washington Education Association might well have draped in black the statue of Governor John R. Rogers in front of the Old Capitol. The populist from Puyallup was the architect of the landmark 1895 act to fund public schools.[*]

EARLY IN 1928, Noah D. Showalter, a member of the State Board of Education, announced he would oppose Preston for the Republican nomination if she sought a fifth term. Showalter, 59, was an associate of King County Superintendent Albert Burrows, still bitter over his loss to Preston in the 1912 GOP primary. The pair had long been critical of her administration. But they were no fans of Governor Hartley. In 1926, the seldom-smiling Showalter resigned as head of the teachers' college at Cheney to protest the governor's directive to its trustees to withhold expenditure of $26,000 appropriated by the Legislature. Showalter was still "expected to be the beneficiary of the Hartley forces' three-year war" against Preston, *The Seattle Daily Times* said.

Preston declared she would run on her record of "integrity, efficiency and economy" while overseeing "a state school system recognized nationally" as a leader

---

[*] Engraved at the base of the statue in Sylvester Park is a quotation that sums up Governor Rogers' Populist credo: "I would make it impossible for the covetous and avaricious to utterly impoverish the poor. The rich can take care of themselves."

in promoting educational excellence in "both city and country schools"—a record she said her political opponents had "sought in vain to discredit…through devious methods." Preston had recently enhanced her staff by appointing Elizabeth Russum, Idaho's former superintendent of public instruction, to oversee elementary-school education, particularly in rural areas.

Showalter, a widely respected educator, appears to have walked a tightrope during the campaign. Clearly "out of sympathy" with the governor's policies, Showalter was viewed by Hartley as by far the lesser of two evils. He would benefit from the Hartley machine's support, including allegations Preston branded dirty tricks.

A few weeks before the primary, rumors began circulating in solidly Republican Lewis County that Preston was in opposition to the junior college movement. Centralia College, founded in 1925, was the state's second community college; others were being planned for Skagit Valley, Yakima and Grays Harbor. In a campaign stop at Centralia, Lewis County's largest city, Preston emphasized she was an early proponent of community colleges. Her position was that before the movement gained more steam "a definite plan for financing these institutions should be legalized by the Legislature" because common school funds could not be diverted to support higher education. Preston also faced renewed criticism over alleged political bias in educational materials. During the 1924 campaign, opponents revealed she had received a total of $150 over the course of six years for "incidental expenses" in connection with vetting a series of pamphlets about the state's industries. A private-industry group supplied some of the information distributed in schools. Preston said it was only after the issue generated "political attacks" in the previous campaign that she learned some of the information was viewed by public power supporters as "thinly veiled propaganda for private ownership of public utilities." Other pamphlets made the case for public power, she said, dismissing the furor as "ridiculous."

The Seattle Daily Times, the state's largest newspaper, endorsed Preston's re-election in a front-page editorial:

> Ever since Mrs. Preston took up the duties and heavy responsibilities of her department, she has been periodically opposed by men educators. They have sought to belittle her achievements and to decry her effectiveness, but without appreciable result. …The fine record made by Mrs. Preston is apparent to everybody. It would be a serious mistake to interrupt her work. Mrs. Preston deserves another term. She should be nominated and re-elected.

Nevertheless, public power advocates joined the Hartley/Showalter forces. Badly outspent and dogged by negative publicity, Preston was trounced by Showalter, who captured 62 percent of the 1928 Primary Election vote. There being no other candidates, Showalter was all but elected then and there. The Showalter campaign spent $3,812—80 percent of which was donated by a committee. Preston raised and spent $720. Running on her record wasn't nearly enough.

A few weeks later in Washington, D.C., Preston addressed the Federal Trade Commission, which was conducting hearings on the power industry. Though it had "already exonerated her of any suggestion of impropriety," she asked for the chance to testify about her conduct in connection with the pamphlets. She categorically denied accepting payments from power companies or public utilities. Published inferences that she had been summoned to appear before the commission were "contemptible, as has been the whole political campaign against her," *The Times* said in another blast at Governor Hartley.

At the end of her testimony, there was a tidbit that might have been payback: Preston said the pamphlet had been approved by the president of one of the State Normal Schools. If that was a dig at Dr. Showalter, he had no comment. Nor did research turn up evidence it was he who reviewed the pamphlet.*

State Superintendent Noah D. Showalter. *Washington State Archives*

PRESTON MADE HER OFFICE AVAILABLE to her successor to expedite the transition. And on January 17, 1929, as Showalter took office, she turned in a final report on her 16 years as superintendent of public instruction. She pointed to higher teacher salaries, the landmark act mandating equal pay for male and female teachers; a teacher retirement fund; modernized curriculum; music and vocational programs. And, dear to her heart, dramatically better rural schools. Preston italicized the finding that Washington was now one of the top five states for teacher certification standards.

Incorrigible as ever, Governor Hartley ordered the state printer to omit from Preston's biennial report a four-page introduction that mentioned his vetoes of bills to improve the public schools, including the 1925 measure to assist handicapped students, and the 1927 funding equalization measure to aid needy rural districts.

---

* Governor Hartley was re-elected. But most of his other enemies were, too. When the Depression hit, Hartley took a broadax to the state budget. It was a singular "pleasure" for him to see the UW regents cut $1 million from the budget, allegedly "without reducing in any way the efficiency of the institution." Hartley's detractors cheered his defeat in the 1932 primary, one of the preliminary events to a national Democratic landslide that swept Herbert Hoover out and Franklin D. Roosevelt in. Superintendent Showalter was one of the few Republicans to survive the backlash. His only general election opponent in 1932 was the Farmer-Labor Party's Alfa S. Ventzke.

Newspapers around the state took note of Preston's official goodbye:

George Washington University

> After having been identified with educational work for the last 36 years in Washington, as a classroom teacher, a county superintendent of schools and superintendent of public instruction, it would be impossible for me to discontinue my activities in the educational field. After taking a much-needed rest, I shall devote the greater part of my time to writing and speaking on educational subjects. My heart will ever be in the upbuilding of the State of Washington …and I am deeply appreciative of the opportunity the people have given me for public service.

She was 55 years old. Education had been her passion from the day she was drafted at 14 to help teach the younger children of Otter Tail County.

As she left office, the Associated Press reported that the federal Department of Education once again rated Washington's schools best in the nation.

11: Belle's Ball

Always frugal, Preston had enough savings and retirement income to support herself and assist her mother. They moved to the summer cottage, "Memory Lodge," purchased years earlier at Burton, a serene waterfront settlement on Vashon Island in Puget Sound. When Mrs. Corliss returned from an extended stay in California in 1929, her daughters had a Christmas surprise: They had added a new wing to make her more comfortable.

Preston joined the Daughters of the American Revolution and the local chapter of the League of Women Voters.* She spent a semester at Columbia University in 1930, and was in demand for several years as a speaker and consultant—addressing the American Association of University Women in New York and attending National Education Association conferences as a life-member past president. Increasingly, however, she stayed close to home, nursing her bedridden mother, who died at 80 during the winter of 1933.

Later that year, *The Seattle Times*' influential society columnist, Virginia Boren, spotted Preston in the crowd at a women's literary luncheon in the posh Georgian Room of the Olympic Hotel. Despite the hard times "there were many exquisite orchids quivering on luxurious furs," Boren wrote, demonstrating her mastery of the genre. Publishing companies were once again buying books, another "good barometer of improved conditions" under Franklin D. Roosevelt. Preston was greeted warmly by old friends—Seattle club women who had rallied to her campaign in 1912. "She tells us there's a writer's club over on the island," Boren wrote.

BY 1937, Preston was back in the classroom, teaching in Maple Valley in rural King County and often filling in as school principal. Her career had come full circle.

When her old friend, State Representative Belle Reeves, an ebullient Democrat from Chelan County, was appointed Secretary of State in 1938, Preston had her last major public hurrah. The first woman elected to statewide office in Washington was the toastmistress at a gala reception and banquet honoring the second. Nearly 500 men and women from all over the state converged on the Hotel Olympian.

Preston, looking well in a dark blue dress with a silver-sequined collar, was seated next to tuxedoed Governor Clarence Martin at the head table. The governor said

---

* Preston was the regent of the DAR's Elizabeth Bixby Chapter on Vashon Island from 1950-52. Her Patriot ancestor was Timothy Emerson of Methuen, Massachusetts, who served as a private in 1777-78.

Josephine Corliss Preston, at left with Governor Clarence Martin, as the toastmistress at a 1939 banquet honoring the new Secretary of State, Belle Reeves, right. *The Morning Olympian*

of Secretary Reeves, "No hall in the state is large enough to hold those who wish her well." Bertha Knight Landes, the first female mayor of Seattle, was there, together with State Senators Pearl Wanamaker, Mary Farquharson, Lulu Haddon, Kathryn Malstrom, Nellie Tucker and an array of other elected officials, including the chief justice. Future congresswoman Julia Butler of Cathlamet, who would soon announce her candidacy for the State Legislature, was there, her mother Maude having been one of Preston's deputies.

Preston's "clever" remarks were noted in all the write-ups. Like a seasoned teacher managing a classroom, she kept the speeches short. But she allowed herself a point of privilege: Glancing around the room, she observed that the women of Washington had come a long way.

It was a long way from Fergus Falls, too.

Josephine Corliss Preston died of cancer at 85 on December 10, 1958, in a Renton hospital. Undaunted by the diagnosis, she had attended the National Education Association convention in Cleveland a few months earlier. *The Seattle Times*, her champion 30 years earlier, relegated her obituary to Page 45. The story didn't even note that her victory in 1912 was a first for a woman. Too many had forgotten she was unquestionably the architect of Washington's modern school system and a formidable politician who believed that every child—and every vote—counted.[*]

John C. Hughes
Legacy Washington

---

[*] Preston bequeathed her assets to Carleton College in Minnesota, Whitman College and her nieces and nephews. She is buried at Mountain View Memorial Park in Lakewood, Washington.

Dr. Seagrave, right, and her friend Florence Denny Heliker wore their French uniforms at a 1919 dinner in their honor at the Women's University Club of Seattle. Seagrave is wearing the silver medal she received from the French government for her heroic service. *Bushnell photo/The Seattle Times*

MABEL SEAGRAVE, M.D.

LIVING UP TO THE MOTTO

Mabel Seagrave, the "lady doctor" from Seattle, wasn't rattled by the gruesome battlefield wounds she saw in France in the long, cruel summer of 1918. Her surgical skills and bedside manner impressed everyone. In the months to come, however, *Madame la doctoresse* admitted to being overwhelmed at times by a deluge of refugees suffering from the deadly "Spanish flu." The highly contagious respiratory virus ravaged the immune systems of young soldiers in the trenches and thousands of hapless, undernourished civilians fleeing the fighting. The hunchback from a nearby village "was the nearest to an able-bodied man they could get to bury the dead."

At great peril of becoming ill herself, Dr. Seagrave stayed on after the November 11th armistice to work at a Red Cross hospital. Awarded the silver *Médaille d'honneur* as a token of France's gratitude, she had "labored as a superwoman to check the plague and relieve suffering," another volunteer said. Carrie Chapman Catt, president of the National American Woman Suffrage Association, presented Seagrave the group's Merit of Honor award, saying she had demonstrated that strength, courage and patriotism were not just male attributes.

War hero, influential surgeon, lecturer and raconteur, Mabel Seagrave would qualify as a remarkable woman in any era. In hers she was extraordinary. She was one of the first Seattle women to attend elite Wellesley College in Massachusetts. After graduating from the Johns Hopkins School of Medicine in 1911, she spent 18 months as the house physician at the New York Infirmary for Women and Children before returning to Seattle.

Judging from photos, you'd never guess that Seagrave—somber in a mannish starched white shirt and necktie—could switch from an OB-GYN lecture to show-stopping impersonations of Teddy Roosevelt, Benito Mussolini and the bawdy actress Mae West at the "Stunt Nights" staged by the Women's University Club of Seattle in the 1920s. She loved fun, fast horses and adventure.

WORLD WAR I was at its apex when Dr. Seagrave and her Wellesley chum, Florence Denny Heliker, were sent to France by the National American Woman Suffrage Association to staff a refugee hospital. Both were ardent suffragists. Heliker, in fact,

Dr. Seagrave treats a soldier with an injured foot at a field hospital in France in 1918. *University of Washington Libraries, Special Collections, UW39542*

was a granddaughter of Seattle pioneer Arthur A. Denny, an early champion of gender equality.[*]

Donning khaki uniforms, Seagrave and Heliker rejected Victorian gender norms of faint-hearted femininity. "All the male members of my family who could serve their country in the Revolutionary and Civil Wars did so," Seagrave told a reporter as she and Heliker boarded a troop ship. "As there were few men in my family able to enlist in this war, it was plainly up to me to 'carry on.' " The head of the Suffrage Association's overseas hospital unit, Dr. Caroline Finley, told a reporter that the women doctors and nurses were doing "a fine thing for suffrage." Seagrave also jumped at the chance to enhance her skills in a battlefield setting. Surgeons would be confronted with "unusual wounds" and split-second decisions, she enthused, adding:

> Just to see such cavities opened up will give the surgeon a chance to demonstrate things which heretofore have been more or less experimental. Experience gained now is going to make it possible to introduce great alleviations of suffering to the race. Military surgery in France today is of the greatest educational value, and an opportunity all surgeons must covet.

The Women's Oversea [*sic*] Hospitals, U.S.A., which sent 78 women physicians to Europe during the war, saved countless lives, Seagrave told *The Seattle Daily Times* when she arrived back home in 1919. "Not a man in the outfit," she said of the hospital where she and Heliker worked 18-hour days. "Indeed, we scarcely saw

---

[*] At the first meeting of the Territorial Assembly in 1854, Arthur Denny proposed that "all white females over the age of 18" be allowed to vote. The amendment was defeated by one vote. Washington women had to wait 56 years to achieve permanent suffrage.

Doctors, nurses and ambulance drivers at a Red Cross field hospital in France in 1918. The photo is from an album that belonged to Seagrave. *University of Washington Libraries, Special Collections, UW39907*

men at all at first. All the French males were at war, save a few tottering graybeards. We had to do all our own heavy work …including making coffins. Our plumber was a former New York actress. Our carpenter was just out of a fashionable girl's school. Our chauffeurs were all girls."

Like Seagrave and Heliker, many of the "girls" had attended prestigious women's liberal arts colleges that challenged graduates to make a difference in the world. At Barnard, Bryn Mawr, Smith, Wellesley and Vassar, sisterhood was steeped in idealism. Heliker, who could have been a Seattle society lady pouring tea at book talks, volunteered as an X-Ray technician with Seagrave's unit after undergoing weeks of training. When the ship carrying her equipment was torpedoed by a German U-Boat, Heliker "turned her hand to any and all tasks," Dr. Seagrave said. "Sometimes she was an undertaker; sometimes she assisted in the operating room." Heliker insisted that her friend was the real hero, noting that Seagrave came down with pneumonia before they departed for Europe but would not hear of being left behind. Nothing could stop her, Heliker said.

On arrival in France, they were temporarily pressed into service at a battlefield "evacuation" hospital where 12-stretcher ambulances were arriving hourly. Then, at an overwhelmed refugee hospital near Labouheyre in southern France, they discovered there were only two other physicians. Moaning, feverish people were dying, literally left and right. At the peak of the war, an

Mabel laughs as another volunteer shows off her baggy pants. *University of Washington Libraries, Special Collections, UW39906*

estimated 10,000 refugees swarmed the area around the previously "sleepy little village." Seagrave also traveled 40 miles twice a week to oversee village clinics. Her "strength was marvelous," Heliker said.

The Red Cross field hospital where they volunteered after the armistice was in an overrun town called Foug in northeastern France—the Western Front during the war. The shooting had ended, but typhoid and dysentery were rampant and the flu was more deadly than war. More American Doughboys died from diseases, primarily the flu, than were killed in combat.* The virus would claim at least 50 million victims worldwide—some say twice that. In America, an estimated 675,000 people died in one year, including Donald J. Trump's grandfather. Franklin D. Roosevelt, a young assistant secretary of the Navy, nearly died of the flu after touring the battlefields.

ANOTHER AMERICAN RED CROSS volunteer from the Pacific Northwest, Marion Randall Parsons, was convalescing at the hospital on the afternoon of November 11, 1918, when Dr. Seagrave arrived from a visit to the village. "They've signed the armistice!" she shouted. "Hurrah, the war is over!" The mayor wanted everyone to join in the celebration. And what a celebration it was, Parsons wrote in a letter home:

> We went just as we happened to be nurses in uniforms and white veils; the pharmacist in a blue apron—the cook drying reddened hands on hers; the doctor with her cap on one side, and the convalescent from Mont de Marsan with her ankles swathed in woolly white socks of trooper size. …

"Come, walk beside me," said the mayor. "I want Americans around me today."

The crowd was already gathering, drawn by the wild and joyous clangor of the church bells … A drum and a trumpet, which was spasmodically sputtering out the notes of the Marseillaise, swung into line too, and in a moment every voice in the crowd was signing, or shouting "Vive la France!" …

---

* 63,114 deaths from disease vs. 53,402 in combat

> All the crowd went with us back to the mayor's house. …"We must sing the Star Spangled Banner," I said. So we gathered together on the mayor's steps, fourteen American women, and sang with all our strength.

Seagrave remembered it as one of the great moments in her eventful life. No one who knew her was surprised by the courage and determination she demonstrated in France. She made it to Johns Hopkins on pure merit, and left a successful medical practice in downtown Seattle to volunteer for the overseas hospital. Public service was the hallmark of her medical career. She always said her goal in life was to live by Wellesley's motto: *Non Ministrari sed Ministrare*. "Not to be ministered unto, but to minister."

MABEL ALEXANDRIA SEAGRAVE was born in Cheyenne, the cattle-town capital of Wyoming, in 1882 to Arthur A. and Selina Stone Glass Seagrave. Arthur Amasa Seagrave, a descendant of Massachusetts Bay Colony Puritans, was a construction engineer for the Union Pacific Railroad. After a stint as a Wells-Fargo agent in Portland, he arrived in Seattle in 1885 and dabbled in real estate. The following year, tragedy struck the family. Selina Seagrave, only 38 years old, died of an illness. Mabel was motherless at the vulnerable age of 4. Happily, the precocious child acquired a "notably kind and devoted" stepmother two years later when her father married a Seattle woman, Sarah Chatham.

Seagrave around the age of 8 in 1890.
University of Washington Libraries, Special Collections, SOC9751

Shortly after Seattle's great fire of 1889, Mabel's father built the Seagrave Hotel, followed by a bigger and better one near Pioneer Square. It was the fourth Seattle hotel to be named the Occidental. The Seagraves lived in the five-story hotel throughout Mabel's childhood. She was an inquisitive girl who loved talking with hotel guests from far-flung places. In the summer of 1897, when Mabel was 15, Seattle became the gateway to the Klondike gold fields. Nine-thousand prospectors and suppliers departed the city's docks in the space of eight weeks. And in the months to come Seattle became a haven for returning miners. The city's hotels and boarding houses were sleeping six to a room. An estimated 20,000 newcomers arrived in 18 months. Arthur Seagrave, while "making no pretension to being a Sunday school scholar," prided himself on running an upstanding establishment. There was no "saloon bar" at the Occidental, he noted, and the "uncouth" characters flooding the city could look elsewhere for lodging, newly rich or not.

Mabel Seagrave spent her grade-school years at Denny School, an impressive new two-story building that opened in 1884 on Battery Street, between 5th and 6th Avenues in Belltown. She was an exceptional all-around student, excelling in math, biology and chemistry. She loved acting in school plays.

In 1900, at the outset of her senior year at Seattle High School, Seagrave's skill as a horsewoman was reported in a *Seattle Post-Intelligencer* feature on the growth of the Seattle Riding Club. One event—a mock "hare and hounds" chase—took place on a Saturday in September near what is now called the Central District. The chase started at the intersection of 18th Avenue and Madison Street, with the rider playing the hare galloping down 18th to the place where the pavement ended. With club-member "hounds" in hot pursuit, the hare entered "a tangle of wood roads and bypaths." Some hounds were "greatly confused." But Seagrave stayed on the hare's tail. "There was a splendid run down 17th Avenue to the flag, with a spectacular finish," the *P-I* wrote. "Miss Mabel Seagrave, mounted on her swift horse Frank, led all the way down the avenue" until Herbert S. Upper, vice president of the club, finally nudged past her "and won with scarcely eight feet to spare. So close was the finish that by unanimous sentiment of the club, the honors were divided between Miss Seagrave and Mr. Upper."

Mabel hated losing. Frank probably did, too.

Seagrave at Wellesley College around 1904. She was active in athletics and the Republican Club. *Wellesley College*

SEAGRAVE WAS CO-VALEDICTORIAN of the 65-member Seattle High School Class of 1901. Her address on the role of 20th Century women was warmly applauded by a standing-room-only crowd of 2,000 at the city's Grand Opera House.

Wellesley College, striving to geographically diversify its enrollment, may have recruited Seagrave. Likely this came at the recommendation of Florence Denny, who had matriculated at the prestigious Massachusetts school the year before. Whatever the case, the sturdy, bespectacled young woman from Seattle was a good fit. She was studious but sociable, with a puckish sense of humor. She tried her hand at everything. At the college's 1902 Field Day, Seagrave won the first low-hurdles heat and placed second overall, helping secure the championship for the Class of '05. "But no one who wandered about over the grounds through that long, golden, Indian Summer day, watching and cheering one sport after another, could help realizing that Field Day meant something besides points and class rivalry," the student newspaper said. It was a day to "rejoice in the open world of Wellesley, and take a long breath in the midst of a hurrying, restless life." Seagrave may well have written that. She was a literary editor of the *College News*, as well as treasurer of the Executive Board of Student Government. She was practically fluent in German, conversational in French and solid in Latin.

When an illness claimed her stepmother in 1903, Seagrave withdrew from college for a semester to return to Seattle and comfort her father. She was back on campus in the fall of 1904 and an enthusiastic member of the Republican Club, boosting the candidacy of President Theodore Roosevelt. With her gift for mimicry, Seagrave portrayed Roosevelt's Secretary of War, Elihu Root, at a torchlight rally. The *College News* offered a stirring account:

> "Rah, Rah, Teddy!" was the rally call that announced the assembling of Republican forces on Monday night. Such a parade, such costumes, such yells and cheers, such torch lights and illuminations, such political enthusiasm, surely have never before been known at Wellesley! … Nor were the Freshmen to be outdone, for "Roosie's Rooters" from the Noanett [dormitory] were all present in workingman's blouses and red neckties, each with a dinner pail swinging at her side. It would be impossible to tell of the costumes and cheers of all the houses.

Teddy Roosevelt was depicted on the cover of *Puck* magazine courting suffragists.

Roosevelt was handily elected. Seagrave's impersonation of the "Rough Rider," complete with bushy mustache and nose-pinching *pince-nez* spectacles, would delight friends for decades to come.

After graduating from Wellesley in 1905, Seagrave taught math at Seattle's new high school on Broadway for two

Seagrave is #34 in the 1911 class photo at Johns Hopkins Medical School. There were only seven women among the 89 graduates. *The Alan Chesney Medical Archives of the Johns Hopkins Medical Institutions.*

years before matriculating at Johns Hopkins Medical School in 1907. In order to meet the Baltimore school's stringent entrance requirements she took an intensive Physics laboratory course at the University of Washington.

A pioneer in clinical training, Johns Hopkins was also a gender-equality pioneer. Throughout the 1880s and early '90s, "women were generally considered too frivolous and delicate to handle full-strength medical education, with its gory emphasis on human anatomy and disease," historians at Johns Hopkins wrote. "So people were understandably shocked when word spread in 1893 that there were three women in Hopkins' first medical school class. The step was revolutionary. Except for a few women's colleges, very few American medical schools of any stature then allowed a woman to take a degree."*

Seagrave was one of seven women in Hopkins' 89-member Class of 1911. In 1910, women represented 2.6 percent of American medical school graduates. It wasn't until 1970 that women made up more than 6 percent of any medical school class in the United States.

In 1928, Seagrave was one of two women admitted to the prestigious American College of Surgeons. (It initiated 600 men that year.) The news made headlines throughout the West. The ACS, which admitted its first woman in 1913, initiated no more than five a year until 1975.

Fast forward to 2019: The U.S. has a serious physician shortage, yet women doctors still face career barriers. Medical association surveys and media reports point to blatant pay inequities and inadequate support for their family responsibilities, especially childcare. Women doctors say they get less respect than their male colleagues. They're second-guessed more often and subjected to slights they're supposed to shrug off. "Women physicians are all too accustomed to having the

---

* In 2018, 57 women and 63 men entered Johns Hopkins School of Medicine. Its admission rate was 3.9 percent.

Dr. Seagrave when she was establishing her successful practice as an OB/GYN specialist in Seattle. *University of Washington Libraries, Special Collections, UW39540*

title 'Doctor' left out when introduced by colleagues or addressed by staff members and patients. They're more likely than male physicians to be called by first name only at medical conferences and in clinical settings," Lisa Esposito, a writer for *U.S. News & World Report*, wrote in a 2018 study of the challenges women physicians face.

Imagine what Mabel Seagrave faced in 1911 when a female doctor was a novelty. Female physicians in her era stuck together. Seagrave wrote her father in 1910 that the female physicians of New York offered her $1,000 as an inducement to locate in Manhattan after she received her medical degree and studied abroad.

Though she loved the work, after 18 months at the New York Infirmary for Women and Children, Seagrave headed home to rapidly growing Seattle. She was impressed that Washington women had won the right to vote two years earlier, in 1910. Seattle's female physicians were among "the hundreds of thoroughly educated professional women of the city" who campaigned for the suffrage amendment approved by nearly 64 percent of the voters. Building on that decisive victory, they were now redoubling their efforts for national suffrage, outraged that the men who made the laws seemed to regard "the vote of the lowest class of their own sex …including loafers, drunkards and jailbirds …as superior to that of the highest class of women."

Seagrave, 31, was warmly welcomed by Seattle's established female physicians. Among them were Maude Parker, a dedicated suffragist, and Lillian Irwin, Sarah Dean, Mariette Marsh Armstrong, Mary Skinner, and Harriet Clark, who would serve with the Red Cross in Greece during World War I. Those women were among the seven founding members of the Medical Women's Club of Seattle, which was organized in 1906. Their ranks grew to 24 with the arrival of Dr. Seagrave in 1912. In all, there were 450 physicians in Seattle. The city's population would grow by nearly 33 percent to 315,000 between 1910 and 1920.

Seagrave's energy registered immediately as the Medical Women's Club reached out to female physicians around the state. And in Oregon and Idaho as well. The goal was creation of a Tri-State Women's Medical Society. Nena J. Croake, a Tacoma doctor elected to the Legislature in 1912, was an enthusiastic supporter of their efforts to advance the standing of women physicians. Croake, was vice president of the Washington Equal Suffrage Association, and had been active in the suffrage movement since 1889.

DR. SEAGRAVE'S JOHNS HOPKINS degree and overseas exploits opened doors. Her sheer competence and force of personality—together with the lingering frontier character of the Northwest in her era—also helped her gain entrée denied to women doctors in the East. In her study of women physicians and the profession of medicine from 1850 to 1995, Ellen S. More writes:

> [W]omen who did become physicians faced extremely limited opportunities for internships, residencies, hospital staff positions, medical school faculty appointments, specialty society memberships—that is, for entrée to the profession's upper tiers. Many women physicians continued to work as generalists in private practice or in community health long after male physicians began joining the ranks of hospitals, medical schools, and specialty societies.

The Brooks Brothers shirts and neckties Seagrave wore early in her career likely were part of her doctor "uniform" to counter gender bias. Or perhaps they suited her fine. Seagrave may have been a trailblazer in that regard as well. By the mid-1920s, however, when she was a revered member of the King County Medical Society, she wore dresses. The women's news pages of *The Seattle Daily Times* remarked on the blue lace gown, accented by an orchid corsage, she wore at a high-society wedding reception.

She was "Dr. Mabel" to her friends. Her patients, especially children, loved her "gentle, reassuring smile." To have "a little chat with her was to get a sunnier slant on life," the *King County Medical Bulletin* wrote.

Seagrave volunteered early on with the Children's Welfare Division of the Seattle Health Department, overseeing dental clinics for underprivileged children. Her Wellesley and Soroptimist Club friend, Florence Denny Hellker, was now a probation officer with the county Juvenile Court. Seagrave volunteered to help there, too, as well as at Seattle's new Children's Orthopedic Hospital.* Her OB-GYN practice thrived. Her lectures on infant care drew crowds of women to the Bon Marché department store. She reported on child-care facilities in Seattle.

Seagrave was accorded privileges at all of Seattle's hospitals and became chief of staff at Seattle General Hospital. The hospital's internship program for nurses and physicians was one of her abiding interests. She gave lectures warning against the over-prescription of morphine, and in 1926 delivered an address to the State Conference of Social Agencies on the underlying causes of "sex delinquency" among young girls—a hot topic in the "Roaring Twenties." Seagrave was simultaneously liberal and conservative, freely offering her married patients advice on contraception,

---

* The Dr. Mabel Seagrave Guild of Children's Orthopedic Hospital was organized in 1937 by her friends and admirers.

yet also worrying that too many young people were "in a modified way having trial marriages." She wrote:

> The ease with which contraceptives are purchased at cigar stores and drug stores has given youth a false sense of security from possible infection and conception, and in the absence of any idealism about marriage and home many have in their own language "gone the limit."

The era had become so promiscuous, she added, that some "more or less steadily employed" young women were occasionally having sex "for monetary gain, but more commonly in exchange for a good time. In fact, these girls consider themselves quite apart from prostitutes for three reasons: first, they have other means of support; secondly, they have only one or two men with whom they have intercourse; thirdly, they charge no fee. They feel no inferiority." Worse, Seagrave wrote, she was seeing increasing numbers of freewheeling young women coming to her for pregnancy tests, having been "told by their men friends that everyone has abortions—that there is nothing to that." Her conclusion was that "the pendulum" had swung too far to the side of "lawlessness and individual freedom."

IN 1921-22, Seagrave headed the committee that oversaw construction of the impressive new home of the Women's University Club. Wearing the caps and gowns of their alma maters, the club's present and past trustees, each carrying a lighted candle, descended the staircase into the drawing room and placed the candles on the fireplace mantel. To signify hospitality, Dr. Seagrave lit the fire with "a great green candle."

She was a patron of the Cornish School of Music and the Seattle Art Museum, as well as regional director of the Soroptimist Clubs, dedicated to improving the lives of women and girls around the world.

Never married, Dr. Seagrave shared her home with her father, who died at the age 85 in 1927. "For a year I tried to go on living at my old home, but it was too lonesome," she told the Johns Hopkins alumni bulletin. She rented out the house and moved in with a dear friend from Wellesley's Class of 1909, Willye Anderson White, the widow of a prominent Seattle financier. Dr. Seagrave became an honorary aunt to her friend's three children—Fred, 18, Horace, 16, and 9-year-old Willye Jr. In January of 1929, the five of them set sail from San Francisco on an ocean liner for a trip around the world. They spent three months in Vienna, where Seagrave met with noted surgeons and visited hospitals. From there they rented a motor car and roamed Eastern Europe. The "trip of a lifetime" included a flight from Paris to London. "I highly recommend the air to all," Seagrave wrote.

Seagrave and White were having a quiet Sunday dinner at home when the doctor suffered a cerebral hemorrhage. She died at 53 on November 10, 1935.[*] It was the day before the 17th anniversary of the armistice that ended the suffering "she had worked to alleviate with skill and valor," one eulogy said. A few days earlier, Dr. Seagrave had attended a symposium on World Affairs.

"She was a woman of fortitude," the *King County Medical Bulletin* wrote. "Her passing was as she would have chosen. There was 'no sadness of farewell.' There were no long days and nights of illness and failing strength; there was no time at which she was not at her accustomed post of duty in service to others." Fifteen Seattle physicians were honorary pallbearers. Ironically they were all men.

Dr. Seagrave bequeathed a diamond ring to White; $1,000 to her office nurse and $500 to the Children's Orthopedic Hospital. Most of the rest of her estate, estimated at $15,000 to $20,000 overall—$275,000 to $350,000 in 2018 dollars—was left to Florence Denny Heliker and White's daughter.

In a letter to their Wellesley friends, Willye White wrote that Seagrave gave away more money than anyone knew. "She was always putting some youngster through college and I suppose never turned down anyone who asked for help. That's who she was."

John C. Hughes
Legacy Washington

---

[*] Dr. Seagrave's death certificate was signed by her friend and personal physician, Minnie B. Burdon, another OB-GYN specialist who had been active in the suffrage movement.

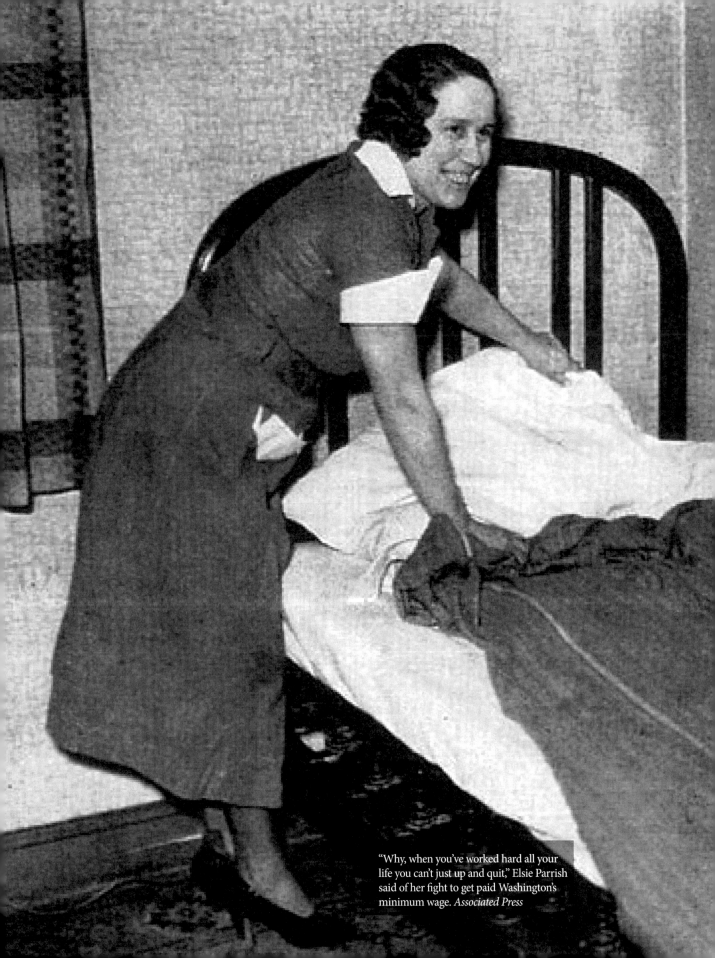

"Why, when you've worked hard all your life you can't just up and quit," Elsie Parrish said of her fight to get paid Washington's minimum wage. *Associated Press*

ELSIE PARRISH

WORKING CLASS SHERO

Elsie Parrish had reached her limit. No stranger to perseverance, she was a toddler when her father died in a gruesome farm accident. She was married at 15 and bore seven children. As a chambermaid, she scrubbed toilets and changed bed sheets for a living. And in the spring of 1935, she just wanted what she was owed for working at Wenatchee's splendid Cascadian Hotel.

With the countryside pink in the fragrant blush of its signature apple orchards, Elsie walked to the handsome Doneen Building, a block from the Cascadian, and the law office of Charles Burnham Conner. Her question was simple: Why shouldn't the hotel owners pay her what state law required?

Washington was the fourth state in the union to adopt a minimum wage law for women. And Elsie knew she wasn't paid the prescribed minimum of $14.50 for a 48-hour week.

Yes, she had cashed her deficient paychecks in the depths of the Great Depression, when Wenatchee's unemployment rate stood at a stubborn 24 percent. "I took what they gave me because I needed this work so badly," she said. Still, it gnawed at her that the hotel, over the course of a year, had shorted her $216.

Her gumption appealed to Conner, a part-time justice of the peace known as "C.B." He agreed to take her case, even though she couldn't afford to pay him. He would soon learn the hoteliers didn't dispute Elsie's job performance. Or the chambermaid's math. And they were versed in state law. They just believed it was unconstitutional.

The U.S. Supreme Court had famously ruled several times against state regulation of wages and work conditions. The white male justices, seemingly frozen in a 19th century view of laissez-faire economics, had decreed in 1923 that a minimum wage violated a woman's right to make her own contract with an employer.* That was a Constitutional liberty, they opined, no matter how callous an employer might be.

By a narrow majority, the high court once again reached that conclusion just six months before they took up Elsie's complaint, when they considered the case of Joe Tipaldo, a laundry manager. Tipaldo admitted he had only pretended to pay his

---

* In 1923's *Adkins v. Children's Hospital of D.C.*, the U.S. Supreme Court ruled a minimum wage violated the Fifth Amendment's due process clause.

women employees New York's minimum wage. In fact, Tipaldo forced the laundresses to kick back one-third of their wages to him.

Even then, the court once more invoked a woman's right to contract while invalidating New York's minimum wage. "The sacred right of liberty to contract again," scoffed Secretary of the Interior Harold Ickes. "The right of an immature child or a helpless woman to drive a bargain with a great corporation."

In its conservative interpretations, the court

Wenatchee's apple orchards blooming in a 1928 photo by Asahel Curtis. *Washington State Digital Archives*

had also swatted down a dozen of President Franklin D. Roosevelt's New Deal proposals aimed at economic relief and recovery. "After slaughtering practically every New Deal measure that has been dragged before it," one national columnist wrote, the court's halls were "as in the last act of a Shakespearean tragedy, strewn with the gory dead."

This is what Elsie, a grandmother without a gray hair, was up against.

When all the lawyers were done deliberating, to the nation's surprise, the chambermaid's case would take a stunning turn. And she played a pivotal role in a profound change in the justices' thinking.

The victory won by this "ordinary Washington citizen benefited millions of other low-income Americans," says Gerry L. Alexander, former chief justice of the Washington Supreme Court.

"Not only did it give the green light to the states to pass minimum-wage laws, which are ubiquitous today," Alexander says. "But it quickly opened the floodgates to other New Deal legislation, such as the Social Security Act, which has had a huge effect on just about everyone in our nation."

As one historian put it, Elsie Parrish "detonated" a revolution in how American courts viewed the Constitution.

Surprisingly, history's gaze was never really trained on the 38-year old grandmother. Instead, attention dwelled on why Justice Owen Roberts reversed his position and shifted the court's teetering balance in a new direction.

The chambermaid's legacy is so overlooked and untold that many of Elsie's descendants had no idea she was at the center of a landmark lawsuit. Among the clueless was Barbara Roberts, her grandniece and Oregon's first woman governor. Roberts only recently learned about Elsie's landmark victory from Helen Knowles, a professor in New York writing a book about Parrish.

ELSIE DELIAH MURRAY was born in 1899 in Penalosa, Kansas, in the south-central part of the state, about 60 windswept miles west of Wichita. Elsie's family had come to America from Ireland in the early 1700s. They eventually made their way west to Illinois and then on to the sparsely populated Great Plains where bison and Indians roamed just several decades before.

Elsie's father, Ed Murray, was "one of the most highly respected citizens of the county." When Elsie was 15 months old he was killed in what the *Wichita Eagle* called "one of the more deplorable and horrible accidents which ever has occurred in Reno County." Murray was walking on top of a thresher that separated grain from stalk when he slipped and stepped into its rotating cylinder and blades. His leg was almost torn from his body. "With almost superhuman strength he struggled from the machine and had pulled himself free…before any help reached him." He died a few hours later.

Elsie's oldest brother drowned the next year. Her mother was left with a 160-acre farm and six children under 14 to care for. Emma Murray soldiered on as a single mother until she remarried in 1907.

Elsie married her first husband, Roy Lee, and had her first child when she was 15. *David Buck*

Family members, including Elsie, later migrated west to homestead in Montana. So did the Lee family, whom the Murrays knew, from a neighboring Kansas township. Both the Murrays and Lees ended up living near Coffee Creek, Montana. Elsie married Roy Lee, nine years her senior. She gave birth to their first child in 1915, five days shy of her 16th birthday.

Details are scant about their lives in Montana. In 1927, their 8-year old son died. It's not clear how, says Knowles, a political science professor at State University of New York at Oswego.

With the Depression gripping the country, the couple and their six remaining children trekked to Neppel, Washington. (With a population of just over 300, it became Moses Lake in 1938.) When Elsie and Roy arrived, Neppel's sizable lake supported some agriculture and fishing. Disputes over water rights kept the community from growing much until the 1940s when the Grand Coulee Dam provided

Elsie worked at the Cascadian Hotel on the day of her wedding to Ernest Parrish.

irrigation to the arid landscape. It's not clear how the Lees survived in Neppel, but their marriage did not. Elsie divorced Roy, finally unable to tolerate his alcoholism.

By 1933, Elsie had moved about 70 miles west to Wenatchee, a crossroads city of river and rail transportation ambitious enough to proclaim itself "Apple Capital of the World." Elsie, a single mother, started working at the Cascadian Hotel for 22½ cents an hour. The next year, she wed Ernest Parrish, who listed "orchard work" as his occupation on their marriage license. She worked a full shift, court records show, on the day of her wedding.

The Cascadian was part of a growing chain that would become Seattle-based Westin Hotels. An imposing mix of Art Moderne and Beaux Arts styles, it was the tallest building in Wenatchee, with 184 rooms and amenities such as air conditioning. It remains the city's tallest building.*

Two decades before the Cascadian welcomed its first guests, the 1911 Triangle Shirtwaist Factory fire had spurred reforms in work conditions. New Yorkers, including FDR's future Labor Secretary, Frances Perkins, watched in horror that Saturday afternoon while smoke billowed from a 10-story Greenwich Village building. Factory owners had locked some doors so they could check workers for stolen goods before they left the premises. The factory's single fire escape collapsed due to heat and overloading. Forty-seven workers, mostly young immigrant women, jumped from the 8th and 9th floors to their deaths. In all, 146 workers died

The Triangle Shirtwaist Factory's only fire escape collapsed in a blaze that killed 146 workers and spurred labor reforms. *Kheel Center, Cornell University*

* Financially troubled, the Cascadian was converted to subsidized apartments for the elderly in the 1970s.

HATS OFF TO THIS WAITRESS

MISS ALICE LORD.

Alice Lord organized Seattle waitresses to lobby for minimum wages and an 8-hour day. *The Spokane Press,* June 4, 1910

in New York's most lethal workplace tragedy until the terrorist attack on the World Trade Center.

In Seattle, reformer Alice Lord had already organized the Waitresses Union, Local 240, to lobby for better conditions for women who tended to be single, worked nights, served strangers and were eyed with suspicions of immorality. Lord pushed for an eight-hour day, six-day work week, and a minimum wage. She was also a suffragist, helping women in Washington win the right to vote in 1910, a decade before the 19th Amendment extended suffrage to female citizens in all states. Soon, Washington lawmakers would pass a minimum wage for women—with a twist.

The 1913 Legislature featured the state's first two women representatives, Frances Axtell of Bellingham and Nena Jolidon Croake of Tacoma. Both women had campaigned for a minimum wage. But it was Croake, a physician, who sponsored a bill to that effect. Her version languished until the final days of the session, when it was voted down.

A minimum wage for women wasn't unpopular. Its supporters included Progressive movement reformers, women's clubs, the state labor federation, and others who worried that poverty was the "parentage of prostitution." Washington didn't have much in the way of sweatshops then, but many advocates saw a minimum wage as a preventive measure to protect women's virtue and health, while stabilizing society and lifting morals.

Business leaders in Washington were largely indifferent to the idea. Their apathy, in part, owed to the fact that women accounted for just 4 percent of all the state's employees in manufacturing. Business leaders also knew they faced a zealous coalition. Newly armed with the vote, "an unprecedented number of women flocked to the Capitol to lobby." One legislator said they made an opponent "look like a mangy kitten in a tiger fight."

Male lawmakers said they disagreed with Croake's proposal to set a specific floor of $1.25 per day for women's pay. Instead they overwhelmingly supported a bill by state Senator George Piper of Seattle that created a state Industrial Welfare

State Rep. Nena Jolidon Croake proposed a daily minimum wage of $1.25 for women in 1913. *Washington State Archives*

Commission to determine wages for women and children. Some said the commission's deliberations would be more legally defensible than Croake's flat wage for all.

Governor Ernest Lister quickly appointed three women commissioners to survey wages around the state.* A newspaper editor in Everett called the trio "emissaries of His Satanic Majesty in the guise of halo-lighted angels of philanthropic regard." In early 1914 the commission set minimum weekly wages in different industries: $8.90 for workers in manufacturing, $9 for laundry and telephone operators, $10 for mercantile and clerical employees.

In 1918, the commission increased the minimum to $13.20 in all industries, and eventually to $14.50 by the time Parrish filed her lawsuit.

Passed first in Massachusetts, then Oregon, Utah and Washington, minimum wage laws didn't sweep the heartland because of the "decidedly hostile treatment that the first round of laws received at the U.S. Supreme Court."

Starting with the *Lochner* case in 1905, a narrow majority of the justices ruled that state regulations of work conditions ran afoul of 14th Amendment protections against state deprivations of "life, liberty, or property, without due process of law." This logic was applied to wages in 1923's *Adkins v. Children's Hospital*, a decision against the District of Columbia's minimum wage law.**

Despite the odds, Elsie Parrish was determined to take on one of Wenatchee's biggest employers even if it meant risking job prospects in her adopted hometown.

ON JUNE 10, 1935, Charles B. Conner tossed the rock that would start a judicial avalanche. He filed *Ernest Parrish and Elsie Parrish, his wife, vs. West Coast Hotel Company* at the Chelan County Courthouse. (Washington's community property law did not then allow married women to file lawsuits in their own names.)

Conner's motive for taking on such a long shot—at some expense—appears to come from a sense of social justice, Professor Knowles says. Conner believed charitable work was a lofty calling, Gerry Alexander points out.

"I would be false to myself did I think of compensation from this case as is measured by money," Elsie's attorney wrote. "Working women are receiving better wages, children have more food and better clothes. May I not have a reason to hope that I have served my country and in this thought receive a very handsome remuneration indeed?"

Back in Wenatchee, Parrish and Conner were quickly dismissed by Superior Court Judge William O. Parr, who relied on the *Adkins* precedent in his October 1935 ruling that the state minimum wage was unconstitutional.

---

* The first three commissioners were Theresa McMahon, an economics professor at the University of Washington, Florence Swanson, a social worker, and Mrs. Jackson Stillbaugh, prominent in women's clubs.

** Because *Adkins* concerned the District of Columbia—governed by Congress, not state officials—the court relied on the Fifth Amendment's "due process" guarantee. In cases of *state* law, the court cited the 14th Amendment.

Conner would not quit.

He appealed to the state Supreme Court. He argued Parrish's pay was a matter of statewide concern. He insisted her cause "reaches into every home where the woman does or may have to perform labor for the purpose of feeding herself and children."

The Cascadian's lawyer, Fred Crollard, a former Wenatchee Chamber of Commerce president, stuck to the U.S. Supreme Court's arguments against minimum wage laws.

The state Supreme Court issued a unanimous decision on April 2, 1936.

It was written by Chief Justice William J. Millard, a Republican. Millard had worked in railroad yards and was a proud member of the Brotherhood of Locomotive Engineers. During his 1936 election campaign, he gave his view of a jurist's role: "I don't consider cases as much as a judge as like a human being. The law should be used to further progress, not block it."

A minimum wage would counter the "harsh and greedy employer," said Washington Supreme Court Chief Justice William J. Millard. *Washington State Digital Archives*

In upholding the minimum wage, Millard said low-paid employees, "are prone to accept pretty much anything that is offered" given their circumstances. "They are peculiarly subject to the overreaching of the harsh and greedy employer," he continued. "The evils of the sweating system and of the long hour and low wages which are characteristic of it are well known."

Good quotes for the newspapers, but the chief justice stood on shaky legal ground. Because the *Adkins* case involved the District of Columbia, Millard concluded that the high bench had not explicitly shot down a *state* minimum wage law. "The same Constitution applies" to states and the District of Columbia, former chief justice Gerry Alexander, notes.

Crollard later asked Millard how he could have reached such a decision in light of what the U.S. Supreme Court had said in *Adkins*.

"Well," the justice replied, "let's let the Supreme Court say it one more time."

THE HIGH COURT's rulings against minimum wages were largely the work of a group of conservatives known as the "four horsemen." Depending on your politics, their nickname referred to Notre Dame's fearsome football backfield of the era or the Biblical heralds of apocalypse, Alexander says. The four were Justices George Sutherland, Willis Van Devanter, Pierce Butler and James McReynolds, "the latter generally being considered the most curmudgeonly person ever to sit on that court." (McReynolds was so anti-Semitic that he refused to speak to fellow Justice Brandeis.)

The horsemen were old in age and old world in their thinking. Only Butler

The U.S. Supreme Court in 1937. Front: Justices Brandeis, Van Devanter, Hughes, McReynolds and Suther-land. Back: Justices Roberts, Butler, Stone and Cardozo. *United States Supreme Court*

was born (1866) after the Civil War. Their average age was 74. "They were also, in a philosophical sense, 19th-century men who regarded laissez-faire—the principle opposing governmental interference in economic affairs—as enshrined in the Constitution," Alexander says.

A trio of reliable liberals often stood against them. These "three musketeers" were Louis Brandeis, Benjamin Cardozo and Harlan Fiske Stone. This left Chief Justice Charles Evans Hughes and Justice Owen Roberts as the swing votes.

Roberts, the youngest member of the court at 61, was best known as a prosecutor in the Teapot Dome scandal that tainted the presidency of Warren G. Harding. Roberts often rode with the four horsemen, giving them the edge in many cases scrapping planks of the New Deal. The conservative majority rejected farm debt relief, coal industry regulations, municipal bankruptcy relief, industrial rules aimed at lifting wages, and more.

It was, some complained, "government by judiciary."

Nevertheless, in June 1936, Justice Roberts stuck with the four horsemen again in the Tipaldo decision against New York's minimum wage, while Chief Justice Hughes sided with the liberal minority. That 5-4 alignment seemed to spell doom for Parrish even though that notorious decision (known in legal circles as *Morehead v. N.Y.*) was "among the most unpopular ever rendered by the Supreme Court."

It came at a time when populist movements, led by the likes of Father Charles Coughlin and Huey Long, were barnstorming for social justice, labor rights and redistributing wealth. Newspaper editorials pilloried the court's cold narrow vision. Even FDR foes said the court had stooped to extremism. Conservative Congressman Hamilton Fish said the justices handed down a "new Dred Scott decision" condemning three million women and children to economic slavery.*

The negative publicity filtered down to Tipaldo. "After the court decision, business looked good for a while," the laundry manager told a reporter months later. "I was able to undercharge my competitors a little on what I saved in labor costs."

Then business started to fall off. "My customers wouldn't give my drivers their wash," he said.

The Parrishes adopted one of Elsie's grandchildren, Darald, who decades later told his daughter that Elsie fought for women's rights, all the way to the Supreme Court. *Debbie Stewart*

Before the summer was over, the Bright Light Laundry folded and Tipaldo was unemployed. "I'm broke now," he confessed. "I couldn't stand the gaff."

The public shellacking seemed to have bruised the court, as well. Just months after the New York decision, the justices agreed to revisit minimum wages by taking an appeal from the Cascadian's owners, which became *West Coast Hotel Co. v. Parrish.*

Shortly before the justices heard arguments, a newspaper reporter and photographer caught up with Elsie in her new job at a hotel in Omak, 90 miles north of Wenatchee. They said they wanted the story of her life. "My goodness," she said, thinking they were mistaken. They pumped her for details of her early marriage, her grandchildren, and her willingness to help her husband "keep the wolf from the door" while raising six children.

"Why, when you've worked hard all your life, you can't just up and quit," she said. In one of the few pictures ever published of her, Parrish smiles, making a bed in her crisp uniform and low heels.

With the time and cost of traveling to the nation's capital sinking in, her attorney sought help from state officials, pleading "the welfare of the whole state is at stake." Conner even wrote a letter to state Attorney General Garrison Hamilton saying that supporting Parrish would help Democratic candidates win elections in 1936. Arguments for Parrish's case were scheduled for mid-December. A state assistant attorney general, Wilbur Toner,

---

* The 1857 Dred Scott decision "upheld a slave's status as a piece of property that could be carried from state to state, including free states."

Parrish's Supreme Court victory made headlines, although history's gaze didn't focus on the plucky chambermaid.

already had plans to be in Washington, D.C., at the time. Toner would argue Parrish's case before the high bench, sparing Conner the long trip. While Parrish awaited the justices' decision—which wouldn't be announced for three months—President Roosevelt stunned the country. Infuriated at the "horsemen" for trampling his ideas, and emboldened by his 523-to-8 electoral vote margin in 1936, FDR flexed his power like no other chief executive. He wanted to alter the very foundation of the nation's judicial system. On February 5, 1937, Roosevelt proposed that the president could appoint a new federal judge for every judge over 70 who was not retired. Because the current Supreme Court was the most aged in history, Roosevelt would be able to add as many as six new justices to the bench. While many Americans might not grasp the labor rights detailed in FDR's Wagner Act, they could understand his mighty grab for judicial power.

MARCH 29th CAME during the Easter holidays, with the capital resplendent in cherry blossoms. On that Monday morning, tourists and children filled the steps of the Supreme Court building. They lined up in record numbers to enter the marble palace, opened two years earlier, with "Equal Justice Under Law" chiseled above its columns. It was to be the first day of rulings handed down since FDR had suggested packing the court. Newshounds would not be disappointed.

Chief Justice Hughes, who narrowly lost to Woodrow Wilson in the 1916 presidential election, was known for leading the court with the skill of a symphony conductor. The silver-bearded judge began his analysis by stating why Parrish's case called for "fresh consideration" of the court's *Adkins* decision.

There was the "importance of the question" to states with minimum wage laws like Washington's, Hughes said, and the narrowest of margins in the *Adkins* ruling.

But more important were the economic miseries of the Depression and the court's reliance, while striking down state wage laws, on the doctrine of freedom to contract.

"What is this freedom?" Hughes asked. "The Constitution does not speak of freedom of contract."

He turned to women's welfare. "What can be closer to the public interest than the health of women and their protection from unscrupulous and overreaching employers?" If protecting women was in a state's interest, he said, it only followed that a minimum wage was legitimate.

Hughes then added an "additional and compelling" argument. The exploitation of "relatively defenseless" employees not only injured women, it burdened the larger community. What "these workers lose in wages," he reasoned, "the taxpayers are called upon to pay."

He called that burden "a subsidy for unconscionable employers."

The scales of justice were tilting left. With Roberts joining the liberals this time in a 5-4 majority, the Chief Justice confessed an earlier error by the court. Hughes concluded that *Adkins v. Children's Hospital* "should be, and it is, overruled," and the Washington state Supreme Court judgment on behalf of Elsie Parrish "is affirmed."

Some two years after Parrish last swept rugs in the Cascadian, the Wenatchee chambermaid was to receive her $216.19 in back pay.

Some ardent feminists argued that women shouldn't enjoy any special privileges, including a minimum wage. But most reformers hailed the *Parrish* ruling as a proper response to grim times when it had become clear the "market and states had found the crisis beyond their competence."

The court's reversal in Parrish—really Justice Roberts' reversal—could be seen as reflecting changes in ideology across the legal profession in 1937, Bernard Schwartz wrote in *A History of the Supreme Court*. In this transformed thinking, unregulated markets were not meeting minimum needs of human welfare. If there ever was a need for the federal government to exert power, it was aroused during the Depression.

On the day *Parrish* was decided, the Court also upheld the rights of railroad workers to unionize and affirmed a revised version of a law that made it harder for banks to repossess farms. (Justices had struck down the original one in 1935.) The court's shift hinted at massive changes to come.

Two weeks later, the court again marched in a new direction. In another 5-4 vote, with Roberts joining the liberals, the court validated the Wagner Act. Called the "Magna Carta of the American labor movement," it guaranteed workers' rights to bargain collectively and strike, while barring paid goons from interfering.

In the following month the justices turned aside challenges to the Social Security Act. In doing so, they gave broad authority to Congress to tax and spend for the public welfare, including on unemployment insurance created by the act. It marked a new role for government.

Thanks to the "constitutional revolution" Elsie Parrish helped spark, Secretary of Labor Frances Perkins, the nation's first female presidential cabinet member, got most of her ambitious agenda, including a federal minimum wage, passed.*

DID THE THREAT of FDR's court-packing plan cause Justice Roberts' critical conversion? Some had presumed so, giving life to a twist on the saying about thriftiness that a "stitch in time saves nine." After Roberts' reversal in *Parrish*, it became "the switch in time that saved nine"—referring to the nine justices being spared from FDR's proposal.

Frances Perkins became a work-place-safety investigator after she witnessed the Triangle Shirtwaist Factory fire. It "was the day the New Deal was born," said Perkins, who was President Roosevelt's Secretary of Labor. *Frances Perkins Center*

On closer examination, though, many historians have discounted that theory. The Parrish case was argued on December 16 and 17, 1936. Justice Stone, a stalwart liberal, was in the hospital then. In their closed-door conference on December 19, justices were deadlocked four-to-four on Parrish, with Roberts deserting the conservatives. Hughes persuaded the justices to hold off announcing their decision until Stone returned. But the justices knew how he would vote. In effect, Parrish was already decided, some six weeks before FDR unveiled his court-packing scheme. The public didn't know that.

"It is too facile to state that the 1937 change was merely a protective response to the Court-packing plan, to assert, as did so many contemporary wags, that a 'switch in time saved Nine,'" Schwartz wrote. Evidence supports Chief Justice Hughes' later statement that the "President's proposal had not the slightest effect on our decision."

It's possible that Roberts' heart and mind had finally been opened to laissez-faire's inability to meet the Depression's pressing problems.**

History will never know for certain what motivated Roberts' change of mind, says Gerry Alexander, who has written about the Parrish case for the State Historical Society and Washington Bar Association. Roberts was a private man and closemouthed about the matter for the rest of his life. "Judges are like everyone else," Alexander says. "We aren't the same all of our lives. I think he just changed his mind."

---

* Perkins would see all of her New Deal priorities become law except for one: universal access to health care.

** Justice Cardozo, a virtuoso of persuasion, had been steering the court to new thinking that the law was not immutably Newtonian. "To him, the law was neither an *is* nor an *ought*; it was also an endless *becoming*."

PARRISH's UNAPPRECIATED legacy still echoes around modern Washington. In 2018, Washington had the highest minimum wage of any state, $11.50 per hour. California and Massachusetts joined Washington at the top in 2019, with hourly minimum wages of $12.

Shortly after her Supreme Court victory, Elsie Parrish disappeared from the public eye. Later accounts and records had her toiling in Omak, where her husband worked at a lumber mill, then they moved to Snohomish County, and on to southern California. Although her case later "launched a thousand law review articles," she was never the story. She was not prominent in feminist or labor-history literature—or even in family lore.

Elsie's grandnephew, Bill Murray, a Washingtonian, says he reached out to a number of relatives after learning of her lawsuit from the Wenatchee Valley Museum and Cultural Center in 2013. "Other than one distant cousin, who had a newspaper clipping about the trial in her grandmother's keepsake box that she always wondered about, no one was aware of Elsie's Supreme Court adventure," Murray says.

He did recall meeting Elsie at a couple family gatherings when he was a boy. If his parents ever discussed her lawsuit with him he doesn't remember.

Ernest and Elsie Parrish settled in California in the 1940s. *Wenatchee Valley Museum and Cultural Center*

Barbara Roberts, the former Oregon governor, thinks Elsie's legacy took a back seat in the male-dominated clan. "Hers was a female and legal story in a family of mostly farmers and ranchers. You have to have the right people to get stories told."

Debbie Stewart, a great granddaughter, says Elsie was a big part of her upbringing in Southern California and bought her a middle-school graduation dress. Stewart's father, Darald, was actually Elsie's grandson, the son of her oldest daughter Vera. But Ernie and Elsie adopted him as their son and Stewart knew Elsie as her grandma. Stewart recalls Elsie as sweet but stern, fond of crocheting and gardening, with a "you kids got it easy" toughness forged in the Depression. One afternoon in April 1980, after going to see her newly-born great great grandson, Elsie came home, took a nap, and died in her sleep, Stewart says.

Stewart, also a Washingtonian, says her father told her about the legendary lawsuit, but she never talked about it with Elsie.

Elsie did finally get some recognition decades later when author Adela Rogers

Debbie Stewart, on hobby horse, recalls Elsie, her great grandmother, as sweet but stern. *Debbie Stewart*

St. Johns tracked her down in Anaheim, Calif. Then the plucky chambermaid was elevated to royalty in St. Johns' 1974 book, *Some Are Born Great*, a feminist version of John F. Kennedy's *Profiles in Courage*.

Parrish came to the door "looking much younger than I had expected, dressed in something pink and fresh-washed and ironed," St. Johns wrote of Parrish, then a septuagenarian like the author. Parrish said she was surprised that few women seemed to pay much attention to her historic triumph.

"I had to do it," she told St. Johns, herself a trailblazing female journalist. "What they did wasn't *right*."

The author was astonished at the possibility that "the women of Lib and let Lib do not know the name of the woman who won this early big victory for them, bigger than the Vote, which of course was inevitable?"

There are questions about the accuracy of St. Johns' tribute to Parrish. In a few pages, St. Johns says four times that Parrish stood before the Supreme Court justices in Washington, D.C., to plead her case.

Court rules did not then, and do not now allow litigants to address the justices. Only attorneys may. In her book about Parrish, Professor Knowles says the courageous chambermaid never journeyed east of Montana after she filed her lawsuit. "There is no evidence that she ever traveled to Washington, D.C., and she certainly never 'stood alone' before the justices of the Supreme Court," says Knowles, whose book is scheduled for publication in 2020 by the University of Oklahoma Press.

She also notes that St. Johns was a "celebrity 'sob sister' journalist" and fiction writer who worked primarily for the sensationalist Hearst publications. In language that would have suited one of her Hollywood screenplays, St. Johns rendered Parrish's case a clash of Biblical proportions, Knowles says.

"But that is beside the point, because even though St. Johns knew full well—as we do today—that she was writing with a heavy dose of dramatic license, her basic observation was still valid. The constitutional victory achieved by Elsie Parrish would have monumental socio-political and legal implications."

Bob Young
Legacy Washington

After her book *Marriage, A History* was published in 2005, Coontz was playfully photographed for Evergreen's magazine in a kitchen, 1950s style. *Martin W. Kane/The Evergreen State College (TESC)*

STEPHANIE COONTZ

THE WAY WE NEVER WERE

Stephanie Coontz was off her daily diet of research and writing in late June 2015 while she was vacationing in Hawaii. After a Friday of hiking, body-boarding at the beach, and snorkeling out to a rock where turtles gathered, she checked her email. Waiting was a flurry of messages from excited colleagues. They wanted to know whether Coontz, a Washington historian, had caught the news. The U.S. Supreme Court had just announced its landmark ruling on same-sex marriage. The court's 5-4 opinion cited Coontz twice. Just after Confucius and Cicero.

A longtime faculty member at The Evergreen State College, Coontz had made a big impression on the country's top legal minds. "Like national, epic-historical big," said columnist Danny Westneat in *The Seattle Times*. Her writing about the evolution of marriage from an unequal property contract to a gender-neutral bond of love had influenced the court's thinking, the law of the land, and millions of lives.

It wasn't the first time the limelight reached Coontz. She had chiseled a niche as the nation's leading fact-checker on matters of family and marriage.

Her 1992 book, *The Way We Never Were*, took a trenchant look at American nostalgia for the good old 1950s. Coontz brought a basket of hard-boiled reality to the picnic of soft-focus memories. Rates of poverty, child abuse, marital unhappiness, and domestic violence were higher in the 1950s than in subsequent, more-libertine decades. The prosperity of white men was tied to government subsidies, high rates of union membership, and unequal treatment of women and minorities. Reviews of her book inspired "Ozzie and Harriet Lied" headlines.

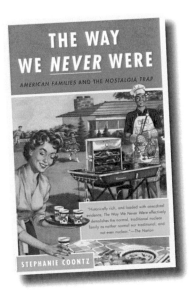

With impeccable timing, Coontz hit shelves as a national family-values debate raged. Vice President Dan Quayle made coast-to-coast news for suggesting that TV character Murphy Brown's decision to become a single mother made her the kind of tramp who was driving the country into a ditch.

When it came to myth busters, talk-show bookers knew who to call. And there was the Evergreen educator on TV, telling Oprah, "*Leave It to Beaver* was not a documentary."

Debunking has kept Coontz busy ever since. She was drawn back into the "nostalgia trap" by President Donald Trump's "Make America Great Again" campaign. She sees some Trump supporters embracing a particularly noxious strain of nostalgia. But you're not likely to change their minds by hurling insults at them, she says. "Some of them can be won over, at least on a few important issues. Others can be redirected toward less divisive topics—but not if they are demonized."

That perspective is consistent with her long-standing approach. Protests she led against the Vietnam War were known for civility. And she kept a practical goal, even in the face of people who got screaming-mad at her politics. "I believed strongly, radical though I may have been," Coontz says, "that you start to reach people where they are, not where you want them to be."

COONTZ WAS "perhaps the best-known radical woman in the Northwest" in 1970. But the "petite co-ed doesn't look like a revolutionary," *The Seattle Times* said. In

phrasing hard to imagine today, one reporter wrote that she was a 108-pound "charmer," demure in a magenta dress with a fringed hem, who had to stand on tiptoes to reach microphones. And she was a "good cook."

As a University of Washington student protesting the Vietnam War, Coontz started making news in 1968 (almost always written by men).* Unlike many of her peers, she wasn't rebelling against her parents. "My dad was a big supporter of labor unions. Both of them were active in the NAACP. My mother was executive secretary of the ACLU in Salt Lake City," she says.

---

* Coontz didn't mind the details about her appearance, although sexist, because the writers took her ideas seriously. She thought they aimed to counter "hostile" images readers were likely to conjure about radicals.

Little did young Stephanie know that she would teach at a college whose mascot is a geoduck. *Stephanie Coontz*

Born in Seattle, she was quickly uprooted. Her father, Sidney Coontz, a labor organizer, used the GI Bill to go to college and become an economics professor. That took young Stephanie to academic outposts in California, Idaho, England, New York and Utah. Her mother, Patricia McIntosh, was an "ambitious, independent" student at the UW before marrying Coontz's father. She tried living the mid-century role of wife as stay-at-home nurturer, booster and mother. In time, she came to feel something was missing. She and her husband divorced. She restarted her studies. She became an English professor at Eastern Washington State College and a founder of the Cheney school's Women's Center.

Coontz's mother credited her awakening to Betty Friedan's 1963 book, *The Feminine Mystique.* "It was as if someone had sucked all my insides out, as if there was nothing in there but emptiness... as if marriage and that supposedly admirable self-sacrifice that goes with it had robbed me of personality, brains, determination, guts, really." After reading Friedan she thought, "my God, that's it, that's the answer." Friedan's radical idea? That women could restore meaning to their lives through education, work and community involvement.

Coontz, who would later write a book about Friedan's impact on a generation of women, graduated from high school a year early and took off for undergraduate life in Berkeley, California. She was soon involved in civil rights campaigns, then the free speech, and anti-war movements. Her activism had been partly driven by an anti-communist film, *Operation Abolition.* It was the *Reefer Madness* of the red-baiting era, when the Boston Public Library came under fire for displaying a copy of the *Communist Manifesto* and public librarians in Seattle and Ephrata were fired for not taking anti-communist loyalty oaths. The film "was so clearly a work of propaganda that it did for a young person like me the opposite of what it intended," she says.

Her mother later recounted the drama of talking to her daughter on a pay phone during a 1964 campus demonstration that led to mass arrests. Police were grabbing students, who purposefully went limp, "by the feet and pulling them down the stairs." She could hear over the phone "the bumps as their bottoms hit the floor."

Then Coontz said she had to go and the phone went dead. Her mother read about the arrests of some 800 demonstrators. More than student bottoms were thumping the stone stairs of Sproul Hall. "One conscientious reporter counted the

Coontz spoke at an anti-war rally crowd of more than 2,500 at Seattle Center in 1970. *The Seattle Times*

marble steps as he followed a girl whose head jarred sickeningly as she was dragged down. There were ninety." Coontz initially went limp to be dragged out. But she got up and walked when she saw people's heads whacking the stairs. "Always felt a bit chicken," she says decades later, "but in retrospect I no longer feel guilty about it!"

Coontz (center) led a joke "invasion" of Fort Lewis, complete with toy guns and peace-sign flags. *Stephanie Coontz*

After a brief expulsion, Coontz went on to win a Woodrow Wilson Fellowship that allowed her to pursue graduate studies in history where she wanted. She chose to come home. Her mother's pioneering side of the family had deep roots in the Olympia area.* They settled in Washington decades before it became a state. Coontz's widowed grandmother lived alone in the Seattle area. Coontz decided to study at the UW so she could help her.

SHE PLAYED a leadership role in the Seattle anti-war movement, which swelled as the draft call escalated on its way to inducting 2 million American men. In 1968 she was part of a group that was booted from Fort Lewis, where they went to ask soldiers to join a newly formed GI-Civilian Alliance for Peace. Costumed as a cigar-chomping general, Coontz led a return the next year in a joke "invasion" of the Army base.

---

* Coontz's grandparents Albert and Helen (Eastman) McIntosh lived in a Tumwater house, between where the historic Crosby and Henderson Houses stand above Tumwater Historical Park.

The Seattle Times soon reported that "the dark-eyed girl with the clear voice and a quick smile is unquestionably a successful politician." The grad student with a 3.75 GPA didn't speak in the "strung-out, strung-together jargon of the New Left." ("I never used the word 'pig,'" Coontz says about an epithet some protesters spat at police officers.) Her socialism was tempered. She condemned bomb-throwing and window-smashing. Given a stage and bullhorn, she called for peaceful change. Democracy was a desirable way to govern, she said. But it didn't do black people much good to be able to eat at an integrated restaurant, if they couldn't pay for the food. Economic changes were also needed.

As an undergraduate at University of California, Berkeley in the 1960s, Coontz was involved in the free speech movement. *Stephanie Coontz*

To some, she was still a freeloading troublemaker. "Here we have a 25-year-old woman in her sixth year at tax-built and tax-supported universities doing her level best to destroy this country," said Seattle's Daryl Hogan in a 1969 letter to the editor, "and she is presented as some kind of prima donna...Yet she has contributed nothing to support this society that has so amply endowed her."

TV reporter Don McGaffin told Coontz his station got more hate calls when she appeared on-air than any other Seattle radical. McGaffin's theory: because she looked like a sorority girl, viewers were more inclined to give her a listen rather than leave the room or change the channel when they saw another scraggly peacenik on the screen. They stayed for Coontz. And they got mad as hell hearing the well-spoken socialist's pitch for sharing the wealth.

"I always thought, 'Isn't that wonderful?' If you present yourself as someone who is not trying to show how different you are, or how radical you are," she says, "they might listen to you. And maybe they'll not like you, but maybe some will actually listen to you."

UW students lashed out in a stormy week of protests in May 1970 after National Guard troops shot and killed four students at Ohio's Kent State University. Coontz led thousands of students in daily rallies. Many spilled onto Interstate 5 and blocked the freeway on successive days.

The next week Coontz was walking down stairs in the UW Communications Building when two men "dressed like radical students or hangers-on" jumped her and punched her several times. She was kept overnight in the health center for observation but not seriously injured.

A 6 The Seattle Times   Friday, January 3, 1975

Ex-war resister gets Evergreen faculty post

Stephanie Coontz

Coontz ran for Congress that year on a Socialist Workers Party ticket, urging a 100-percent tax on war profits and polluting industries. One headline captured the election results in four words: "Minor parties remain minor." Coontz received 2.6 percent of the vote.

She moved to New York City to work for the National Peace Action Coalition. She never did finish her Ph.D. But she secured a teaching job at Evergreen four years later, a rare hiring chronicled by a headline: "Ex-war resister gets Evergreen faculty post." Her mother earlier had applied for a faculty post at the unconventional Olympia school.* "Although Evergreen didn't have disciplines," Coontz says, "they told her they didn't really need another person in English literature. They were actually looking for a historian. At which point, my mother said, 'My daughter is an historian' and encouraged me to apply. And to my surprise I got it."

A FEMINIST PUBLISHER asked Coontz, who had been an editor for the publishing arm of the Socialist Workers Party, if she wanted to write about women's history. She started digging. She wasn't thrilled about what she found. There were lots of books coming out. But they all seemed to be about what had been done to women through the ages, or what a few women had accomplished despite what was done to them.

Coontz looked for an opening that involved men and women interacting on a regular basis. "Suddenly, it was like, 'the family, duh.' "

But family and social history were not very respectable fields of study then. "So thank god for Evergreen," she says, "and not having to publish or perish." She spent parts of 12 years researching and writing *The Social Origins of Private Life: A History of American Families 1600-1900*. She now calls the

Coontz poked at Hollywood's fictional "misty water-colored memories of the way we were." *TESC*

---

* Evergreen faculty don't have titles such as "professor." Coontz says one colleague called the school "Plato's Republic with electricity."

book pompous in its use of big words. But it built a foundational expertise and academic credibility.

With her focus freed from mortality rates of colonial families and other grim facts of the 18th century, she looked around the real world and saw the values debate erupting, with women leading groups trying to restore what they considered "traditional" family norms. "Neither they, nor the liberals opposing them actually knew very much about what family history was really like," she says.

Until two centuries ago, "marriage was considered too important to leave up to the emotions of two people," Coontz wrote. *Jay Takaaze/TESC*

She set out to write a book called *Myths and Realities of American Families*. Then an editor saw one of Coontz's chapters and said "that's the title of the book!" With a push from the Murphy Brown squall, the values debate stormed into the 1992 election season. *The Way We Never Were*, with its title poking at fictive Hollywood romance, poured high-octane "fuel in the sound-bite fires."

She was back in the public eye, this time as a full-fledged academic.

Now it was *The Seattle Times* book reviewer praising her, and without a mention of her weight or wardrobe. Instead Mary Ann Gwinn produced 27 incisive paragraphs on the way Coontz "takes a measured, reflective stroll through history to demonstrate how the 'simpler time' we long for was never so simple." Step after step was built on bricks of data: In 1957, the teenage pregnancy rate was almost twice as high as it was in 1983; at the end of the 1950s, an era of economic expansion, a third of all children were considered poor; domestic violence was more common than in subsequent decades.

A myth buster was born.

She crisscrossed the country, basking in Oprah Winfrey's nationally-syndicated attention and debating Pat Buchanan on CNN's Crossfire. When she didn't hear creative solutions emerge from the ruckus, she spun off a sequel in 1997, *The Way We Really Are: Coming to Terms With America's Changing Families*. *The New York Times* found it layered with "pragmatic optimism."

Remedies in the book started with a better understanding of history. Government supported families in the 1950s with subsidies for college education, home-mortgage loans and massive transportation projects. Strong labor rights led to high union membership. Businesses were more inclined to invest in stability than funneling profits to shareholders.

Even if families were to return to 1950s form—dad bringing home the bacon, mom cooking it up with a smile, kids saying grace—government and business were unlikely to follow. Government had shifted benefits from workers to businesses and the wealthy. Corporate tax breaks and subsidies cost three times what Americans spent on all welfare programs.

For many workers that spelled eroding benefits, constant worries about layoffs, and a move into "casualized" work, as part-timers and subcontractors, while companies prioritized the bottom line. It was absurd for James Danforth Quayle III to blame mothers for working. Many did so, even when married, to keep their kids out of poverty. Coontz saw child care, parental leave, and limits on work as compelling new health and safety regulations, every bit as vital to the public interest as meatpacking safeguards were a century before.

SOME CRITICS THOUGHT Coontz really hit her stride in 2005's *Marriage, a History: How Love Conquered Marriage.* "She's no chatty pop-prof," one reviewer said. "This is a thorough examination of the history of marriage." In tracing the evolution of matrimony from cave dwellers to computer programmers, Coontz found most of that time could have been themed, "What's Love Got to Do With It?"

Until roughly two centuries ago "marriage was considered too important to leave up to the emotions of two people." It was about economics and politics, gaining property and strategic alliances. Or as Coontz likes to put it: "Marriage had as much to do with getting good in-laws and increasing one's family labor force as it did with finding a lifetime companion and raising a beloved child."

Coontz is grateful Evergreen emphasizes undergraduate education rather than the "publish or perish" pressure faculty often face in academia. *Shauna Bittle/TESC*

But then heterosexuals began to change it. Marriage became rooted in love and free choice. And then equality instead of fixed gender roles. And it was decoupled from procreation and child-rearing. It became clear marriage responded to changing times.

The Supreme Court embraced Coontz's logic that once heterosexual marriage was unmoored from strict gender roles, it couldn't legally be denied to same-sex couples. (Justice Antonin Scalia's dissent called the majority opinion "profoundly incoherent," and compared its logic to the "mystical aphorisms of the fortune cookie.")

Supreme Court Justice Anthony Kennedy embraced Coontz's view that the history of marriage is one of both continuity and change.

Coontz was flattered by the citations of her work in Justice Anthony Kennedy's majority opinion.[*] But when she read his decision, she realized he didn't fully grasp her book, or chose to ignore key parts of it. Kennedy argued that gays and lesbians deserved to marry, in part, because matrimony had always "promised nobility and dignity to all persons."

That was not the history Coontz excavated. "For thousands of years, marriage conferred nobility and dignity almost exclusively on the husband, who had a legal right to appropriate the property and earnings of his wife and children and forcibly impose his will on them."

She had a point. In Washington state, husbands could use physical force to legally rape their wives until the law was changed in 1983.

AS THE 21st CENTURY took hold, an old problem lingered. Some women were cracking glass ceilings, but many were "still stuck in the basement looking for an up escalator." Gender equity had stalled. American women were still being paid less than men for similar work. Progress had slowed so much that women were not expected to achieve pay parity until 2058. The forecast was even worse for African American women and Latinas.

When a woman stopped working to have a baby, she tended to fall further behind, compounding the pain. The lack of family-friendly work policies and affordable child care, combined with men's higher wages, encouraged many women to cut back when work conflicted with family obligations. And that only reinforces gender inequality, Coontz says.

"On average, when a woman leaves the workforce for a year to care for a child, she loses almost 20 percent of her lifetime earnings power. If she spends three to four years away, it reduces her potential lifetime earnings by 40 percent."

And yet if moms don't quit work, they're also penalized. "Studies show that employers are less likely to hire or promote mothers than childless women (or fathers) on the assumption that they are less committed to work."

With her usual optimism, Coontz points to the good news: men have come a long way, baby. "Since 1965, husbands have doubled their share of housework and tripled their share of child care."

---

[*] Kennedy twice cited *Marriage: a History*. Coontz and 25 historians also submitted a "friend of the court" brief in the case, *Obergefell v. Hodges*, which legalized same-sex marriage. Kennedy cited the historians' brief as well.

"Our founders did want to build a wall," Coontz says. "Between church and state." *Shauna Bittle/TESC*

Unfortunately, when men have tried to help out in child care, seeking paternity leave or a more flexible schedule, they've met with resistance because of the breadwinner mentality. "So your discrimination against men comes when they ask for flexibility," she says. And that only perpetuates the problem with women stepping out of the workforce.

What's needed? Coontz says new corporate polices, affordable child care and preschool education, and family leave. If women were paid the same as men for comparable work, that would slash the poverty rate in American families. Men, women and children would benefit if the U.S. adopted job-protected, subsidized family leave. Of 193 countries in the United Nations, only a few—and the U.S. is among the outliers—do not mandate paid maternity leave; almost half of all countries also offer paternal leave. "Again, this is where we recruit men," she says. "We have to show them paternity leave is in their interest as well." (Ahead of the curve, Washington in 2020 will become the fifth state to offer paid family leave; it is also considered to have one of the strongest pay-equity laws in the country.)

Norway has implemented paternity leave and child care, she says, with interesting results. "They've found that men who take paternity leave do end up earning a little less over the course of their lives than they would if they hadn't. But their wives earn so much more over their lives that the family as a whole is better off." And household tensions are reduced. A study in Norway found a 50-percent drop in domestic spats about housework and child care after men had taken paternity leave because they were more aware of what was done around the house.

It's not an easy sell to conservatives. Former Fox TV host Bill O'Reilly yelled at Coontz that he wasn't going to pay for child care for single mothers. "I want society to tell people you're on the road to destruction if you're a single parent," O'Reilly said. Coontz, a single mother for much of her son's life, laughed it off and quoted statistics to reinforce her arguments.

COONTZ RETURNED to the nostalgia beat in 2018 with a fresh angle for the *Harvard Business Review*. A 17th-century Swiss doctor had mixed two Greek words to coin the term "nostalgia," she wrote. It described the "algos," or pain, felt by people who left their native home, or "nostos." During the American Civil War,

Union Army doctors reported 5,000 serious cases of nostalgia.* Physicians were soon debating how to treat this homesickness.

Their concern abated near the end of the 19th century when modern industry and communications made people more open to change and less susceptible to the disease. Researchers later identified a milder strain—a longing for a feeling once shared with friends and family, not a literal return to another place or time. "This kind of nostalgia makes people feel warmer themselves and act more warmly toward others, including strangers," Coontz says.

But in the run-up to the 2016 election we saw a more pernicious form, what Coontz calls "past-sickness." This is a longing to reproduce an idealized piece of history, rather than personal feelings. And when people are collectively nostalgic for an idealized era, they "start to identify more intensely with their own group and to judge members of other groups more negatively." They become more hostile to those perceived as outsiders; they deny diversity and social injustices of the past.

When politicized, this nostalgia can lead to delusions about a golden era in the homeland, supposedly ruined by interlopers. "And when people get scared and think they're losing and see themselves as under attack, they get into this sort of pathological nostalgia," she says. Make America Great Again enthusiasts appear to idealize the 1950s, when real wages were rising for working-class white men, and America emerged from World War II as the only major industrial power that had not been decimated, setting the stage for the U.S. to play an outsized role for several decades.

Like nostalgia outbreaks of the past, Coontz says this one was triggered by an understandable sense of loss. For roughly three decades—1947 to the early 1970s—men with high-school educations saw their earnings, adjusted for inflation, steadily rise, and outpace what their fathers had made at the same age. And over that same time, the vast majority of the country's income growth went to the bottom 90 percent of the population.

But this prosperity was an exception, powered by government subsidies and expanded labor rights, not the norm. And the trend, it turns out, was an aberration. Profit motives reasserted their supremacy. Economists declared that corporations were responsible only to stockholders. Jobs were shipped overseas. Union ranks sank. CEO salaries soared to such heights that they averaged 300 times what their workers made.

And wages sagged for blue-collar men. Between 1980 and 2007, median real earnings of young men with a high-school education declined by 28 percent. They worked hard, and then harder with fewer benefits. And they still saw their paychecks shrink.

---

* In her 2011 book *Homesickness: An American History*, historian Susan J. Matt says 74 Union soldiers died of nostalgia between 1861 and 1866. Units barred bands from playing melodies such as "Home, Sweet Home."

During that same period, the top 10 percent of all earners received 95 percent of income growth.

But rather than blame the forces and fat cats who drove down their wages, shuttered their factories, and gutted their pensions, Trump supporters have scapegoated others, particularly immigrants.

Too often, America's working class has been pitted against one another, Coontz says. In colonial America, "Irish indentured servants and black slaves worked so closely together that the Negro spiritual was a blend of the Irish ballad and African folk song." But plantation owners felt threatened by the prospect of interracial alliances. "And that's how they started giving special treatment to indentured servants who reported slaves who had accumulated any property. It was a very conscious attempt to divide."

The absence of effective leadership makes it easier for some to see the solution as going after someone their own size instead of the big guys. "I see this as a huge obstacle but not an insurmountable one," Coontz says, pointing to the New Deal and desegregation as examples when blue-collar Americans were less divided. (Frustrated at what she saw as Hillary Clinton's aloofness, Coontz says she watched TV during the 2016 campaign and yelled at Clinton's speeches: "Would you EFFIN' name a truck driver or a farmer? Would you add one of them please?")

She doesn't dispute evidence of racism in the 2016 election. But she draws a distinction between active defenders of white supremacy and those who appear less conscious of their biases. She points to blue-collar timber counties in southwestern Washington— Cowlitz, Grays Harbor and Pacific— that voted for Barack Obama in two elections and then turned around and voted for Trump. Those counties don't seem inherently racist,* she observes. But some residents were likely upset by liberalism (environmentalism having dramatically impacted logging) they saw as threatening the security that

Ever optimistic, Coontz points to good news in marriages: husbands have doubled their share of housework and tripled their share of child care. *Karissa Carlson/TESC*

traditional family, religion, race and culture had provided. Others may have been sexist, or just anti-Clinton. They were ripe for the "angriest" candidate, all the more so if he promised a return to tradition. "So I don't think it helps at all to label them with

---

* Trump did not bring out droves of new voters in those three counties; 2016 turnout was lower in all three counties than it was in the 2012 and 2008 presidential elections. And Clinton did not come close to reaching Barack Obama's 2008 and 2012 vote totals in the three counties.

the same thing," Coontz says.

She points to her husband's experience. "When he was working in the airline industry and his fellow workers would say something racist, he had a way of handling it that I thought was really good. He would say, 'You know, personally I'm not prejudiced.' And no one wants to be prejudiced, but it's not as red flag as 'you're a racist.' " His co-workers would say they weren't prejudiced either. "And then they'd get into a really good discussion about it."

COONTZ IS NOT WORKING on a new book. She's reluctant to start one now because there's so much watchdogging to do on recycled and redeveloped myths. ("Our founders *did* want to build a wall," she says. "Between church and state.")

Coontz's family has deep roots in Thurston County, where she lives on farm property that belonged to her great grandfather. *Stephanie Coontz*

She also gets offers to write shorter, newsy pieces about marriage and family. NBC asked her to weigh-in on the feuds of Kellyanne and George Conway. Kellyanne is a senior counselor to President Trump; George is an outspoken critic of the commander-in-chief. Trump, the third wheel in this awkward imbroglio, has called George Conway "a stone cold loser" and "husband from hell." Coontz couldn't find a historical precedent for this odd couple, but she saw trouble brewing. In her view, George's contempt for Kellyanne's boss, and by extension, her work, combined with Kellyanne's defensiveness, amount to a formula for d-i-v-o-r-c-e.

Coontz' other "big passion" is helping researchers—be they historians, psychologists or sociologists—explain their findings in ways people can use and understand. "Too often they've just been kept in the ivory tower," she says. To help them avoid mistakes like the kind she made with ponderous writing, she'll point out things like "this paragraph you buried on page eight is what people are dying to know about how marriages work."

She is faculty emerita, effectively retired from Evergreen. Much of her recent work has been in service to the Council on Contemporary Families, where she is director of research and public education. Based at the University of Texas at Austin, the council is a nonpartisan, nonprofit association of family researchers.

Coontz and her husband live on an organic farm—property first acquired by her great grandfather—in Thurston County. Still a good cook, she's known to whip up a homegrown meal for guests of arugula and fennel salad, nettle risotto, fried green tomatoes, Angus beef, and applesauce.

When asked how to characterize the politics of a '60s radical-turned-*Ladies Home Journal* marriage consultant, she says, "I don't feel comfortable calling myself a socialist at this point. I have begun to really appreciate the value of free markets—although ironically our current version of capitalism seems to be pretty much destroying those. Mostly I'm out to figure out what are the most pressing injustices we see…and what can we do to make this society a better place for everyone. So I don't have a name for it anymore."

As for the letter writer who said back in 1969 that she contributed zilch to society, a bunch of folks—students, readers, historians, judges, and newlyweds—would beg to differ. Bill O'Reilly might too.

Although O'Reilly berated Coontz's arguments for expanding child care and parental leave, they have become orthodoxy for Democrats seeking the 2020 presidential nomination. O'Reilly, meanwhile, left Fox News in the wake of *New York Times* reporting that the network had paid out $13 million in settlements to women who alleged he engaged in sexual harassment and other inappropriate behavior. O'Reilly dismissed the stories as "crap."

Discussing her penchant for taking a very long view of history, Coontz recalls a movie she saw about a rebel in the Spanish Civil War. "There are two things he says you need to make revolutionary change: Patience. And a sense of irony."

Bob Young
Legacy Washington

LOCAL
1225
SUPPORTS
COMPARABLE
WORTH

I SUPPORT COMPARABLE WORTH

On a snowy day in 1985, state employees and supporters held a rally for comparable worth at the state Capitol.
AFSCME Council 28

PIONEERS IN PAY EQUITY

CHRIS GREGOIRE'S "MOST UNIQUE CASE"

A few days after flinging her Husky mortarboard into the air, Chris Gregoire began her career in state government typing and filing in a Seattle probation and parole office. It was the summer of 1969. Her training as a teacher kindled her interest in juvenile justice and she applied for a promotion. A supervisor told her he didn't need a "token" right then. Unfulfilled and underpaid, she quit and staked her future to Gonzaga Law School, where the vast majority of her classmates were men.

In 1982, just five years out of law school, she was arguing a case with national importance and huge implications, particularly for the gender gap in pay. Women were then earning about 62 cents for every $1 men made. But Gregoire, who had been named Washington's first woman deputy attorney general, was not locking arms with feminists. Her job was to fight a union lawsuit alleging discrimination in state salaries for women.

"There was nothing about this case that wasn't fraught with controversy," the former governor remembers.

The lawsuit was rooted in an innovative argument. Union attorneys said employers needed to go beyond the existing doctrine of "equal pay for equal work." That 1963 law rarely applied because men and women didn't often perform the same work. They were segregated by occupation. Engineers were men, nurses were women; same with plumbers, librarians and more. The idea unveiled in Washington was called "comparable worth." It hung on the notion that jobs of *similar value* to an employer should be paid the same.

Former Governor Chris Gregoire, the state's first female deputy attorney general, felt "constant mixed emotions" about her role in the comparable worth case. *Washington Attorney General's Office*

The concept would migrate from the country's mossy northwest corner to the marbled halls of Congress and the Supreme Court. It would propel the idea of pay equity, while boosting women's activism, wages and self-respect. And it would ultimately fall short of sweeping the nation, stalled mostly by conservative thinking in business, politics and especially the courts.

The union was "very strategic," Gregoire says, in choosing Washington as the laboratory for testing comparable worth. It was betting on the state's reputation as a leader on women's issues, from suffrage to equal pay. If the lawsuit didn't prevail in court, the logic went, then women workers could still win in the court of public opinion, and pressure lawmakers that way for pay parity.

Comparable worth proved to be "the most unique case" Gregoire ever handled. It was rivaled in complexity, says the former three-term attorney general, only by the $206 *billion* tobacco settlement on which she led the negotiations for 46 states that had sued the industry.*

But she wore a white hat and sheriff's badge in the tobacco showdown, while squaring off against mustache-twirling villains. Comparable worth was more ambiguous—and rife with conflict. "On this one, I had constant mixed emotions," Gregoire says. "It was trying and difficult for me."

From her own experience she knew women working for the state were underpaid. From her expertise, she knew that didn't mean the state was guilty of illegal discrimination. The state had set salaries by following an elaborate survey of 2,700 jobs in the private market. How was that unlawful?

Her job was to represent the state's elected leaders. When it meant arguing against comparable worth, she did that with focus and firmness. If it meant negotiating a deal to raise pay for women, she applied the same determination.

"I happened to be a woman on a case, doing a lawyer's job," she says—albeit no ordinary case and no easy job. Four governors juggled the political grenade. Two future U.S. Supreme Court justices dealt sharp body blows to the cause. The President of the United States mocked it.

At different stages of the case, Gregoire would lose badly, win thoroughly, and then draw. The final result, a $500 million settlement between the state and union that brought raises to 35,000 employees, was the most satisfying to her. "I had been a clerk-typist. I knew how low my income was. And I had a college degree. And I didn't know how people could have a family on my salary," says the state's second woman governor.

While the historic settlement in Washington amounted to progress, it did not completely implement comparable worth. And a stubborn gender gap in pay remains in Washington, and around the country.

---

* The costliest settlement in U.S. history, it also banned the Marlboro Man, Joe Camel and other cigarette advertising.

But The Evergreen State is again ahead of the curve. It is one of seven states with a strong pay equity law, according to the American Association of University Women, thanks to a 2018 bill that revives elements of comparable worth.

COMPARABLE WORTH was born in Washington, christened in 1973 by Larry Goodman, a union representative for state workers. Goodman gave a speech in Seattle that landed on the front page of the *Post-Intelligencer*. In his talk, he accused the state of perpetrating "sex discrimination in pay practices." It tended to pay women less than men, even when their work seemed as important or difficult as a man's. Assessing the "comparable worth" of different jobs was not radical, he said. Consulting firms did it for corporations. (Although they hadn't applied such evaluations to gender bias.)

Norm Schut, executive director of the Washington State Federation of Employees, was a member of the Washington Women's Council. *State Federation of Employees*

In Olympia, Goodman's boss picked up the morning paper and nearly dropped his coffee mug. Fortunately, Norm Schut, director of the Washington State Federation of Employees, had a good relationship with Governor Dan Evans. And on November 20, 1973, after Schut cooled down, he sent Evans a letter saying that discrimination was baked into state salaries because they were based on sexism that "permeates through the private sector." To start on a road to redress, Schut requested an analysis of wage disparities based on gender. The Washington Women's Council, of which Schut was a member, also advocated a study.

Evans, it turns out, was familiar with a study that used comparable worth principles to assess the value of state elected officials and appointed managers. (Elected officials earned less than managers, the study found, and both made far less than private sector peers.) In other words, you could compare truck drivers and secretaries by assigning numerical scores to key facets of their work, such as skills and responsibilities. When the metrics showed jobs to have equivalent values, their pay should be the same.

The governor nudged the ball forward. Evans responded with a letter saying if state salaries were biased "then we must move to reverse this inequity."

The governor paid consultant Norman Willis to conduct a study of 121 female-dominated and male-dominated "benchmark" jobs.* Willis concluded that

---

* Because the state had more than 3,000 job titles, personnel officials set salaries for a much smaller number of "benchmark" jobs. Salaries of related positions were "indexed" or adjusted to those benchmarks. "Secretary III" was a benchmark title; other secretarial jobs, above or below it in class, would be scaled accordingly.

the women's jobs were paid an average of 20 percent less than men's for work of comparable value.

Jim Dolliver, a former Evans aide who went on to become a Washington Supreme Court justice, would later testify that the studies showed that "sex seemed to be the only" factor in the pay disparities.

It's one of the oldest stories in history, says Barbara Reskin, a University of Washington professor emeritus. "According to the Old Testament, women's work has been undervalued for at least 3,000 years, which is approximately when Leviticus wrote that a male servant was to be valued at 50 shekels and a female at 30 shekels," says Reskin, author of six books about gender and race in work.

HELEN REMICK moved to Washington in 1975 and became director of affirmative action for women at the University of Washington.

"I thought I had gone to heaven," Remick says, recalling when someone gave her one of the state studies on comparable value.

She had faced discrimination as a young faculty member in California. She was interested in feminism and found it resurgent in Seattle during the 1970s. The Seattle-King County chapter of the National Organization for Women was as brash as Remick. The group famously created a poster of Israeli Prime Minister Golda Meir with the caption, "But can she type?"

The Seattle-King County chapter of NOW created a famous poster of Israeli Prime Minister Golda Meir.

With her Ph.D. training as a developmental psychologist, Remick was comfortable with computers long before desktop PCs existed.

She jumped in with a paper analyzing Washington's trailblazing study, which was eye-opening. The female-dominated position of Secretary III required an array of skills, from shorthand to managing an office, plus a high school diploma and two years of experience. The male-dominated "traffic guide"—essentially a parking attendant—required little more than a valid driver's license.

The traffic guide's pay was slightly higher, although

Helen Remick, University of Washington's director of affirmative action for women, was an expert witness for both sides in the federal comparable worth lawsuit. *Helen Remick*

the Secretary III post tallied more than twice as many points, 210 to 89, in value.

The findings were a revelation. Washington was the first employer to apply point-system evaluations specifically for gender bias, Remick reported. "Before the comparable worth study, women *felt* they were being underpaid," she says. "The study provided the hard data to *show* the salary differences. Before, academicians made hypothetical arguments to support their beliefs about sex discrimination in employment. After, there was at least one set of data to study: a management tool, with management-accepted standards, showed systemic gender inequality within the workforce of a single employer."

Remick would spend the next decade immersed in comparable worth as the concept gained traction with unions, feminists and academics. (While the terms "comparable worth" and "pay equity" were used interchangeably, some have viewed pay equity as the larger issue or goal, and comparable worth as a tool for achieving it.) She wrote papers and spoke at conferences in the U.S., Canada and Sweden. She appeared as an expert witness for both sides in the federal legal case over comparable worth. And she played a part in devising the eventual settlement between the union and state.

Along the way she would get to know Jennifer Belcher, who started her state work in the Evans administration and would specialize in women's issues for Evans' successor, Dixy Lee Ray, when the struggle took an unexpected turn.

BELCHER WAS a 23-year-old administrative secretary for Evans' planning director, Richard Slavin. She typed, filed, set up appointments, played gatekeeper, and even prepared her boss's lunch. She too felt stung by discrimination. She played a key role, she felt, in her boss's success. Her boss also had an aide who was a young attorney. "He didn't do half of what I did and got paid more. He was an administrative assistant. I was an administrative secretary. You couldn't be a woman in work those days and not feel discrimination," she says.

Jennifer Belcher started as a secretary in Governor Dan Evans' office. She later chaired the Legislature's joint committee on comparable worth. *AFSCME Council 28*

Belcher's mentor was Jo Garceau, Evans' liaison on women's issues. Garceau invited Belcher to tag along with her to meetings. "I got to sit in on executive pay issues," Belcher says. "Then when comparable worth came along, it was a natural interest."

She recalls that near the end of Evans' 12 years in office he gathered staffers and asked them to think of three things he should

Governor Dixy Lee Ray said comparable worth was like mixing "apples with pumpkins and a can of worms." *Washington State Archives*

do before he left office. In his proposed budget for 1977, Evans included $7 million to begin implementing comparable worth. He hoped it would be gradually carried out so it wouldn't prove disruptive to state budget-writing.

Then the state's first woman governor was elected. The iconoclastic Dixy Lee Ray quickly put the kibosh on Evans' plan.

Belcher was one of Ray's few holdovers from the Evans' administration. She was office manager and represented Ray on women's issues. "It was a tough place to be," she says.

Ray didn't know much about comparable worth. Based on what she had heard, she said it was like mixing "apples with pumpkins and a can of worms." She wiped out Evans' $7 million appropriation from her budget, even though the state enjoyed a surplus of funds. "The ultimate irony is that she was the first woman governor in the state's history and that's one of the things she eliminated," Evans later said.

On her way out of office in 1980, Ray expressed a change of mind. She told the Legislature "the cost of perpetuating unfairness, within state government itself, is too great to put off any longer." But new Governor John Spellman and lawmakers— facing a billion-dollar budget deficit—appeared either unfazed by the warning or paralyzed by the prospect of acting on it.

FED UP WITH THE INERTIA, the state federation of employees and their powerful parent union, based in Washington, D.C., prepared for action. The legal team of the American Federation of State, County and Municipal Employees' was led by Winn Newman. As attorney for the electrical workers' union, Newman had won groundbreaking anti-discrimination settlements for women employees at Westinghouse. Newman modeled his arguments on those of civil rights lawyers. He had gone to work for AFSCME because the union was committed to significant spending on pay equity struggles.* More than half of its 1 million members were women. And pay issues had percolated up through the ranks. A committee on sex discrimination was created at the union's 1972 national convention. Its survey of members found that pay inequity for women was their most pressing issue.

But how Norm Schut and his union of state employees came to comparable worth as a solution was more nuanced. Schut later explained that the union's progression had started in the late 1960s by looking at workers in state psychiatric

---

* Martin Luther King Jr. was slain in Memphis after going there to support striking AFSCME sanitation workers who said they were underpaid because most of them were black.

hospitals who had, by far, the most contact with patients. They were usually ward attendants and nurses. And they were paid less than the carpenters, painters and truck drivers who had no direct contact with often-difficult patients. Schut came up with the idea of paying nurses and attendants "on the basis of how important their job was to the mission and the role of that institution."

Those workers soon got significant raises. So the union's focus turned to determining the value of one job in comparison to another in a given program or workplace. Meanwhile, administrators and other women professionals at Washington State University and University of Washington "were stirring it up," Schut said, over gender disparity in pay. But the women lacked a political strategy. "We needed something we could sell, that was defensible, that would attract the minds of the people, the Legislature, make good media copy, too," he said. The union could articulate the new concept of comparable worth, give it legitimacy, and press levers in the legislative process to make it a reality.

Progress had been slowed in the 1970s by economic stagnation. Conservatives began to make public employees a favorite scapegoat for rising government budgets. President Ronald Reagan delivered a blow felt in union halls around the country when he fired 11,000 air-traffic controllers for illegally striking in 1981.

Schut also faced resistance from Jerry Wurf, the powerful national president of AFSCME. Wurf was worried comparable worth would detract from the civil rights movement, with which he was deeply involved.

But by late 1981 Wurf had died and his successor, Gerald McEntee, was more receptive. AFSCME steered into the storm. It filed a complaint with the federal

The union's comparable worth lawsuit featured eight women plaintiffs, including, from left: Willie Mae Willis, Penny Comstock-Rowland, Peggy Holmes, Helen Castrilli and Louise Peterson. George Masten, director of the State Federation of Employees, is third from left. *AFSCME Council 28*

Equal Employment Opportunity Commission, a necessary first step before going to court. The EEOC did not respond in the allotted 180 days. Just as that deadline passed, President Reagan appointed Clarence Thomas, a future Supreme Court justice, to head the commission. Thomas would prove dismissive of comparable worth in subsequent EEOC cases.

By July 1982, when Newman and AFSCME filed a discrimination lawsuit in U.S. District Court, more than 100 state employees were paid so little they received welfare checks. Most of the workers were clerks and single mothers with take-home pay of less than $1,000 a month.

The union lawsuit featured eight women plaintiffs. Soon, AFSCME had more public relations people than lawyers working on comparable worth. The plaintiffs' stories made their way into newspapers and the airwaves.

Helen Castrilli, a medical secretary at Western State Hospital, felt her blood pressure rise whenever she looked out her office window at the gardeners. Castrilli knew the gardeners made $300 more a month than she did working in a pathology lab, where she was required to transcribe autopsy and surgical reports, order supplies and schedule tests.

"I'm not talking horticulture," she said about the gardeners. "I watch these guys work. They mow, they dig up flower beds, they do minor pruning—the kind of thing my son did to earn money to buy his first car."

Castrilli studied business at Tacoma's Lincoln High School. She wanted to be a secretary because her dad spoke about how helpful his office secretary was. That sounded "pretty neat" to her. She started as a clerk-stenographer at the hospital in the late 1950s when many women worked just to supplement their husband's income.

She worked until she had children. "I wanted to stay home and raise them—that's what women did in those days—but I was out for only five years when inflation drove me back." In 1970 her income was needed to help pay basic bills. She and her husband, Louis, a forklift operator, owned a three-bedroom home with a recreation room, fireplace, and small above-ground pool. They had two children and Castrilli worried about how to pay for their college education.

"We knew we were making history," said Helen Castrilli, president of the local union at Western State Hospital. *AFSCME Council 28*

As the union was gearing up for a lawsuit, she became president of the 1,200-member local at the hospital. When she was asked to be a plaintiff, Castrilli, in a quiet but firm voice, said, "You betcha."

At the time of the union lawsuit, more than 100 state employees—mostly women –were paid so little they received welfare checks. *AFSCME Council 28*

She became a leading spokeswoman for the cause. "Through the union, I've learned how to fight back, stand up for my rights, get things done and help other people. But I could never had done it without my husband's support."

She said she felt like a trailblazer. "It's a revolution. We knew we were making history. I've been on a high since the day I became involved, because I'm convinced it's so right."

A tailwind was starting to swirl behind comparable worth. The 1982 elections gave Democrats control of the state Legislature. Belcher had spent a good part of the previous year stumping for the National Women's Political Caucus, encouraging women to run, while also explaining comparable worth to Kiwanis Clubs and women's groups around the state. Helen Sommers and Shirley Galloway, both elected to the Legislature in the 1970s, recruited Belcher to run for a seat in the House. She beat a moderate Republican and became a representative for most of Thurston County. Comparable worth was a top priority for her.

CHRIS GREGOIRE GRADUATED from law school in 1977 and interned with the Attorney General's Office in Spokane. She was preparing her resume when Slade Gorton, the state's attorney general, called.

Washington Attorney General Slade Gorton hired a handful of Gonzaga School of Law graduates to work in his Spokane office (from left): Craig C. Beles, Gayle M. Ogden, Christine O'Grady-Gregoire, Peter J. Bezek and Gary D. Keehn. *Washington Attorney General's Office*

Gorton, she says, realized private law firms were still reluctant to hire women. "He came to the conclusion that if you were a woman in law school and doing well, then you had to have a special bit of gumption and capabilities," she says. And he figured the state could capitalize on the private sector's sexism. She joined Gorton's staff as an assistant attorney general.

Gorton's successor, Ken Eikenberry, promoted Gregoire to head his Spokane office. Then Eikenberry, a Republican like Gorton, made her the state's first woman deputy attorney general. She hadn't heard much about comparable worth. A more pressing problem, she thought, was the kind of in-your-face discrimination she encountered earlier when she applied to be a probation and parole officer.

"I scored high on the test. The regional administrator told me at the end of my interview that he didn't need a token then. But when he did, I'd be among the top on his list," she says. "It was that kind of inherent discrimination that was more concerning at that time than anything other than equal pay."

Now ensconced in Olympia, her subordinates included the team assigned to defend the state against the AFSCME lawsuit. After getting briefed by the team, she met with Eikenberry and his chief deputy Ed Mackie.

"You've got trouble," she told them. "You don't have a trial lawyer on your team."

They looked at her, she says.

Now they did. It was her.

"A huge number of things went through my mind," Gregoire says.

She felt honored that they trusted her with such a big case. But was she up to it? Was it against her personal values?

She requested some time to consider the challenges. But Eikenberry and Mackie weren't asking. She served at their pleasure. And as she later realized, having a woman as the lead attorney on the case was politically astute.

IN BRIEFS and in the Tacoma courtroom of Judge Jack E. Tanner, Gregoire and her team argued that the state had not intentionally discriminated. It had only tried

Federal judge Jack Tanner ruled in 1983 that the state was guilty of "institutionalized discrimination" against employees. The state appealed Tanner's decision. *U.S. District Court*

to reflect the marketplace. What's more, the state's good intentions were evident in its "active, successful affirmative action program" for women in state jobs.

Gregoire also stressed that Washington was a leader in studying "a unique and novel theory of compensating employees—comparable worth." State leaders shouldn't be punished for their bold curiosity, she said.

But the new theory had a flaw, she noted, one that hadn't been addressed scientifically. Comparable worth required subjectivity in scoring jobs. How could you objectively score whose work conditions were more difficult: the nurse who had to put her hand in vomit, or the mechanic sticking his mitt in axle grease?

"At trial we were very clear that attributing points was fraught with bias," she says.

In the end, Gregoire said, the decision of how to pay employees should be left to the people's representatives in the Legislature.

Tanner, who had served in a segregated Army unit during World War II, wasn't buying it.

Contrary to Gregoire's arguments, Tanner said that comparable worth was a reasonable way of setting salaries, and federal civil rights law did extend to the concept. That, in effect, decided that discrimination did occur.

"We were dead on arrival," Gregoire says.

It was no surprise. She felt Tanner, a former Northwest-area president of the NAACP, had made up his mind before the trial. "In my opinion," Gregoire later said, "the judge was acting as a legislator. He was saying, 'This is the right policy; I think they should be paying comparable worth.' "

That notion was reinforced by Tanner's intimidating style. He refused to allow a number of state witnesses to testify, saying he wasn't interested in their perspectives. "And the judge has been unmerciful in the barbs he has directed at the state's attorneys for what has been a

Diana Rock, AFSCME's director of women's issues, was part of the union team that negotiated a $500 million settlement. *AFSCME Council 28*

muddled strategy and stumbling presentation of the state's case," *The Seattle Times* reported.

On September 16, 1983, Tanner ruled that the state was guilty of "direct, overt, institutionalized discrimination."

Tanner rejected the claim that his decision would impose a crushing burden on the state budget. He pointed out that the state had failed to correct the discrimination when it had a budget surplus under Governor Ray. Tanner ordered back pay and raises for 15,000 state workers in female-dominated jobs. The tab was estimated at $840 million.

The union, most of whose members worked in mental health care, social services, transportation, corrections and higher education, was flying high. From coast to coast, Tanner's ruling catapulted an obscure, oddly-named policy to a cause celebre.

Critics blamed Gregoire. "When the state lost at trial, the attorney general got telephone calls from the business community highly critical of me," she said. "Their assumption was that we had lost the trial because I was the lead attorney and I was a woman and therefore I had thrown the case because I wanted the plaintiff women to win." (She insists she would never do that.)

After Tanner's ruling, both the union and Gregoire's team focused on building their records for an appeal. "In fact, appeal is always on everybody's mind in Tanner's courtroom," wrote Doug Underwood, covering the trial for *The Seattle Times*. Some of Tanner's major rulings had been modified or reversed by higher courts.

Phyllis Schafly, a leading opponent of the equal rights amendment, saw comparable worth as "a new rallying point against the ERA." *Library of Congress*

THE NEW YORK TIMES' first edition of 1984 carried the headline, "A New Push to Raise Women's Pay."

Comparable worth had entered the national political arena. Walter Mondale, John Glenn and other Democratic presidential candidates had declared support for the theory. For Phyllis Schafly, a leader in the battle against an equal rights amendment, comparable worth "provided a new rallying point." Schafly's supporters saw comparable worth as "ERA through the back door." Schafly herself sounded an alarm against creeping feminism, elitism, socialism and federalism—all wrapped up in comparable worth.

Schafly came to Washington, D.C., to testify against a study of gender-based pay disparity among federal workers. That analysis was proposed by Dan Evans, a Republican supporter of the ERA and abortion rights, who had moved from the governor's office to the U.S. Senate.

"Let's be blunt," Schafly said. Comparable worth was as an attempt to have wages "set by compensation commissars." A commission overseeing the study would be loaded with advocates, she said, and its bias "so outrageous that one wonders how it could be supported by anyone with a straight face."

Senator Evans' face remained straight, reported Eric Pryne in *The Seattle Times*.

Schafly rose to leave.

In a 1985 exchange with Phyllis Schafly, Dan Evans, then a U.S. Senator, said comparable worth was another step in a continuum that began with the 1963 federal equal pay-for-equal work law. *Washington State Archives*

Just a minute, Evans said. Fortune 500 companies evaluated jobs using techniques similar to what the commission would use, he said. Are they biased?

And about those "commissars," Evans continued. President Reagan would appoint two; Senate Majority Leader Bob Dole would choose another. Would those staunch Republicans select "commissars?"

And what about collective-bargaining agreements? Evans asked. And pay scales set by the Civil Service Commission? Would those exist if the free market was, as Schafly suggested, perfect? And if the market was infallible, wouldn't that call for repealing equal pay for equal work, as well as all wage-and-hour regulations?

"Comparable worth did not come out of the cosmos like Haley's Comet," Evans said in an earlier debate. "It is simply one step in a continuum which began… with the debate over equal pay for equal work."

As the deadline approached for submitting arguments to the U.S. Court of Appeals for the 9th Circuit,* Gregoire was in the hospital delivering her daughter Michelle, "which of course brings all kinds of emotions to the fore." The state had applied for an extension in filing briefs, but union lawyers argued against it, saying her pregnancy was not an unforeseen circumstance.

"The federal appeals court not only granted us the extension we asked for, but more," she says. "I thought, 'Thank goodness someone understands that being a brand-new mom and doing this case can be a bit challenging.'"

In early 1985, the 9th Circuit Court was still months from a decision. Conservatives were rallying against comparable worth. President Reagan called it "cockamamie." Clarence M. Pendleton Jr., chairman of the U.S. Civil Rights Commission,

---

* The U.S. Court of Appeals is divided into 13 circuits by geography. The 9th Circuit includes Alaska, Arizona, California, Hawaii, Idaho, Montana, Nevada, Oregon, Washington, and Guam.

said comparable worth amounted to "middle-class, white women's reparations." In Congress, Republicans lambasted the study of federal workers proposed by Evans.* "The Sexist Socialism Act" and "Feminist Folly," they called it.

EVEN SOME LOCAL PROPONENTS said comparable worth was losing ground. "Those who used to be in the middle of the road are now skeptics. And those who were opponents now seem to have all the arguments on their side," said House Ways and Means Chairman Dan Grimm, a Democrat.

Some men also stood to benefit from comparable worth if data showed they were underpaid in their positions. *AFSCME Council 28*

Again and again, critics returned to the idea that you couldn't compare apples and oranges—or archivists and astronauts. "You tell me how to set up a system outside the marketplace that objectively compares rock musicians and brain surgeons," one attorney said, "and I'll tell you whether nurses and plumbers should have comparable pay."

Advocates such as Belcher and Remick countered that one could indeed count nutritive values of apples and oranges. There are "general characteristics of fruit, such as the number of calories, the vitamin and mineral content, and so on, that make it possible to compare specific apples with specific oranges," Remick said.

In an important development, Booth Gardner ran for governor in 1984. A Democrat with a Harvard Business School degree, he told AFSCME members at their annual convention he was committed to negotiating a settlement for comparable worth. "And we had it on the record, in writing, on tape," says George Masten, then executive director of the state federation. Gardner defeated Jim McDermott, chairman of the state Senate Ways and Means Committee, in the Democratic primary. He reiterated his support for a settlement, criticizing Governor Spellman, who was seeking a second term. "We have to drop the law suits and put on our negotiating suits," Gardner said. Come November, he won 53 percent of the vote.

Three months into his first term, union leaders knocked Gardner for not following through on his campaign promise. Helen Castrilli, head of the union's women's committee, said she was disappointed "with the unwillingness of governors and legislators to put the state's money where their mouths are."

---

* The Senate bill was sponsored by Evans and Alan Cranston, a California Democrat. The House companion bill's chief sponsor was Mary Rose Oakar, an Ohio Democrat.

Just three weeks before the 9th Circuit issued its opinion, Gardner held a press conference to again state his support for the "basic fairness" of a settlement. He also said he hired a trio of private-sector attorneys, including Susan Agid of Seattle, to lead negotiations.

Legislators appropriated $100,000 for Gardner's negotiators. "We wanted the

Governor Booth Gardner with some of the women he appointed to state government. *Mary Faulk Riveland*

governor to hire someone who hasn't been involved (in the case) to truly act as a mediator," said Jennifer Belcher, who chaired the Joint Select Committee on Comparable Worth Implementation. Gardner's negotiators had to beat a January 1st deadline set by lawmakers.

Negotiations between the union and state were to start September 9th, 1985.

Union chief Masten saw the talks as strictly for unionists, not activists. He understood the value of having women outside the union support the cause and apply pressure on lawmakers. But at this critical juncture he'd take input, and no more, from women's groups and their leaders. They wouldn't have a hand in negotiations or press conferences. "I'll admit I had blinders on," he says. "I did not let these outside groups interfere with where the organization was headed."

He couldn't afford to, says Gary Moore, who succeeded Masten in late 1985. Once the union had committed its resources to litigation it had to stay disciplined and stick to its strategy. "You couldn't run the risk of having others screwing it up," Moore says.

AFSCME v. STATE of Washington was heard by a three-judge panel. Their decision, issued five days before scheduled settlement talks, was written by Anthony Kennedy, who would become a U.S. Supreme Court justice in 1988.[*]

"Feminists groaned" at his 9th Circuit opinion.[**]

The three male judges totally reversed Tanner's decision, finding it flawed on legal principles. In sum, Kennedy said AFSCME failed to show the state intended to illegally discriminate. The state was following the market, he said. "Neither law

---

[*] President Reagan nominated Kennedy for the high court.
[**] The 9th Circuit ruling came on September 4, 1985.

Attorney General Ken Eikenberry was a critic of comparable worth, but didn't interfere with Gregoire's legal work on the case. *Washington State Archives*

nor logic deems the free market system a suspect enterprise."

Washington lawmakers could choose to enact a comparable worth policy, he said. No one was stopping the state. But the law "does not obligate it to eliminate an economic inequality it did not create."

As for the specific findings of the state's comparable worth study, Kennedy added, "we reject a rule that would penalize rather than commend employers for their effort and innovation in undertaking such a study."

In the pathology lab at Western State Hospital, plaintiff Castrilli said, "You've got to be kidding."

The 9th Circuit decision brought another round of criticism for Gregoire. This time Eikenberry "got calls saying it was wrong for a woman to have abandoned the women employees of the state of Washington," she says.

Gregoire had been confident the state would prevail on appeal. But she expected the 9th Circuit would find flaws in Tanner's methods and reasoning and send it back to the trial court for reconsideration. "That was a surprise that we won in court outright," she says.

She immediately understood that the ruling leveled the bargaining table. Before the appeals court decision it had not been in the state's interest to settle, she told the governor. State leaders held a weak hand under Tanner's edict. But now the state had some leverage. In Gregoire's mind, she hadn't delivered a crippling blow to comparable worth. She had corrected for Tanner's heavy thumb on the scale. What's more, Gardner *wanted* to raise women's pay. And she had argued in court that policy on salaries was best made by the governor and the Legislature. Now it seemed the 9th Circuit ruling might produce the best outcome in Washington.

While its spokesman vowed that the union had another round left to fight at the U.S. Supreme Court, Gregoire didn't think so. Her prescient quote was that "the decision we have today is the ultimate opinion we will have in this case."

AFSCME attorney Newman didn't want to settle, says Masten. "He wanted his trial at the U.S. Supreme Court." But Masten didn't know how long that would take, never mind what the outcome might be. "And our people wanted some resolution," he says. It had been 11 years since Washington's historic study, eight years since Governor Ray wiped out proposed funding for comparable worth.

He called AFSCME national President Gerald McEntee and got Newman fired.

FACING THE DEADLINE imposed by the Legislature, Gardner wanted to steam ahead toward a settlement, but was wary of the state's top lawyer.

Eikenberry sounded almost giddy after the appeals court decision. "I'm delighted with the result," the attorney general said. "It really devalues the union's position." Gardner assumed the Attorney General's Office was not going to be all that dedicated to brokering a deal.

Becky Bogard, a key Gardner aide, met with Gregoire. "I was suspicious of

Booth Gardner said Gregoire's work on comparable worth led him to appoint her head of the Department of Ecology. *Washington Attorney General's Office*

Chris at first because she worked for a Republican and I worked for a Democrat," says Bogard. The two intended to talk over a glass of wine. "And we drank a bottle," Bogard says.

The more Bogard talked, the "more open and honest she became about how skeptical they were about me," Gregoire says. In turn, she made it clear that state attorneys worked for their clients. And if the governor and Legislature wanted a settlement, then "we will settle, and we will do it right."

True, Eikenberry had publicly stated his opposition to the concept of comparable worth. But he was able to set his personal opinion aside. "To Ken's credit, he had me go do my job as a lawyer and he never interfered with me."

Gregoire and Agid became a formidable team—and good friends. Likewise, she and Bogard, who served as treasurer on her first campaign for attorney general.

With the clock ticking toward deadline, negotiators for the union and state signed a deal on the afternoon of New Year's Eve. It called for an estimated $482 million in raises for state workers. But no back pay. And the union agreed not to take the case to the U.S. Supreme Court. The negotiating teams celebrated with Champagne in the governor's office.

The national press had differing views of the proposed raises of at least 2.5 percent for 35,000 state workers, mostly women. A *Chicago Tribune* headline hailed the deal as a "Major Victory for Comparable Worth." AFSCME's McEntee called the Washington workers "pioneers" and said their deal would renew pressure on state and local lawmakers.

On the other hand, a *Los Angeles Times* story predicted that opponents, including President Reagan and business leaders, would see the settlement as a victory

Eleanor Lee, a Republican state senator, was an outspoken supporter of comparable worth. *Washington State Archives*

because it would leave Kennedy's 9th Circuit ruling untouched and the law of the land.

But the agreement still had to be ratified by the Legislature, where "tears of rage" would flow.

THE $482 MILLION DEAL was expected to pass the Legislature. But the Democratic majorities in both chambers were narrow. And approval wasn't certain, particularly with business leaders opposing it.

The Association of Washington Business, Safeco and Boeing lobbied against the bill, afraid that if state workers won pay equity it would create pressure for a similar policy in private industry. Boeing lobbyists "worked frantically." Two of them camped out in an office used by GOP Senate Leader Jeannette Hayner, convenient for buttonholing lawmakers. Opponents succeeded in delaying a Friday vote until the following Monday, giving them more time to massage senators.

"I didn't expect Boeing to break their pick on this," said Mark Brown, spokesman and lobbyist for the Washington State Federation of Employees, adding that the weekend delay left him a "nervous wreck."

Under the strain, Senator Eleanor Lee of Burien lashed out. A feminist and comparable worth advocate, Lee said she openly wept in a meeting with fellow Republicans, because she was so appalled at their tactics. Lee accused Hayner of threatening to cut her off from campaign contributions from "our friends" if she voted for the settlement. Hayner denied the charge, saying Lee was carried away by her own emotions.

When the vote was called, two Democrats, A.L. "Slim" Rasmussen of Tacoma and Brad Owen of Shelton, voted against the deal. Five Republicans, including Lee voted for it; three others, including Hayner, did not vote. The final tally was surprisingly lopsided, 30—16 in favor of the settlement.

Three months later, raises started showing up in paychecks, along with a dash of self-esteem.

Castrilli was ecstatic about the extra $106 a month she'd get. She said it would go to bills and her daughter's UW tuition. And the raise put a bounce in the secretary's step. "Sure it feeds the ego," she said. "There's nothing wrong with that."

Not all women faulted Gregoire for her role in the appeals court ruling, which would prove damaging to the national comparable-worth cause.

"Gregoire did take flak," said Remick, who went on to become UW's assistant provost for equal opportunity. "I know she was supportive of women's issues at the time, but as a lawyer that was not the issue. She did a good job."

After a testy start, union leaders came to see Gregoire as playing a key role in negotiations. At first, Masten did not want her involved—or even in the room. "We were negotiating with the governor, not the attorney general," he says. "But as things went on she became an important part and positive. She became more of an advocate for implementing comparable worth rather than opposing it."

She had more background and expertise than anyone on Booth Gardner's team. And as Brown, the union spokesman, understood it, when the management team met, "she was a driving force to bring them along and get them closer to where the union was and bridge the gaps."

Belcher believes Gregoire didn't want to carry the fight to the U.S. Supreme Court, where the state appeared to have a good chance of killing comparable worth. "Chris is a settlement person," Belcher says. "She likes the finality, I think, of being able to direct things to happen rather than just hope it happens." If you go to court, you may come away empty-handed, or the other side might. "My guess is she was person who helped make (the settlement) happen so that the state didn't win or lose, but everybody won," says Belcher, who later became the first woman elected Commissioner of Public Lands.

Gardner was impressed by Gregoire's team and its ability to pivot from legal critics of comparable worth to dealmakers granting the biggest pay-equity raises in history. So impressed was the governor that he would soon ask Gregoire to head the state's Department of Ecology. Litigation had stalled progress at the agency, Gardner said, and he needed someone to stop the lawsuits "so we can get things done." She accepted the assignment.

"So the fight moves on," says Gregoire about the persistent gender gap in pay. "Because inherent, as Ruth Bader Ginsburg would say, is a bias sitting in there. All the time." *Washington Governor's Office*

She ran for attorney general in 1992 and won by beating respected King County Prosecuting Attorney Norm Maleng. Three years later, a headline about her asked, "The attorney general: Governor in waiting?"

Gardner later said that if he hadn't spotted and promoted Gregoire she "wouldn't have been governor."

Gregoire agreed. Unequivocally.

THE SETTLEMENT amounted to real progress, Remick said. But it didn't fully implement comparable worth. It only got the state close to that goal.

The agreement required the state to bring salaries up to 95 percent of a line between the average of men's and women's wages by July 1993. That line was plotted by Remick, using computer punch cards to run a statistical regression analysis.

The federal General Accounting Office later analyzed the settlement's outcome. GAO looked at a sample of 109 "benchmark" jobs used in drawing the salary line. Well over half of the jobs that had been below the line moved up to it in almost five years.* The state expected full compliance by July 1992. After compounding the expense over time, the GAO estimated the cost of the settlement at $571 million.

Comparable-worth campaigns surfaced beyond Washington's borders. AFSCME members in San Jose, Calif. won pay adjustments after going on strike in 1981. *Walter P. Reuther Library, Wayne State University*

The impact of the AFSCME case spread far beyond Washington's borders, says Michael McCann, a University of Washington professor and author of *Rights at Work*, a well-researched assessment of the pay equity movement in the 1980s.

By 1989, an estimated $450 million had been spent on raises addressing pay disparity. Twenty states accounted for most of that. Seven of those states, including Washington, were considered to be implementing comparable worth. Related studies, research and data collection were underway in 44 states. Some $6 million more was spent in 112 counties, including King County. Another $60 million was paid in raises to public employees in 50 major cities, from New York to Los Angeles.

And the benefits of litigation amounted to more than money. McCann's research showed a steep spike in national coverage of comparable worth after *AFSCME v. Washington*—the "biggest bang" of all the pay-equity lawsuits—went to court. That publicity, in turn, helped raise consciousness and invited others to join the cause. Some of the 140 activists McCann interviewed said comparable worth's greatest achievement was changing hearts and minds. Women said they gained confidence and felt a newfound sense of solidarity.

For most of those 140 activists, Washington was the catalyst. "It all of a

---

* GAO found that 44 of the 109 jobs were below the designated salary line before the settlement; only 19 were below it as of January 1991.

sudden looked like the issue of the future," one said. A flurry of action followed the case. A Massachusetts special committee on comparable worth credited the Washington lawsuit with "enormous social and political impact."

But that impact cut both ways. The 9ᵗʰ Circuit decision was a harbinger, the tip of a huge iceberg bearing down on comparable worth.

By 1986, powerful forces were coalescing. The U.S. Chamber of Commerce and the Business Roundtable fashioned themselves as sophisticated counterbalances to unions and liberal movements. The Reagan Administration had sent strong signals against workers' rights— from firing air traffic controllers, to appointing Thomas to head the Equal Employment Opportunity Commission. Reagan and allies began employing a new tool—the argument that anti-discrimination campaigns were about installing "racial and gender 'quotas,' " says McCann. Never mind that the quotas claim was fantasy, he says. It stuck.

AFSCME's loss in the court of appeals was a clear signal, McCann says, that judicial support for comparable worth claims was waning. Kennedy's arguments would be echoed by other judges.

The U.S. Supreme Court's 1989 decision in *Wards Cove Packing v. Atonio* all but sunk the cause. It was a 5-4 decision, with three of the justices in the majority appointed by Reagan. The majority reprised 9ᵗʰ Circuit arguments by Kennedy, who by then had joined the high court. The justices also expanded the business defenses to the point that, as one feminist put it, "discrimination is all right if everyone else does it." After the ruling sunk in, it was widely seen as "the death of pay equity claims," says McCann, who is writing a book about the case involving Filipino cannery workers.

During the life of Washington's comparable worth settlement, the national gender gap in pay narrowed. When the agreement kicked in, women earned 64 cents for every $1 earned by men. Seven years later, by 1993, women were up to 71.5 cents. The gap had shrunk by a penny a year.

By 2002, progress had slowed, with the gap at 76.6 cents. Then it stalled. Fifteen years later the gap seemed stuck at 80 percent. At the current rate, women would not achieve pay equity until 2058.

"That sounds pretty optimistic," Remick says.

THE WHITE HOUSE convened a National Equal Pay Task Force in 2013. It reported a bevy of advances.

Women were earning a majority of Bachelor's, Masters' *and* Doctoral degrees. In 1960, roughly 15 percent of managers in the workforce were women; four decades later almost 40 percent of mangers were women. Almost one-quarter of women earned higher wages than their working husbands. Women were increasingly working in the fields of science, technology, engineering and math (known collectively as STEM).

But there was plenty to offset those gains.

The narrowing pay gap had as much to do with declining men's wages as it did with rising women's salaries. And most of the increases in women's earning power were reserved for those with a college degree. "Women with less education saw much smaller or even no changes in earnings." And over half of all women were employed in lower-paying sales, service and administrative support positions.

Women might have been busting glass ceilings, but a gap still existed for women with advanced degrees and corporate positions. A 2008 study of newly trained doctors, "even after controlling for the effects of specialty, practice setting, work hours and other factors," found the women physicians earned $17,000 less a year.

Job segregation also remained a reality. Women were still more likely to enter occupations where the majority of workers are female, such as health care, education and human services. Segregation was not just a simple matter of women's choices, the Task Force said. Historical "patterns of exclusion and discrimination paint a more complex picture."

The President's Council of Economic Advisors issued a 1998 report in which they said about 40 percent of the gender gap in pay couldn't be explained by factors such as skills, experience and union status. Discrimination, they concluded, likely accounted for that 40 percent. Evidence of alleged discrimination played a part in EEOC charges and multi-million dollar settlements with corporations such as Allstate Insurance, Boeing, Coca Cola, General Motors, Morgan Stanley, Texaco and Wachovia.

As solutions, the Task Force suggested policies that would expand protections for workers who share salary information, as well as those that would revive principles of comparable worth. But bills featuring those policies lanquished in the GOP-controlled Congress in recent years.

In 2018, Washington adopted one of the country's strongest pay-equity laws when Governor Inslee signed HB 1506. *Washington State House Democrats*

Not waiting any longer for Congress, the Washington Legislature pursued those policies through passage of a bill known as HB 1506. Washington joined an elite group of states with strong pay equity laws in 2018, according to the American Association of University Women, thanks to its new law.

The law allows employees to talk about their earnings with co-workers and ask for equal pay, without fear of retaliation. It also marks a comeback for principles of comparable worth. Washington's 1943 Equal Pay outlawed lower wages for women "similarly employed" to men. But the pioneering law didn't define "similarly employed." The new law defines it as jobs that require similar skill, effort and responsibility, performed under similar work conditions—the essential criteria used in comparable worth. California adopted the same standards in 2016.

And while Washington previously banned discrimination in promotions, its new law expands protections against depriving an employee of "career advancement opportunities" that would be available but for an employee's gender. In that realm, Washington goes further than California and federal law.

All the more reason, Remick says, that comparable worth shouldn't be viewed as a failure. Other state and local governments used the approach to examine and change their pay systems. The issue raised awareness, galvanized women and spurred them to organize. It sparked serious research. It led some private employers to examine and alter their practices. And the term "pay equity" lives on as a reminder of continuing segregation and discrimination.

Comparable worth is now memorialized in state collective bargaining law. It forbids any proposal "that would be inconsistent" with the landmark comparable worth agreement.

Another state law requires that job classifications and salaries for state workers can only be changed for a few reasons. One reason is "inequities," defined as similar work in different job classes. State officials say they frequently review job classifications for proper compensation, and comparable-worth considerations are integrated into those review processes.

"So the fight moves on," Gregoire says. "Because inherent, as Ruth Bader Ginsburg would say, is a bias sitting in there. All the time. And we have to keep fighting that inherent bias that leads to the kind of outcomes which brought the comparable worth lawsuit in the first place."

Bob Young
Legacy Washington

In a society racing toward a high-tech future "while still mired in a racially divided past," Trish Millines Dziko was in a position to make a difference. She quit Microsoft to create the nonprofit Technology Access Foundation in 1996. *Benjamin Benschneider/The Seattle Times*

TRISH MILLINES DZIKO

"YOU HAVE IT, YOU SHARE IT"

Sit with Trish Millines Dziko and you can still feel the passion that drove her to walk away from serious money in order to teach computer skills to minority children. It's in her gaze, her candor, her words. *Evolutionary. Revolutionary. Generational change.*

Dziko (pronounced "Zeeko") has been at it since 1996, when she turned her back on more Microsoft stock options to create the nonprofit Technology Access Foundation. "We've been very lucky," she said when she retired from Microsoft at 39, a millionaire. "And one of my first instincts as a person who grew up fairly poor is: You have it, you share it."

An African American woman who rose from programming to prominence in Puget Sound's largely white male geekocracy, she has been anything but retiring. She remains committed to changing the world one kid at a time.

In her vision, that also means one teacher at a time, one principal, one superintendent, one school board, one PTSA, and one archaic policy at a time. While she's at it, why not try to transform the culture of philanthropy?

And *do* get her started on diversity. "It's become a multi-billion dollar industry with very little to show for it," she says. The tech industry is still primarily male and white. And it's hardly alone. Nonprofits whose constituents are mostly people of color tend to be run by white people. A survey of the largest nonprofits and foundations in the U.S., including 180 organizations working in education, youth development, and social welfare and justice, found that 87 percent of all executive directors were white.

"They don't look like me. But they're serving people like me," Dziko says.

Her nonprofit, staffed mostly by women and minorities, started as an after-school program culminating in technology-related internships and $1,000 scholarships. It has morphed into a model for teaching in public schools. In its history, the foundation—or TAF, as it's known—reports that it has served some 19,000 students resulting in a 95-percent high school graduation rate and a 100-percent college acceptance rate for those who applied.

Now, after two decades of challenges, frustrations and lessons, Dziko strides through the sixth- through 12th-grade public school that TAF runs in partnership

Originally an after-school program culminating in technology-related internships, Dziko's foundation—known as TAF—has partnered with the Federal Way and Tacoma public school districts. *Technology Access Foundation (TAF)*

with the Federal Way public school district north of Tacoma. Called TAF@Saghalie, it has adopted Dziko's philosophy, which means weaving science, technology, engineering and math into child-centered and project-based learning. That, in turn, has led to variances in district policy to allow students to use the internet and email during school, and to read *The Hate U Give*, a best-selling young-adult novel about a 16-year-old girl who witnesses a police officer shooting her childhood friend.

Dziko, who played college basketball, still moves with the grace of an athlete. She stops to drape a friendly arm around a boy and exchange a few quiet words with a girl. Then she glides down a hall showcasing college acceptance letters and pops into a ninth grade biology class where students and their teacher, Brandon Carlisle, contrast the evolutionary theories of Charles Darwin and one of his contemporaries, Jean-Baptiste Lamarck. The walls are decorated with student-made posters of science heroes. They're not just the usual suspects like Tesla and Einstein. There's also Neil deGrasse Tyson, the astrophysicist of Puerto Rican and African American descent, and Shirley Ann Jackson, a physicist and first African American woman to be awarded the National Medal of Science. Dziko is quick to credit teachers and others for TAF's success. "We are the product of people who work here and we wouldn't be anything without them." They're people like Sherry Williams who joined TAF when it was four months old as an administrative assistant. Williams now oversees its operations.

But as TAF's executive director, Dziko is still the point guard, directing the team, guiding strategy, doing the bulk of the big fundraising, her raptor vision looking for opportunities for others. And she remains the public face of the foundation. It's a role that's somewhat uncomfortable for her.

Dziko (pronounced "Zeeko") and her team won the 2018 "Geeks Give Back" award from the tech news site *Geekwire*.

"Sometimes I feel the pressure of living up to the way people think I am. People think I can solve anything. I really appreciate that people trust me. But the expectation is that I will always be on-point. But I'm not always. I'm just like everyone else. I have challenges like everyone else."

She does promise this: "I am always who I am. No matter what the situation, you get Trish. I certainly know how to tailor my speech. But you will get the truth no matter what."

THERE IS NO QUESTION where Dziko got her drive, vision and selflessness. "That comes directly from my mother," she says. "Everything that I am as a person has to do with how she raised me and the things that I observed with her and the things she was able to accomplish as a woman who cleaned houses for a living. You can't get any better of a role model than her."

Pat Millines, Dziko's mother, was born in 1906 in rural Putnam County, Georgia. She and her family migrated to New Jersey and settled in Belmar, a small seashore town just south of Asbury Park, which would become renowned for launching Bruce Springsteen's career. (Springsteen's E Street Band is named for a spot in Belmar where they used to practice.)

In Manhattan, Pat Millines cleaned the residences that the Warner brothers of Hollywood fame kept in the Pierre Hotel, on the doorstep of Central Park.* Millines would pocket cab fare they gave her and take the bus home. She did the same with lunch money. And she worked 51 weeks a year, cleaning two homes a day. That kind of thriftiness allowed her to buy her own house in Belmar. And then another.

She was a single woman in her early 50s and childless when she adopted Trish. "I knew I was adopted but you don't ask, 'Why did you adopt me? ' I have

---

* Trish received the Arthur Ashe Athletic Association Leadership Award for supporting youth in a 1998 ceremony at the Pierre Hotel.

Pat Millines cleaned houses 51 weeks a year, paid all her bills promptly in cash, bought two houses, and stressed to her daughter the importance of going to college. *Trish Millines Dziko*

no idea, but I know I'm grateful," Trish says. Pat raised Trish by herself. She also took in troubled relatives, led drives to start three local Baptist churches, and paid all her bills promptly in cash.

Her mother stressed the importance of Trish going to college. "Well, as a black woman on the East Coast, who grew up in the South," Trish says, "she didn't have a choice, right? You do what you can to thrive to make sure the next generation gets something better than what you had."

The same was true for her cousins. "None of our parents had gone to college but they knew that was the thing we needed to do to be successful."

At around the age of 13, Trish told her mother she didn't really see the value of going to college.

"Another one of my genius moments," she says with a laugh. "So she made me come work for her that summer cleaning houses. That was my job. And it was hard. Two houses a day, and then also the spring, she prepares houses for the people who come down from New York for the summer, so I did that as well, and lesson learned."

AT ASBURY PARK High School, Trish took Swahili for three years and remembers reading a lot for English classes: Hemingway, Hesse, Shakespeare, Solzhenitsyn. Early on, she realized she was way ahead of her classmates in algebra. Her teachers got her into the honors track for math. Only later did it dawn on Trish that school officials had probably assumed she couldn't do higher level math because she was black.

She was "kind of geeky" back then. But there wasn't much to explore in the way of technology, so she carted the film projector around to classes, threaded celluloid through sprockets inside the machine and onto a take-up reel, flipped the bulb on, and watched the device entertain her peers.

When it came to sports, *The Asbury Park Press* ran a picture of her as an 11-year-old at a swimming class. Trish was then known as Pat Millines, the same as her mother. Almost seven years later the newspaper depicted the agile teen in high-top Converse All-Stars shooting a layup in a state championship game. The only senior on the squad, she was at point guard in Asbury Park High School's 57-37 victory.

Pat Millines, the only senior on the Asbury Park team, goes up with layup as Phillipsburg players are left standing flat-footed. Bishop girls won the state title, 57-37, Saturday night.

QUEENS OF COURT — Asbury Park High School's state championship girls' basketball team, which finished a 24-1 season, is proud of its title trophy and the net through which it poured the points last weekend. The starting five, left to right, are Colleen Collins, Pat Millines, Martha Megill, Betty McGuire and Pam Reaves. The Blue Bishops also are prominent on The Daily Register's first annual All-Monmouth County team which appears on page 21.

"It was the sport you played if you liked sports," she says about basketball in the 1970s. There weren't many women role models in the sport then, so she emulated New York Knicks' guard Earl "The Pearl" Monroe, copying his spin move. "I played at the playground in South Belmar. I always played with the boys."

She was Asbury Park's high-scorer in their 1975 championship game. But she really loved feeding the ball to teammates, creating shots for others.

In her senior year, while studying and playing championship-caliber ball, she helped care for her mother, who was bedridden with cancer of the pancreas and liver. Pat Millines died a month before Trish's high-school graduation. Her will stipulated that Trish would not get access to her modest estate until she turned 35. It was another of Pat's efforts to help Trish make her own way.

Alone at 18, Trish entered nearby Monmouth College that fall, the first woman to receive a full basketball scholarship to the school.* "I think if I had done anything different it would have been a huge slap in the face to my mom, a huge sign of disrespect to her. She worked so hard to get me to where I needed to be."

She wanted to major in electrical engineering, but her prerequisite classes conflicted with basketball practice. She switched to computer science. "She was an athlete when she enrolled here, but more of a student by the time she left," said Monmouth coach Joan Martin.

She was invited to try out for the fledgling Jersey Gems of the short-lived Women's Professional Basketball League. But her salary would've been in the

---

* Trish also lettered in volleyball and softball. The school became Monmouth University in 1995.

Dziko's first job out-of-college was writing software to test a new military radar system. "It was really cool," she says. *Trish Millines Dziko*

neighborhood of $6,000. After graduating from Monmouth in 1979, without the benefit of interviewing or negotiating skills, she landed a job at the Computer Sciences Corporation in New Jersey.

Her job was writing software to test a new military radar system. "It was really cool," she says. But then she learned that others had been hired in programming without a background in the field, and they were making thousands more than her. "I'm kind of sorry that I learned about how those things worked, because I was just happily going along," she said after getting a glimpse of sexism and racism in corporate America.

SHE SOON LANDED a job with Hughes Aircraft in Tucson, Arizona. This time she negotiated her salary and moving expenses. She bought a motorcycle, got an apartment, and learned that programming at Hughes was quite prestigious. "You were like, you know, a god."

Even better, she transferred to a team headed by a woman and became a "really good programmer." She made more friends. But Tucson was hot as hate. And it was a college town that seemed to hibernate in the summer. And when you're in your early 20s, like Trish was, you want a little more than stifling heat and sleepy summers. She had visited San Francisco during the first annual Gay Olympics and liked the city.

She decided to move there. Without a job. During an economic recession. She bought a small motor home, about the size of a camper you might see on a pickup truck, she says. She packed her dog and cat. But she couldn't find a job in San Francisco. For six months she lived out of her motor home, parking at a marina and the beach.

"It's not a time that I'm particularly proud of so I generally don't talk about it," she says. "But what I am proud of is that I looked at myself and realized that, 'Okay, you can't keep living like this.'" And she found a job teaching programming.

During Thanksgiving 1984 she visited Seattle and liked the mountains, the water, and the neighborhoods, with their own parks and community centers. She liked that "nobody blinks an eye" at gay and lesbian people. It's one reason she calls Seattle one of the country's best places. "I like that we can go out as a family and everybody already makes the assumption that we are a family, and they talk to us like they talk to the straight couple with kids standing next to us. I love it."

She packed up a U-Haul and moved north in January 1985. But this time she had savings to last six months. She had interviews lined up. She figured she'd work for Boeing, which offered her a job. Instead she went to work for Telecalc, which offered her a better experience as manager of its testing department. There, she was introduced to people who had worked at an upstart company called Microsoft.

ALTHOUGH NOT WIDELY known, there was a time when women flourished in computer programming. Men tended to think hardware was a greater engineering challenge and more lucrative. The first programmable digital computer in the U.S., known as ENIAC held more than 17,000 vacuum tubes. "In contrast, programming it seemed menial, even secretarial," wrote Clive Thompson in "The Secret History of Women in Coding." Women, some believed, were better suited to the precise and repetitive nature of programming—as if it were knitting with numbers.

Women, some believed, were better suited to the precise, repetitious nature of programming computers such as ENIAC (above) the first programmable digital computer in the United States. *U.S. Army Research Lab*

And computers didn't see gender. They didn't care about skin pigmentation.

By 1960, the proportion of women in computing and math professions, classified together in federal government data, was 27 percent and climbing.

By the 1983-84 academic year, 37 percent of all students graduating with degrees in computer and information sciences were women.

Shortly after Trish first visited Seattle, the programming pipeline began to change. Paths in college, and to the industry, and up the chain of command, favored a new type—the teen obsessive, hunched over a keyboard, sporting a pale "cathode ray tan," along with a hard-core attitude.

The tide of girls studying computer science receded. By 2010, the share of women graduating with such degrees plummeted to 18 percent.

Research showed that gender began to matter. From where the first home computers were located (hint: not in girls' bedrooms), to who got one as a gift, to the informal "internships" sons and fathers enjoyed over the new gizmos, to stereotypes of white male nerds in pop culture—all of it gave boys encouragement and an edge over girls.

By the time they got to college, boys were ahead in programming and girls (as well as some minorities) were seen as not committed enough. Women, along with black and Latino students, began to drop out, even though a student's decision to quit computer studies or switch majors "did not seem to be correlated with coding talent." A seminal study at Carnegie Mellon University—which led to the book *Unlocking the Clubhouse: Women in Computing*—found that by the third year of college, women who remained in the field caught up with the "hard-core" boys.

Boys, it turns out, did not have an innate advantage in computer science. But they had gained a cultural one. As more males dominated the college and professional ranks, they tended to hire—and promote—those who were like them.

That's when women really felt they hit a wall.

TRISH STARTED WRITING software for Microsoft in 1988, which broadened her skills. But in time, she came to dislike her manager and his "in-your-face" style that was popular at the company. One day as her team prepared to ship a new product, Trish kept hitting a bug in tests. The bug popped up at different times without a detectable pattern. She and her manager set up computers side-by-side and kept running the test script. They sat together all night trying to figure out the problem. They got to know each other a bit. "And I'm like, well, he's a pretty nice guy."

That guy—who remains her friend to this day—was Bob Muglia, who went on to become a top executive at Microsoft. He hired her as a program manager in 1990 to work on a tool for database management that later would be used by organizations around the world, including most Fortune 100 companies. She was part of a small team. They were young. "We didn't have any lives. We were there, you know, seven days a week, sometimes 15 hours a day." And they "kicked some butt."

She eventually moved to the hardware group where she became program manager for the kids' mouse called EasyBall. "That was a cool project, let me tell you. I have my EasyBall still at home," she says.

On top of that, she was going on recruiting trips for minority applicants, having dinners with candidates of color the company wanted to hire, and playing a part in founding Blacks at Microsoft.

"BAM was created totally out of necessity," Trish says. "We had people coming from historically black colleges, coming from neighborhoods where it was predominantly one race, and coming to the northwest where it's all white, mostly. And coming to Microsoft where it's really, really white. And living on the Eastside." They had questions, such as where to go to church, or for a haircut, or to socialize.

Only about 40 African Americans worked at Microsoft then. BAM organized a Minority Student Day that brought kids from Seattle's Central District to Redmond, gave them a tour, showed them the technology, and basked in their excitement. They fed families at Thanksgiving and bought gifts for them at Christmas. They set precedents for diversity groups at other companies. She doubts any similar group anywhere "had as much fun as we did."

She then decided to leave the familiar harbor of technical work for an opening in the diversity department. She "really, really, really wanted to pursue this whole issue of diversity" and how to recruit more people of color to the company. But she went from a respected job to one that some saw as threatening. She hit waves of resistance.

"You have to get people to really think about their own privileges in the world before they will change for somebody else. And you have to convince them that giving some of that to someone else doesn't necessarily take it away (from them). All the really hard things I couldn't get people to do."

Trish also came to realize that while Microsoft was improving its recruiting, people of color still faced a problem. The tech industry was getting its talent from colleges. And college

B.A.M.! to Honor King on Monday

Next Monday, January 18, is the day set aside to honor Dr. Martin Luther King, Jr. Even though it's not a Microsoft holiday, you can celebrate for an hour or two with B.A.M.! (Blacks at Microsoft).

On January 18, B.A.M.! will be showing video documentaries about King in the Building 21 Columbia Room (1129) from 1-2:30 P.M. Please join us.

The dream lives at Microsoft.
—B.A.M.!

B.A.M.! President Trish Millines beside a poster of Martin Luther King, Jr.

opportunities were limited for people of modest incomes. There was a reservoir of talent in Seattle being ignored, brimming with girls and kids of color. Microsoft and others weren't seeing it because it was at the high-school level.

ON A WINTER DAY in 1996, Trish and her partner Jill Hull, a mental health counselor, were walking their dogs and bemoaning the lack of opportunities for kids of color. In a society racing toward a high-tech future "while still mired in a racially divided past," Trish was now in a position to make a difference. Microsoft's program of providing employees with stock options had created several thousand new millionaires, including Trish, as stock value rose by a factor of 250 in the decade after the company went public in 1986.

But rather than chase more zeros for her bank account, she turned to the gap between technological haves and have-nots and its implications for children of color. She quit the company four months after her turning point conversation in the park with Hull. The duo created the Technology Access Foundation. "It seemed to happen overnight," said Hull, who co-managed the program until she left to have the couple's first child. (They would adopt three more at birth.) "It isn't like Trish to dwell on problems. She's about action."

Trish's action plan for TAF was to flood the technology industry with so many talented people of color that companies could no longer use the excuse that they couldn't find capable young minority candidates, particularly from the most overlooked populations—African Americans, Latinos, Native Americans and Pacific Islanders.

In October 1997, TAF opened in a building in south Seattle. It initially offered after-school technology classes for high-schoolers and classes concentrating on math, writing and problem-solving for kindergarten-through-eighth-graders. The programs required high-schoolers to log six hours of learning a week over the course of eight months. And they imposed strict rules about attendance, grades and apparel.

The William H. Gates Foundation gave $444,000 to TAF just after its first birthday. Trish and Jill would donate $250,000 to the foundation.

In its first year, 27 out of 32 students made it through the "Technical Teens Internship Program." They learned networking, web development, programming, and media production. Of those, 23 were hired for paid summer internships by area companies and agencies. Soon TAF was turning away more students than it admitted.

That same year, on a gorgeous spring day, Trish and Jill dressed in new outfits. Along with family members from New Jersey and Utah, they gathered in Kerry Park for its magnificent views overlooking Seattle. Trish and Jill walked to an altar but neither one could finish their vows because they started crying. Wind blew out candles and swept flowers off tables. The serious became comical. While not yet legally wed, Trish and Jill considered themselves married. They wanted their kids to have the same last name, and not a hyphenated one, so they chose "Dziko," an African name meaning "of the world."

After Washington adopted its marriage equity law in 2013, Trish and Jill contemplated getting legally married. They wondered what it would really mean. And did it matter? So they asked their kids. Their oldest daughter said she already thought of them

Trish and Jill with their kids: Zora is on the floor in front of Trish, who is holding Isaiah; Elise is leaning on Jill's hip, with Langston lying on the floor in front of Jill. *Trish Millines Dziko*

as married. Their oldest son asked if there would be cake.

They rounded up some close friends and marched into the chambers of King County Superior Court Judge Mary Yu some 16 years after what they considered their real wedding and made it official.

AS TAF BEGAN TO COUNT its alumni in the hundreds, Trish Dziko and foundation staff realized the limitations of out-of-school programs. They built a strategy to reach more students by partnering with public schools. TAF then revealed a plan to establish five new public schools rooted in science, technology, engineering and math, known collectively as STEM, in minority neighborhoods. The foundation hoped to provide at least $1.5 million a year in supplemental funds to each of the schools. It hoped to buy a computer for every student, hire more teachers to keep class sizes low, and extend the school day.

Dziko started hunting for grants, donations and school partners. The first TAF academy, or school-within-a-school, was proposed for Seattle's Rainer Beach High School. In state tests, only 27 percent of Rainier Beach 10th graders passed the math portion and just 3 percent passed the science component. TAF would have a say in choosing the school's principal, teachers and enrollment. While the idea was not entirely novel—the Gates Foundation had encouraged specialized academies within public schools—Dziko was "the first African American, at least locally, to offer a transformative plan backed up by millions of dollars."

Computers don't see gender or skin color. Research has shown that boys don't have an innate advantage in computer science although stereotypes have given them a cultural edge in the field. *Trish Millines Dziko*

But Dziko faced community opposition, in part because the school district excluded parents from early discussions about the school TAF wanted to open in 2008. Local activist Sakara Remmu said people "weren't really sure where she comes from or who she is." Some suspected Dziko's plan was elitist, or were put off by her assertive can-do demeanor. Others even speculated that Dziko, who served on a district school-closure committee, recommended shuttering certain schools so she could take them over. At one community meeting the Rainier Beach PTSA president led a walkout.

Dziko's proposal for Rainier

Beach withered. "It was all politics," she says.

Carla Santorno, superintendent of Tacoma Public Schools, was then chief academic officer for the Seattle district. There was nothing fundamentally wrong with TAF's model, Santorno says. "I believe TAF would've worked effectively in Seattle if there had been a disposition of the public to accept it."

On hearing the news about Seattle, Federal Way schools Superintendent Tom Murphy called Dziko. "I liked what I heard," Murphy said.

He and Dziko agreed to a partnership. Their idea would differ from the charter school model—rejected three times by Washington voters—wherein a private group runs a public school with oversight from a school district. TAF's academy would be the first public school in the state managed with a nonprofit.

A deal was signed to bring the TAF Academy to a campus of portable classrooms nestled between Totem Middle School and Star Lake Elementary

A volunteer helps a student build a circuit at the school TAF runs in partnership with the Federal Way district. *TAF*

School. Both are in Kent but part of the Federal Way district. The academy for sixth- through 12th-graders opened in 2008. Former Microsoft executive Paul Shoemaker, a TAF supporter, said it was as if Trish had to leave Seattle "to get it open." Or as she puts it, "You're never a prophet in your own land."

Plans were hatched two years later to create a second academy in Renton.

But in 2012 charter-school advocates succeeded at their fourth try on the ballot. Washington voters approved Initiative 1240 allowing charter schools in the state. Bill Gates gave $3 million to the I-1240 campaign, which won 50.7 percent of the vote. Paul Allen's company donated $1.6 million.

Under the initiative, charter schools have more latitude than allowed by TAF's model of partnering with public schools. Teachers at a charter school, for instance, aren't necessarily covered under the local district's contract; they can have their own salary structure.*

Dziko says she's agnostic about charter schools. Studies have found mixed results about their success. The "reality is that most charter schools don't do even as well as the TAF Academy," *The Seattle Times* reported in 2012.

---

* Both charters and the TAF model are free and open to all students, and receive public funding based on student enrollment just like traditional schools.

In an annual tradition, TAF staff "high five" students on the last day of the school year in Federal Way. *TAF*

Nevertheless, Dziko's plans for academies in Renton and elsewhere fizzled. "All the philanthropic money went to charter schools," she says.

TAF had to regroup and recast its strategy.

THEY TOOK THEIR model of STEM education for children of color, distilled it to its essence, and concluded: "Why not marry the best aspects of public schools with TAF?"

After TAF's success in the Federal Way district, Santorno, the Tacoma superintendent, felt Boze Elementary School was ripe for a partnership with the foundation. Boze needed a boost in student achievement and some attention that would excite faculty and parents, Santorno says. Boze certainly met the foundation's criteria for a partnership; 82 percent of its students were of color and 84 percent were eligible for free and reduced lunch. (Other criteria include having a majority of teachers agree to the change, along with school and district officials.)

"I was always impressed with her vision," Santorno says of Dziko. "Here was a female of color who was really interested in giving back and starting something that was focused on the needs of students, especially students of color."

Josh Garcia, Tacoma's deputy superintendent, worked with Dziko in Federal Way. Garcia stresses that Dziko isn't "doing anything to schools" or the district. She's a partner. "Trish learns and adapts. She's a relentless learner. Trish continues to see different opportunities and truly works in collaboration."

Boze Principal Arron Wilkins embraced the plan, which included bringing instruction coaches to Boze and having its teachers attend TAF's institute during

Dziko tells students they need training or education beyond high school, no matter what they want to be. *TAF*

summers—at no cost to the Tacoma school district. A five-year agreement gave both the district and TAF a say in matters such as staffing. The district and TAF plan to use a similar model at Roosevelt Elementary School.

So what does the TAF model look like in Boze?

The overarching goal, Wilkins says, is an environment where the "students' interests, problems, life and community are what drives what we do and how we design their lessons."

In practical terms, that means the kids start with an authentic question they have about a problem. From there, teachers find ways to weave in relevant content—rather than just covering it because it's required by the state.

Debra Hendrix, a fourth-grade teacher, said her students wanted to know how to help their families prepare for a natural disaster. They studied tectonic plates, tsunamis, volcanology and more. Red Cross workers visited their classrooms. Science, math, social studies, and writing were all embedded in their project-based learning. That learning style also teaches students skills for working together and taking responsibility, Hendrix said.

Using the same model, TAF@Saghalie sixth graders were given a hypothetical $1 million budget, with rows on their spread sheets for college, charitable and housing expenses. Video games and a Dodge Charger might also appear in a student's budget. But hopefully, spending on those items was in sensible proportion to their value, especially after students had received lessons on financial literacy from visiting bank representatives. The idea behind the $1 million exercise is getting students to think about life skills and how math plays into those, Dziko says.

The foundation also petitioned the district to allow TAF@Saghalie eighth graders to read *The Hate U Give* instead of *To Kill a Mockingbird*. Both books are about race and justice. But the former, published in 2017, is much more relevant to students today, Dziko says. (With a woman's false accusation at the core of its drama, *To Kill a Mockingbird*, published in 1960, also complicates the modern "believe victims" movement.)

Obviously, adults have some say in the learning. College readiness starts in kindergarten. TAF's readiness formula for students is awareness, eligibility and preparedness. "Awareness" for kindergarten through second grade means just getting kids to know there is college, and it can benefit them. TAF high-school students and alumni come in to convey that message to kids "just in a fun way."

With third graders, conversations go a little deeper about what it means to go to college, and what it means to be eligible. By sixth grade, students should know they need good grades. The overall goal is to impart the idea that if you're going to make something of yourself, whatever it may be, you need education or training beyond

In keeping with her "you have it, you share it" instincts, Dziko didn't take a salary at TAF for its first five years. *Seattle Business Magazine*

high school. "I like that because that's how I grew up," Dziko says.

TAF wants to export the model around the state. It hopes to transform 60 public schools in Washington in two decades.

WHILE FOUNDATION staff were reshaping their mission, the TAF Academy in Kent was feeling squeezed. The academy's portable classrooms were not ideal for lab work. It couldn't add more classrooms because of sewer-capacity limits. The north part of the Federal Way district, where it was located, faced crowding pressures. Saghalie Middle School in the southern part of the district, was underpopulated. The academy merged with Saghalie in 2017, increasing its number of students from 300 to 700. Students who started at TAF Academy's in Kent as sixth graders got their high-school diplomas from TAF@Saghalie in 2018.

The chief challenge now for Dziko is how to scale up their model to 60 additional schools. "I think our partnership with public education is the way. We just need funders to see it and have some patience and have some faith," she says. "And part of it is having faith in an organization that's led by people of color serving people of color. Philanthropy is not used to that. They're used to giving money to white-led organizations to help brown and black kids."

A 2017 survey of 4,000 people in the philanthropy world found that the homogeneity of nonprofit and foundation leaders contributes to a cycle of unconscious and unspoken racial bias. At the baseline, there's little difference in the education credentials of white people and people of color in the nonprofit sector. And researchers found that minorities were more interested in becoming executives than their white counterparts. But those doing the recruiting and promoting were often biased, ruling out candidates of color based on the perceived "fit" with an organization. That filter often leads to a pale and male applicant pool. Implicit biases, such as the sound of a name, further favor the white candidates.

The result is philanthropists giving most of their money to people they relate to because they have the same background, Dziko says.* "So that's the kind of stuff we have to look at, not just who's getting hired now. It's looking at their trajectory or the potential of them to move up," she says. "It's pretty grim."

But she's not quitting. And she doesn't regret leaving Microsoft rather than hanging in to bank millions more.

"For what? For what?" she says of the forsaken wealth. "Yeah, I would love to have more money. Jill and I have talked about this a number of times when things were getting tight and we're thinking about, 'OK, should I go back to corporate?'" (She didn't take a salary at TAF for its first five years. The couple are paying for two kids in college, with a third ready to start in the fall of 2019.)

But the tradeoff would be too much. She wouldn't feel like her life was her own. She couldn't take off to be with the kids—and family is her top priority. When the tuition bills roll in the question of going corporate resurfaces. "Then I think, OK, I am one helluva happy person. And I have freedom, which is huge. You can't buy that.

"Generational change is my legacy. We need it. I got it with my mom and her siblings doing the work to lift me and my cousins up. I think our generation let the ball drop a little. So I feel really good that I picked it up."

Bob Young
Legacy Washington

---

* TAF funders include Alaska Airlines, Amazon, Boeing, Costco, Comcast, Expedia, FlowPlay, Google and Microsoft.

MARY FAIRHURST

"BELIEVE IN MIRACLES"

There's a Ruth Bader Ginsburg bobblehead and a bowl of "Believe in Miracles" wristbands on Mary Fairhurst's desk at the Temple of Justice in Olympia. A butcher-paper banner that says "Sending BIG Hugs!" is taped to a wall. It's from the Girl Scouts who sold the Chief Justice a lot of cookies.

Robe on or off, Mary Fairhurst is not the chief justice you'd expect from Central Casting. A large woman with a lovely smile, she radiates openness. It's in her gene pool. Her father, Stan Fairhurst, a former Jesuit seminarian, is remembered with affection by hundreds of students he befriended during his years as a teacher and vice president for business and finance at Gonzaga University. Her mother, also a Mary, was the first lay chaplain at Spokane's Sacred Heart Medical Center. Her grandfather, Tacoma lumberman Cyril Jackson Fairhurst, also a Zag, was one of the nation's leading Roman Catholic laymen.

When the chief justice says, "I'm alive for a reason" it's an article of faith as well as a mission statement.

The wristbands say: "Believe in Miracles."
Laura Mott

Mary Elizabeth Fairhurst, 62, is the oldest of seven uncommonly bright, competitive kids. As a volleyball player, she was a fierce competitor who won or lost with a grace that inspired admiration. A magna cum laude graduate of Gonzaga's School of Law, she became the youngest ever president of the State Bar Association. Her cliff-hanger election to the Washington Supreme Court in 2002 created its first female majority. Now, as chief justice, Fairhurst's colleagues call her the conciliator—someone with "a sense of being at peace with her place in the world," as Justice Debra Stephens, a fellow Zag, puts it. "In tense situations, I've heard her say to everyone in the room, 'Let's just breathe.'

She's not lecturing; she's counseling. It's 'Calm down. Be civil. Respect one another's perspectives.' Not many people could do that and come off as effectively as Mary."

With a 6-3 female majority, including the chief justice, Washington is one of 10 states with female high court majorities.* Oregon and California also have female chief justices, and 40 of the 50 states have had female chiefs. Yet America's courtrooms still fall far short of mirroring the nation's diversity.

Undeniably, however, times have changed.

UW Law School class of 1953. Carolyn Dimmick is front row, third from right. *University of Washington*

When Carolyn Dimmick, the first woman to serve on the Washington Supreme Court, passed the bar exam in 1953, the *Seattle Post-Intelligencer's* headline epitomized *oh là là* sexism: "Pretty Blonde Water Skier Qualifies As Attorney." Noting that she was one of only three women in the Class of '53 at the University of Washington's Law School, the story continued in that vein:

> Carolyn Joyce Reaber, 23, blonde and beautiful Seattle water skier with the Ski-Quatic Follies on Lake Washington, will be sworn in as an attorney-at-law this Monday. Last Friday, the day she waited for the bar examiners to announce whether she had passed or not, was the worst day in her life, Miss Reaber said, a lot worse than the day she went up Hell's Canyon Rapids on water skis with a movie camera trained on her.

Fast forward to 1968. The headline this time was "Woman Wields the Gavel." *Post-Intelligencer* reporter Kay Kelly noted that most people would expect a judge to be a solemn, white-haired, 60ish man. But Dimmick—"blonde, attractive, young, pleasant, fun, fashion-conscious and the proud mother of two"—was "a surprise and a treat" on the Northlake Justice Court. She was "also a very competent judge," according to colleagues, one of only three women on the bench statewide. Nevertheless, Dimmick was "reluctant to talk about herself, reluctant to consent to publicity. But why should Kirkland keep her to itself?"

It could not. Few in the Seattle legal community were surprised when

---

* The other states with female high-court majorities are Oregon, Nevada, New Mexico, Ohio, Minnesota, Vermont, Arkansas, Tennessee and Wisconsin, where six of the seven justices are women.

Dimmick in 1981 as the first female member of the Washington Supreme Court. Back row, from left: Fred Dore, Floyd Hicks, William Williams, Dimmick; front row, from left: Robert Utter, Hugh Rosellini, Robert Brachtenbach, Charles Stafford and James Dolliver. *Washington State Archives*

Governor Dan Evans appointed Dimmick to the King County Superior Court bench in 1976.

In 1981, when Governor Dixy Lee Ray's appointment of Dimmick to the Washington Supreme Court made history, her old boss, former King County prosecutor Charles O. Carroll, introduced her as "the prettiest justice on the Supreme Court." Justice Jim Dolliver, who received his law degree from the University of Washington a year before Dimmick, knew she was a lot more than just a pretty face. Dolliver, famous for his wry humor, passed her a note on their first day together on the bench: "Which do you prefer: 1) Mrs. Justice. 2) Ms. Justice. 3) O! Most Worshipful One, or 4) El Maxima?"

"All of the above!" Dimmick wrote back.

NINETEEN-EIGHTY-ONE, the year Mary Fairhurst enrolled in law school at Gonzaga, was a landmark year for women and the judiciary. President Reagan's nomination of Sandra Day O'Connor of Arizona to the United States Supreme Court was confirmed 99-0 by the U.S. Senate. In Judge Dimmick's office at the Federal Courthouse in Seattle, there's a framed photo of her with Justice O'Connor. Born a few months apart, they have a lot in common, including sagacity and a reluctance to be labeled.

Reagan named Dimmick to the federal bench for the Western District of Washington in 1985. Nearing 90 today, her legacy as one of the most respected and influential judges in Northwest history is secure. Mary Fairhurst and Debra

Carolyn Dimmick is now a senior judge on the U.S. District Court in Seattle. *U.S. Courts*

Stephens marvel at the "She's-a-woman-and-a-judge—imagine that!" stereotypes Dimmick endured and the grace with which she handled the pressure and chauvinism, not to mention her formidable intellect.

Judge Dimmick says the idea of appointing a woman to an important office simply because she is a woman is demeaning. That her career path is unremarkable by today's standards prompts this verdict: "That's progress. …It's just been so heartening to see how it's developed. …You're a lawyer. You're not a 'woman lawyer' or a 'lady lawyer.' You're just a lawyer."

Women now make up around 52 percent of law school students in the U.S. and approximately 36 percent of the justices on state courts of last resort. However, they occupy only three of the nine seats on the U.S. Supreme Court. And state supreme courts remain overwhelmingly white and male. On that score, Washington is again ahead of the curve. Two of its newest Supreme Court justices—Mary I. Yu and Steven C. González—personify diversity. Justice Yu, the daughter of immigrants, grew up on the South Side of Chicago and graduated from Notre Dame's Law School. She is the first Asian, the first Latina and the first member of the LGBTQ community to serve on the court. Justice González, an award-winning former assistant U.S. attorney, received his law degree from UC, Berkeley. He is Latino from his father's side of the family tree, while his mother's branches are Eastern European Jewish "and a little Yankee." He speaks Spanish, Japanese and some Mandarin Chinese.

IF THE ARC of the moral universe is long but bends toward justice, as the Rev. Dr. Martin Luther King Jr. posited, there have been bends and roundabouts on the road to judicial diversity in Washington.

Barbara Durham, a distinguished appellate court judge with a law degree from Stanford, became the second female member of the Washington high court in 1985 and the first female chief justice 10 years later. Her judicial career was cut tragically short by early-onset Alzheimer's.

In 1992, "The Year of the Woman," Barbara Madsen became the third woman to serve on the court—and the first to gain her seat by popular election. The former public defender, special prosecutor and Seattle Municipal Court judge narrowly outpolled another highly regarded female attorney, Elaine Houghton, who went on to serve on the Court of Appeals. A record-breaking four female newcomers were elected to the U.S. Senate that year, including Patty Murray, Washington's "Mom in

Tennis Shoes." Future senator Maria Cantwell and Jennifer Dunn were among the 24 female freshmen in the U.S. House, while future governor Chris Gregoire was elected attorney general.

By 2002, when 44-year-old Mary Fairhurst announced her candidacy for the court, Justice Madsen had acquired three female colleagues—Faith Ireland, Bobbe Bridge and Susan Owens. Fairhurst had never been a judge, but she was a widely experienced assistant attorney general. And she knew her way around the Temple of Justice.

AFTER HER GRADUATION from law school in 1984 Fairhurst spent two years as a judicial clerk, working first for Chief Justice William H. Williams and then for Justice William Cassius Goodloe. It would have been difficult to have found two more temperamentally different justices. Williams, a former longtime Spokane County Superior Court judge, was an avuncular fellow Gonzaga Law School graduate who leaned liberal, often casting the swing vote. Goodloe, a former Republican legislator and GOP party chairman, was an avowed conservative. He resigned before the end of his first term to run for the U.S. Senate against fellow Republican Slade Gorton, whom he viewed as too moderate. Working for Goodloe after Williams was an eye-opener for someone like Fairhurst, with her strong Jesuit social-justice upbringing. (Her dad often took homeless men to Denny's; her mom famously instructed one of Mary's six sibs to surrender a pair of brand-new Christmas mittens to a homeless woman dragging a cart down a snowy street in Spokane.) Diplomatic as ever, Fairhurst says Williams and Goodloe were two bright men who had spent decades as trial court judges. "Comfortable in his own skin," Williams instinctively shifted gears to the appellate level, she says, exerting a moderating influence on the court, while Goodloe loved his years as a trial court judge. "I got to see the benefit of the best of both of them." What's more, during Fairhurst's years as a clerk, four new justices came on board, including Barbara Durham. Fairhurst worked with a dozen justices in all.

Next stop was the Office of the Attorney General, working for Republican Ken Eikenberry and his successor, Democrat Chris Gregoire—16 years in all. It was wide-ranging experience: criminal justice, transportation, revenue, labor issues. Fairhurst was chief of the Revenue, Bankruptcy and Collections Division when she ran for the Supreme Court in 2002. The mandatory retirement at 75 of the court's first ethnic minority, Charles Z. Smith, had created an open seat.[*]

"It was like a 2x4 hit me," Fairhurst remembers. "My mom had died of breast cancer; my dad's living with me. He's reading in the paper that Justice Smith is retiring. 'Oh Mary,' he says, 'when are you going to run for the Supreme Court?' Then my phone starts ringing. Justice Madsen and other justices are calling me saying,

---

[*] Justice Smith was born in the segregated South in 1927, the son of a Cuban auto mechanic and a restaurant cook whose grandparents were slaves.

Justice Charles Z. Smith. *Josef Scaylea photo*

'Mary, are you going to run?' I had been Bar Association president and sort of had a statewide reputation. Finally, I said, 'I'm running. I have to run.' I cared so deeply about the court, and I felt that you can't complain about the choir unless you're willing to try out.' "

Fairhurst entered a crowded and competitive field of candidates vying for Justice Smith's seat. Michael S. Spearman, an African American serving with distinction on the King County bench, appeared to be the frontrunner, with Fairhurst neck-and-neck with Jim Johnson, an attorney who had defended Tim Eyman's anti-tax initiatives. Johnson, a Harvard Law School graduate, also had drawn the ire of the tribes for his role as point man for then-Attorney General Gorton during the fallout from the Boldt Decision on treaty fishing rights.

Spearman finished a close third in the primary. Johnson and Fairhurst were headed for a photo-finish.

The State Republican Party, Gorton and the deep-pocketed Building Industry Association of Washington backed Johnson. So did the Farm Bureau and NRA. Fairhurst was supported by the Washington State Labor Council, the Washington Education Association, Governor Gary Locke and former governors Dan Evans, Booth Gardner and Mike Lowry, as well as five members of the Supreme Court and Judge Spearman. On the campaign trail, Johnson and Fairhurst emphasized that the office is nonpartisan, sidestepping the transparent fact that this race was about perceived ideology. "Gender is not the issue I'm hearing," said Cathy Allen, a political consultant.

Come November, Fairhurst was elected to the court with 50.1 percent of the vote a margin of 3,377 votes out of 1.4 million cast. Crucially, she carried King County by 41,719 votes. "I believe it was helpful to be a woman," she says, "and to be willing to give everything during the campaign—leave it all on the field."

The hard-fought Fairhurst-Johnson race—harbinger of several tight Supreme Court races to follow—italicizes the pros and cons of an elected high-court judiciary. Candidates are constrained from promising, if elected or re-elected, to vote one way or another on hot-button issues. Yet they accrue supporters with clear agendas (and checkbooks). As they woo voters, taking care to sound judicious and comply with the canons of ethics, their campaign committees do the fundraising. The candidates aren't even supposed to know who gave or how much—or personally solicit donations, with the exception of contributions from committee members or family. But unlike federal judicial appointees who enjoy lifetime appointments, Washington's Supreme Court justices serve six-year terms. The voters can render their own verdicts at the ballot box.

Presently the longest-serving member of the court is Associate Chief Justice Charles W. Johnson (no relation to Jim Johnson), who paid for law school by working at a Tacoma lumber mill. Johnson had no judicial experience in 1990 when he ousted Chief Justice Keith Callow. Running as a "blue-collar attorney" with a one-man practice, Johnson was given little chance. After the shocking upset, some pundits said the 39-year-old challenger had the advantage, especially in a low-turnout primary, of being named Johnson in a state with deep Scandinavian roots. What's more, another Charles Johnson was a respected King County Superior Court judge and yet another was an anchorman for a Tacoma TV station. "The timing was impeccable," the justice-elect observed, "and my opponent did exactly what he had to do for me to win—exactly nothing."* Callow's overconfidence became a cautionary tale.

Mary Fairhurst's 2002 victory created the first female majority (she joined Madsen, Ireland, Bridge and Owens) in the 113 years since the founding of the court in 1889. The men in the minority were Chief Justice Gerry Alexander, Charles W. Johnson, Tom Chambers and Richard B. Sanders, the court's libertarian maverick. Two years later Faith Ireland did not seek re-election and was succeeded by Jim Johnson—victorious in his second try. Men reclaimed a 5-4 majority.

In 2010 Barbara Madsen succeeded Alexander as chief justice after he stepped down with two years remaining in his term. Alexander, the court's gentlemanly, longest-serving chief (nine years), was nearing mandatory retirement age. "I knew Justice Madsen would be elected, and I told her I would support her," Alexander says. "I wanted to aid in the transition to a new chief."

Fairhurst's election in 2002 created the court's first female majority: sitting from left, Bobbe Bridge, Barbara Madsen, Faith Ireland; standing Susan Owens and Fairhurst. *Washington Supreme Court*

Madsen was re-elected to the court without opposition earlier that year, while Charles K. "Charlie" Wiggins, an ebullient former appellate court lawyer and judge, defeated Justice Sanders in a cliffhanger.

Two years later, with the election of Sheryl Gordon McCloud, a fearless appellate lawyer, Washington's Supreme Court for the first time boasted a female majority *and* a female chief justice. And in 2015, when Mary Yu joined the court,

---

* The lanky, affable new justice quickly demonstrated he was not in over his head. Charles W. Johnson became a constitutional law scholar and adjunct professor, receiving a national award in 2012 for "a lifetime of dedication to the principles and ideals of integrity, compassion, courage and professional service."

female justices achieved the 6-3 majority that still exists at this writing in 2019 on the eve of the centennial of women's suffrage in America. It's notable that Justice Owens, a former District Court judge on the Olympic Peninsula, also served as a chief judge in tribal courts for more than a decade.

JUSTICE MADSEN, reflecting on her 26 years on the court, makes no bones about the attitudes she says she and her female colleagues once endured, and how things have changed:

Retiring Chief Justice Gerry Alexander Alexander swears in Madsen as the new chief. *Washington Supreme Court*

It was when there were finally three women on the court that I actually was listened to. I lived through the era where what I said five minutes ago was now being said by the guy down the bench—and everybody was paying attention to him. But when I said it, it was like maybe I hadn't spoken. I started second-guessing myself. But with three women it was different. It was different because the other women paid attention to what I said and what I said resonated with them. As more women joined the room, suddenly I started to be heard by everyone—and not just the women.

It was 18 years before I became chief justice so I had seen many chiefs. Prior to 1996 the chief was rotational. We'd have a new chief every two years.* I noticed the way I was treated as chief was very different from prior chiefs. I was challenged constantly. That was not true of my male colleagues who served as chief. That said, I was a long serving chief, so I had things I wanted to accomplish. Perhaps I was treated differently, in part, because of that. But I think it was more about gender, since it was the same thing I experienced when I started on the trial court. As a trial judge I was challenged by male attorneys frequently. I had been a trial lawyer myself. I had been a public defender and a prosecutor and was in court practically every day. I saw how attorneys treated judges. That was *not* how I was treated. Later, when I became chief judge I did not have those same challenges. I believe it was because the bench that elected me was evenly divided between men and women.

* By secret ballot, Washington Supreme Court justices now choose a chief to serve a 4-year term.

I've done a lot of diversity training. These patterns I just mentioned seem to be similar for all people of minority communities. It might be a woman of color. It might be a man of color. It might be a person with a disability—the walls you have to climb are higher.

So now, with six [female justices], I don't have to prove anything. With more women at the table I can just be who I am; my ideas are judged on the merits. Making sure women's voices were heard is the chief reason I ran for the Supreme Court.

I really do believe women bring more collegiality to a concerted effort—whether it be a committee or a board or, in this case, an appellate court.

Justice Madsen leans forward, clearly relishing the chance to say some things that have been percolating for a long time:

When a group of women come together they seem very much task-oriented and solution oriented—always bending toward finding a workable solution and less concerned about saying "It was my idea." It's a collaborative effort as opposed to a "me" effort. Of course, it's not true of every woman; it's not true of every man. But my experience is that women are more collaborative, and if it's a whole room full of women, that's more so. When it's a male-dominant room, you see men wanting to stand out as the leader. Women are more inclined to credit someone else's ideas and not reject or ignore them.

Madsen says today's historically diverse court, with an array of intellectual firepower but an abundance of collegiality, is one of the best on which she has served:

I am privileged to serve on the Supreme Court. The best part of the job is when I can really engage on the issues—to debate with other highly intelligent people who have different life experiences. Somehow the answer is better, richer. And then there's the awesome responsibility of putting those decisions into writing that becomes the law. It's really important that there be women and people of color on this court. When C.Z. Smith left there was a deficit.

DEBRA L. STEPHENS, at 54 the youngest justice, entered Gonzaga Law School in 1990 when her daughter was only five weeks old. A former community college debate coach, she is one of the court's most agile debaters and persuasive writers. Writing for the majority in 2012, Stephens authored the landmark, 79-page McCleary Decision that found the Washington Legislature had failed to uphold its

Susan Owens, Debra Stephens and Steven González listen to oral arguments in a 2019 case. *The Columbian*

constitutionally mandated "paramount duty" to adequately fund basic education.

Stephens and Fairhurst look to Barbara Madsen as "the senior Zag"—deeply appreciative that she, like Carolyn Dimmick, poked holes in the judicial glass ceiling. Stephens also points out that Madsen was chief justice during the depths of the Great Recession. "I'll never forget her great quote that 'the animals around the watering hole were starting to eye one another searchingly as the water grew scarce.' "

Stephens, the first Eastern Washington woman to serve on the Supreme Court, is an avid proponent of judicial diversity, adding:

> But the reality is that no more than when there were nine men here do we six women think alike. We're just very different people, and gender is not necessarily defining some personality trait or leadership style or approach to the work. We also come from different experiences. Generationally we're not super far apart—a 16-year gap from me, the youngest woman, to Susan Owens, the eldest, who is also a great friend.
>
> When people ask me what it's like with six women on the court, I always say, "Did anyone ask the men, 'What's that like with nine guys?' "
>
> I think it's equally important that we have people of color on our court. And it's also important to have people from different generations in the room because it makes you ask questions and probe things you might otherwise take for granted. And that holds true on a court. I'm adamant that coming from a different part of the state matters. Coming from Spokane, my sense of what Washington is, is quite different from someone who grew up in Seattle.

EXHIBIT A that not all female justices think alike is the Washington Supreme Court's 5-4 decision in 2006 upholding the Defense of Marriage Act, which denied marriage licenses to same-sex couples. Barbara Madsen and Mary Fairhurst, two Roman Catholic graduates of a Jesuit university law school, held strongly different views. Justice Madsen, writing for a plurality of the majority, wrote that the act was constitutional "because the legislature was entitled to believe that limiting marriage to opposite-sex couples furthers procreation, essential to the survival of the human race, and furthers the well-being of children by encouraging families where children are reared in homes headed by the children's biological parents." Madsen also stressed the limited nature of the court's ruling. There was a rational basis to conclude that the 1998 law passed constitutional muster, she said, adding that the judges should not dictate public policy. The law banning gay marriages might yet change, she said, but not "because five members of this court have dictated it. … We see no reason, however why the Legislature or the people acting through the initiative process would be foreclosed from enacting the right to marry to gay and lesbian couples in Washington."

In a forceful dissent, Justice Fairhurst called the majority's opinion "blatant discrimination," adding: "There is no rational basis for denying same-sex couples the right to marry. … Unfortunately [those in the majority] are willing to turn a blind eye to DOMA's discrimination because a popular majority still favors that discrimination."

Fairhurst says her decision weighed heavily on her because of pressure she was feeling "from the church and from my parish. But I just had to do what I thought was correct under the law. [Afterward] I had people make comments like, 'Well, how can she do that and she's Catholic?' Well, how can I not do it if I'm a judge and it's the right thing?"

Self-described as a less committed Catholic, Madsen was largely immune to church pressure. That said, she quite agrees with Fairhurst on the latter point: "I concluded the law was constitutional. …I'm a judge and I believe I was doing the right thing."

When the fallout cleared, they were still collegial colleagues. Madsen and Fairhurst emphasize that an appellate judge's job is to weigh what the laws say and how they should be applied to the cases at hand. The ambiguities inspire the nuances of dissenting—or concurring—opinions. In the Defense of Marriage Act ruling, "There were so many opinions among the justices that we had to refer to each other by name rather than just by opinion," Fairhurst remembers. "People thought we were really getting in each other's faces. People were like, 'Oh my gosh, they all are falling apart!' Well, we had already gone through whatever sort of emotional roller-coaster experience we were feeling as we were writing and re-writing and editing and amending. So by the time it came out it was all behind us, whereas other people were reading it for the first time and concluding the court was in a crisis. *We weren't.* We were just doing our job. But this case came with a lot of emotion—big crowds in the courtroom. And they're wearing buttons [supporting their passionately held views]. You have to sort through all of that."

"I think Mary is the peacemaker," Madsen says. "She really tries to make sure everyone is comfortable with positions we've taken. And that's not always easy, especially when you're the chief justice."

Gerry Alexander says Fairhurst's "fortitude and faith tell us a lot about who she is as a person and as a judge. Even when I disagreed with her, her arguments were thoughtful and well-reasoned. She has a very good judicial temperament."

Justices Madsen and Fairhurst. *Washington Attorney General's Office*

The former chief points to Fairhurst's wide-ranging experience with the Attorney General's Office and as president of the State Bar Association. "She was one of the first women to head the bar and its first public sector president," Alexander notes. "Being Bar Association president is a *tough* job, but the members had a lot of respect for her."

THOUGH FAIRHURST'S calendar is overflowing right now, she smiles broadly when she talks about being chief justice:

> I love being chief. It's a perfect job for me. But it's a very hard job, as Justice Madsen knows. There are a lot of administrative and public outreach duties. As chief, I'm the spokesperson for a non-unified court system. I'm a co-chair of the Board of Judicial Administration. I run all the meetings of the court conferences. I run the department meetings and the *en banc* meetings where we decide what cases we're going to do and what we're going to decide. Separate and apart from being chief, I'm chair of the Judicial Information System Committee. I speak in many settings—from statewide conferences to the annual State of the Judiciary address. I convene work groups and task forces. I'm dedicated to increasing access to the justice system and working to promote better understanding of the foundations of our democracy. The YMCA's Youth in Government program is very important.

Fairhurst is also dealing with Bar Association discontent over the approval of Limited License Legal Technicians to improve access to the justice system. Madsen

Justice Mary Fairhurst with the Mariner Moose in 2011 after she threw out the first pitch at a Mariners game to celebrate her birthday. *Spokesman-Review*

championed the plan during her term as chief justice. "It was like throwing a hand grenade in the middle of a bowl of soup because it gives people who have legal training but not a full legal degree the right to practice law in a limited scope," Madsen explains. "And why do that? It's because over the years it had become clear to me that the average person cannot access the justice system because they can't afford the cost of legal services and they can't navigate the system without some help from a legally trained person. I wanted to expand the resources available for people who can't afford to access the system, or even are so fearful of lawyers that they wouldn't go to see a lawyer even if they knew they needed a lawyer! I am proud that the court adopted the rule."

Fairhurst agrees: "We're talking about all the people who go into court without assistance, having to be on their own. They have no idea how things work. Sometimes it takes them six or seven times because they don't know how it has to be done. …Then you have all the people who never even had civics in school, and are [susceptible] to people who are purposefully trying to undermine the foundations of democracy."

MAJOR CHALLENGES REMAIN, but in her State of the Judiciary address to a joint session of the 2019 Legislature, Fairhurst was upbeat:

- The justices of the Washington Supreme Court have adopted a new court rule—"the first of its kind in the nation"—making it more difficult to dismiss racial and ethnic minority jurors from a jury panel.
- A new statewide case management system has been implemented for the superior courts and county clerk's offices, "completing a statewide modernization of the state's diverse courts that began with planning in 2005."
- Two reports by the Gender and Justice Commission outline the need for important changes in domestic violence court procedures and treatment "as a guide for addressing the problem of repeat, escalating domestic violence."

More money is sorely needed for court interpreters, Fairhurst emphasized, noting that the number of languages spoken in the state's courtrooms has dramatically increased. Courthouse security, an escalating worry, should be addressed by a task force, she said.

But all things considered, "We're getting better all the time. We're a beacon of hope."

"I want to remind you that time is precious," the chief justice told the crowd of lawmakers and elected officials. "For whatever reasons this is our individual and collective time and place. It is when and where we are serving in the three branches of government. It is when we are deciding what government looks like in *our* Washington. None of us know how many days we have to make a difference. This is again especially true for me."

Then she revealed she is once again fighting cancer—her third bout since an initial diagnosis of colon cancer in 2008. Round two, after the disease spread to a lung, ended in a miraculous victory in 2014. But now, the beast was back—in her lungs and liver. In the parlance of oncology, this is "Stage 4," with five-year survival rates a daunting mixed-bag of maybes.

Fairhurst surveyed the hushed gathering, and in a voice resonant with optimism, she italicized her faith and underscored her determination:

> I am currently undergoing treatment. I will continue working. I still believe in miracles. As Albert Einstein said, there are only two ways to live your life: One is as though nothing is a miracle; the other is as though everything is a miracle.
>
> *Everything is a miracle.* Every day is a miracle. Let's not waste the days we have. Working individually and together on behalf of those that we faithfully serve, we can and are making a difference. Together we will not fail. We *can* change the world to be what we want it to be. And we must ensure that all who seek justice find it.
>
> I would like to close with what my family calls "The Joy Pose." This is what we often do when we are overwhelmed with happiness. Because I am overflowing with happiness, hope and gratitude for you, for me, for us and for the State of Washington.

She raised her arms in a pose of exultation—at being alive and being able to make a difference—and kept them there during a prolonged standing ovation.

Many wept.

But Mary Fairhurst's smile was luminous.

"I don't see it as a death sentence," she said. "I see it as a license to live.

"I'm alive for a reason."

The Washington Supreme Court in 2019: Front row (from left): Susan Owens, Charles W. Johnson, Chief Justice Mary Fairhurst, Barbara Madsen, Debra Stephens; back row (from left): Sheryl McCloud, Charles Wiggins, Steven Gonzalez and Mary Yu. *Washington Supreme Court*

TEN MONTHS LATER, after an exhausting round of chemo, Fairhurst announced "with a clear head and a sad heart" that she had decided to retire from the court to focus on her health. "I don't believe I'm dying. I believe I'm living. You know we're all going to die. The question is 'How are we going to live?' ...I want to live every day to the fullest."

Fairhurst said she is not battling cancer. Rather she is embracing it as part of her journey—one she hopes to continue long after she leaves the bench on January 5, 2020.

"It's been my highest honor to serve the people of the state of Washington as a justice … since 2003, particularly as the Chief Justice for the past three years.

"I'm not going away to die. I'm going away to live."

**John C. Hughes
Legacy Washington**

This is what Fairhurst (center) calls the "Joy pose" with (from left) Sheryl McCloud, Susan Owens, Barbara Madsen, Debra Stephens and Mary Yu. *Laura Mott*

Linea Laird as project manager for the new Tacoma Narrows Bridge. *Washington State Department of Transportation (WSDOT)*

LINEA LAIRD

ENGINEERING HISTORY

Linea Laird's eyes light up when she recalls traversing catwalks and cables, the wind tugging at her hard hat and goggles, as the new Tacoma Narrows Bridge took shape next to its older fraternal twin. As graceful as the Golden Gate, the fifth longest suspension bridge in the U.S. was completed in 2007, under budget and only a few months late despite unforeseen challenges and assorted surprises.

Laird was the project manager for the Washington State Department of Transportation. The bridge was her baby. "It was just a whale of a lot of fun doing it," she says with a grin. What's more, as every structural engineer knows, nothing beats the realization that what you've built likely will be standing long after you're six feet under. Failure, on the other hand, has an unlimited shelf life. The engineers for the ill-fated original Tacoma Narrows Bridge, which oscillated into oblivion in a 1940 windstorm, were haunted by its collapse. Laird's team had to work around the barnacled remains of "Galloping Gertie."

Chances are you've never heard of Linea Laird, despite the fact that she is one of the most accomplished highway engineers in the history of the Washington State Department of Transportation. The limelight isn't her style. Simultaneously self-effacing and self-confident, she likes talking about collaboration, not herself. "I had amazing mentors and great colleagues in my 38 years at WSDOT," she says. "A lot of them were women, but there were also remarkably supportive men."

Up front, in a sort of for-the-record moment, Laird volunteers that she doesn't have a college degree. But neither does Bill Gates. A summer job with WSDOT in 1979 led to the offer of a fulltime job. She decided to forgo her final year of engineering school. Her husband, Mike, whom she met at Montana State University, had already graduated and landed an engineering job at the Puget Sound Naval Shipyard in Bremerton. She decided she wanted to move up the WSDOT career path. The Lairds had a 3½-year-old and another child on the way when, after countless hours of studying, Laird passed the rigorous tests to become a licensed engineer. "I work hard," she says. "I don't like not being on top of a situation."

Laird's career at WSDOT was punctuated by calm oversight of costly, complicated projects, including the Narrows Bridge, the Alaskan Way Viaduct replacement and Highway 99 tunnel. In 2018, when Mayor Jenny Durkan needed an interim director for the beleaguered Seattle Department of Transportation she summoned Laird, who had just retired from WSDOT. A long-planned vacation was postponed.

Laird as administrator of the Alaskan Way Viaduct Replacement Program in 2011. *WSDOT*

"The people at SDOT couldn't believe Linea," says Doug MacDonald, the plain-talking former state Secretary of Transportation. "She came in with a no-nonsense attitude and a sense of collaboration. Engineers who had been horrendously stifled were hugely gratified to find somebody in the corner office who could speak their language and produce answers on an asked-for accountability."

Laird was not among the first women who broke through in the engineering ranks at WSDOT, MacDonald says, but she emerged early on as someone with major potential. Notably, she was preceded by Paula Hammond, who in 2007 succeeded MacDonald as secretary of transportation, and Lorena Eng, the former Northwest Region administrator. As the final financing plans for the Narrows Bridge took shape, Laird also found an ally and friend in Amy Arnis, WSDOT's highly regarded chief financial officer. "Those bright women were among Linea's role models in highways management," MacDonald says. "It's unsurprising that Governor Chris Gregoire became an admirer. ... Linea has a steel-trap grasp of what she's doing—about how to mobilize a team to complete a project. She's a problem solver with a low tolerance for BS. Linea Laird cannot be shined."

"WOMAN NAMED HIGHWAY ENGINEER." The 1993 headline in the *Sun*, Bremerton's daily newspaper, announced Laird's promotion to Kitsap County project engineer for the Washington State Department of Transportation. Twenty years later when Laird became WSDOT's first female chief engineer, that milestone was barely mentioned. To Laird, that's a clear sign of progress, but she emphasizes that she experienced no significant gender discrimination during her years at WSDOT. That may say as much about her competence and confidence as the evolving culture of the Washington State Department of Transportation. Nationally, however, despite the growing demand for science-technology-engineering-math graduates, female engineers still routinely face gender bias in addition to the challenges of achieving work-life balance as working moms, according to recent studies. Stephanie Slocum, an East Coast structural engineer with three young daughters, explores the issue in a 2018 book called *She Engineers*. Slocum stresses the importance of female role models and mentors.

Today, the 26 female licensed engineers at WSDOT represent 24 percent of the total, according to the agency's human resources department. That's on par with the numbers of women receiving engineering degrees nationally, yet in 2018 only 14 percent of the civil engineering workforce in America was composed of women. The good news is that some of the nation's top engineering firms are now aggressively recruiting women. Still, the myth that women are too "fragile" or otherwise temperamentally unsuited to the construction industry lingers.*

John Conrad, Laird's boss when he was an assistant secretary of WSDOT, remembers an incident that occurred a few years ago: "I think Linea may have been the only woman state maintenance engineer in the country—or at least at the national meeting we were attending together. One night at a dinner gathering, the chief engineer from Missouri made reference to me 'and my wife.' I said, 'She's not my wife—she's our maintenance engineer.'"

LAIRD HAS UNDERSTOOD the importance of maintenance since childhood. Born in 1957, she grew up in the heart of Alaska, one of five kids in a close-knit Fairbanks

Lathrop High School, Fairbanks, Alaska, 1973

family that loved camping and fishing. Linea, her sister and three brothers were expected to be resourceful— to have after-school jobs but still do well in school. She worked at a movie theater before landing a job at a grocery store, working before school, after school and weekends. She excelled in math and science.

Her dad was a carpenter. Maybe that's why she likes to build things. Her first car was a second-hand, red '64 Ford Mustang. She learned to drive a stick-shift, change the oil and fix flats. She's feminine and not very tall, 5-3 to be exact, but when she graduated from high school in 1975 and set out to raise money for college, she and a chum went to the laborer's union hall to apply for a job on the Trans-Alaska Pipeline. "We goofed around for a couple of weeks, but when we went back they called our numbers. We looked at each other and thought, 'Oh my!'"

Laird discovered that about 10 percent of the pipeline workers were can-do women. Some may have been the grandchildren of "Rosies" who riveted ships and

---

* Between 2017 and 2018 the number of women working in construction trades—well-paying jobs—increased by nearly 18 percent, "but women remain strongly underrepresented in the trades: fewer than one in 20 (3.4 percent) of construction trades workers in 2018 were women," according to the Institute for Women's Policy Research.

bombers during World War II. "None of the work I did was very technical," Laird remembers. "It might be power washing vehicles. It might be shoveling gravel to leveling out platforms. There was graded area, like a big graving dock, where we tied rebar for metal forms that got set over the pipeline in areas where they crossed rivers. …We were up in the camps eight weeks or more at a time, working 10 to 12 hours a day, seven days a week before we'd get a break. My take home pay was about $750 a week, so I was very lucky to pay my way through college without being a burden on my parents."

Without ever visiting the campus, she chose Montana State University at Bozeman, a compact little city in a picture-perfect valley rimmed by craggy mountains. "I looked at some of the pictures and said, 'Wow, this kind of looks like Alaska! I think I'd be comfortable there.' And I was." Montana State's engineering school was first-rate. One of her fellow students was her future husband.

Her timing was also right when she joined the Washington State Department of Transportation in Kitsap County. It was the 1980s "and there was a big push for women to be hired," she remembers. "It came with a little bit of curiosity and a little bit of angst about whether women were going to be disruptive to an all-male engineering office. But we proved we were capable professionals—good teammates."

Laird loved construction engineering technology, largely a man's world at the time. "I liked the outdoor side of things. I liked the *building* side of things—the surveying and fieldwork. I think it was because of my trades work up on the Alaska pipeline."

For Laird, being state maintenance engineer, was "so much fun." It was—still is—a male-dominated niche, but here and there across America female engineers were demonstrating they understood potholes and expansion joints—or as Doug MacDonald puts it, "She cut her teeth doing the old-fashioned go-get-the-asphalt-laid-on-the-ground deal." Laird smiles when she hears that line. "As a state maintenance engineer, you divvy out the budget to get stuff done. But the people in the regions don't report to you. So you have to use all of your collaborative tools to create the right policy and bring people along. I was not uncomfortable in that world because of the trade work I had done."

IN 1999, as WSDOT's Olympic Region engineering manager for the proposed new Tacoma Narrows Bridge, Laird helped sort out the contract language and plans for the $800 million project. The new bridge generated substantial local opposition. "There were many public meetings during the environmental and design phase—crowds of unhappy people," Laird remembers. "Some did not believe it would solve the traffic issues. Besides, they didn't want to pay a toll. They felt that was unfair. It wasn't about improving the safety of the route with a beautiful new bridge to expedite traffic. It was about disruption. It was about being tolled. Some of the locals felt we were just jamming it down their throats."

Linea and Lloyd Brown, WSDOT's Communication Director, high atop the new Tacoma Narrows Bridge. Catwalks and cables are under construction in the background. *WSDOT*

The project started out as a public-private partnership, with WSDOT as a stakeholder. Then things got complicated in a hurry. After a legislative U-turn, tedious number-crunching and environmental impact statements, the job finally moved forward. It had become, in the parlance of WSDOT, a negotiated "Design-Build" project where the state executes a contract with one firm for design and construction services. But someone from the state still has to be the big boss on site to work with the design-build contractor.

"We executed a contract in the fall of 2002, relying on permits that had already been procured," Laird remembers. "The project amounted to cross walking two worlds between the public-private developer agreements and the negotiated design-build contract. Then Doug MacDonald said, 'By the way, I want you to be the project manager and run this thing.' "

Laird has nothing but praise for Tacoma Narrows Constructors, a Bechtel-Kiewit joint venture, and her WSDOT team.

BRIDGING THE NARROWS for the third time in 60 years involved reviewing historic engineering mistakes to ensure they weren't repeated. In 2017, Craig Holstine, an historian with WSDOT's Cultural Resources Program, wrote an award-winning article on the history of the first span. Here's the genesis of "Galloping Gertie":

> Residents on both sides of Puget Sound's narrowest point between Tacoma and the Kitsap Peninsula had long dreamed of replacing the outdated ferries that crossed the rushing tides there with a bridge. Automobile popularity in the 1920s, along with advancements in suspension bridge technology, fueled interest in a bridge. … As war loomed overseas, defense facilities around Puget Sound grew in size and importance, and a highway connecting Fort Lewis with the Bremerton Naval Shipyards became a national defense priority. But federal funding remained elusive, despite New Deal stimulus.

On August 14, 1937, however, U.S. Senator Homer T. Bone, a Democrat from Tacoma, wrote to Lacey Murrow, the dashing young director of the State Highways Department: "If there is any possible way that we can secure funds for the Narrows Bridge we are going to try to do it." The announcement by the Washington Toll Bridge Authority that Murrow was heading to the other Washington to apply for federal funding prompted "the biggest celebration in Tacoma's history." Funds secured, the bridge was completed in record

The original Tacoma Narrows Bridge opens on July 1, 1940. *Washington State Archives*

time—"barely 19 months, about half the normal construction time for a bridge of its size and type," Holstine notes. An estimated 10,000 people gathered at the span the day it opened, July 1, 1940. Unfortunately, the federal Public Works Administration had rejected as too costly the plan proposed by Murrow's lead engineer, opting instead for "a sleeker, lighter, cheaper design by one of the nation's leading suspension bridge engineers," Leon Moisseiff of New York City. Almost immediately the suspended center span began to vibrate whenever the wind whipping through the Narrows kicked up, which is to say often. New anchoring cables helped a bit. But the clock was ticking on catastrophe. No one has summed it up better than Holstine:

"Galloping Gertie" collapses on November 7, 1940. *James Bashford/The Olympian*

"On November 7, 1940, at 11:02 in the morning, after a half-hour of severe movement in winds over 42 miles per hour, much of Galloping Gertie's main span fell into Puget Sound. A victim not of unforeseen gale-force winds but of design flaws, Gertie became the most infamous failure in bridge history. Its plate-girder deck, acting as a sail in moderate breezes, created a vortex of swirling wind force contributing to a 'torsional flutter'—or twisting motion—that became self-generating. The bridge's extremely light, flexible construction offered little resistance to the torsional forces that a more conventional stiffening deck truss would have provided."

Wartime necessities delayed construction of a replacement span. The new bridge finally opened in the fall of 1950. Though its stability is a testament to the lessons learned from the first span's death spiral, Laird says the designers of the $849 million third span revisited the issue of suspension bridge structural aerodynamics: "We went with the TNC team to Ottawa and put a model of the new bridge in a wind tunnel. The collapse of 'Galloping Gertie' created a whole new segment of engineering."

A stable span was Job One. Aesthetics were also hugely important, Laird says. In constructing a parallel landmark, "we had to have a bridge that could not be an exact replica, because then you diminish the historic significance of the original span. Being a half century newer, it had to meet modern standards but also complement what was already there. That was a darn big deal."

While Gertie's ghost haunts the Narrows, her earthly remains, some 260 feet below the surface, also represented a challenge. The debris field from the 1940 disaster was added to the National Register of Historic Places in 1992. It's now home to "a wide variety of sealife, ranging from giant octopi and wolf eels, to sea bass and salmon sharks."

"We had to take great care to ensure that the caissons (piers) for the bridge towers did not disturb the remains of the original bridge. I had some interesting meetings with the state archeology and preservation director," Laird says.

Meanwhile, each day some 90,000 sidewalk-superintendents in the form of

The second Tacoma Narrows Bridge was built in 1950. *Michael W. Siegrist, State Library Photo Collection, Washington State Archives*

motorists were driving past the project. MacDonald gave the media wide access to the undertaking. "I told her it would be an incredible opportunity to showcase the project," he remembers with a chuckle. "But if something goes wrong there's no curtain to hide behind."

The cables from which the bridge span is suspended are fashioned from strands of wire, each about the thickness of a No. 2 pencil. That facet of suspension bridge technology hasn't changed much from the process invented in the 1870s by John and Washington A. Roebling for the construction of the Brooklyn Bridge.

In 2005, "when they unwrapped the paper on some of the spools from South Korea, they discovered the wire was corroded," MacDonald says. "What do we do now? The public is watching. And you've invited them to watch everything you're doing. You can't say 'Go away for about six months. We have this little problem to deal with!' Linea and her team worked through the problem with Tacoma Narrows Constructors. The long and short of it was that the integrity of the bridge was not compromised. The way she handled that scrutiny was a big evolution in the development of a seasoned project engineer. And when she ended up in Seattle to rescue the tunnel and viaduct program, she brought that experience to a very public project. She played a hugely positive role in those three landmark projects."

Amy Arnis, whom MacDonald describes as "the smartest person in Olympia you've never heard of," was WSDOT's chief financial officer when the tricky financing for the new bridge was being ironed out. "One of the things I came to appreciate about Linea is her attention to detail," Arnis says. "I had so much confidence that she knew that contract inside and out, chapter and verse. I was fielding lots of questions about the project from the State Treasurer and various financial institutions. On the mornings of the bond sales I could call Linea at 6:30 a.m. on my way to the Treasurer's Office and be confident I'd get the answers to the questions I knew I'd be asked. There's another thing, too: Working in the finance end of WSDOT, I didn't get many chances to watch what happened in the engineering office or at a construction site. She invited me to team breakfasts. I got to see how she built her team. I thought that was so cool. And it speaks volumes about what kind of leader she is."

Cutting the ribbon to open the new Narrows Bridge in 2007. Doug MacDonald at right. *WSDOT*

On July 15, 2007, 60,000 people turned out for the dedication of the new bridge. It was the culmination of years of effort from the design-builder and WSDOT. "I was so proud of the teamwork that created a beautiful landmark bridge that will be in place years beyond my lifespan," Laird says.

LAIRD NEXT BECAME WSDOT's state construction engineer, representing the state on national committees for highway planning research and construction. In 2009 she became "intricately involved" in the design-build contract for the controversial Highway 99 tunnel designed to replace Seattle's Alaskan Way Viaduct. The landmark elevated roadway was judged to be vulnerable to a major earthquake.

Some said a tunnel could crack in a quake or become a big-bore inferno if a multiple-vehicle collision ignited gas tanks. Others worried that structures above the route could be damaged by the boring. One study warned that if toll rates were set high enough to foot the bill, thousands of motorists would "avoid the tunnel and cram into downtown streets."

In other words, it was a high-profile political and engineering environment.

"I knew almost as little about tunnels as I'd known about suspension bridges when I started on the Tacoma Narrows project," Laird says, with a sort of here-we-go-again smile. "I mean, it's not like the state digs a complicated, landmark tunnel every few years. And this project is right in *downtown* Seattle. It's incredibly complicated. There is very little room for staging construction equipment, and the project goes right through the heart of the city under an array of complicated buildings. The route included very poor soils. What's more, we didn't own the property underground where this huge tunnel was going to be created, so we had to develop agreements with all the property owners along the way. Meanwhile, the City of Seattle also has a vested interest in the work you're doing and protecting all of its interests. It saw itself as a regulatory oversight body. While projects come and go, the city remains and lives with the results."

While navigating a thicket of contracts, Laird's team worked with the city, King County, worried state legislators, impacted business owners and numerous other stakeholders, including the conflicted public. "Paula Hammond, my boss and mentor for years, was WSDOT's secretary of transportation when the project started, so I knew her door was always open," Laird says. "She's whip smart and so on top of things. She

With "Big Bertha," the gigantic machine boring the tunnel to replace the viaduct. *WSDOT*

FHWA Administrator Victor Mendez, WSDOT Secretary Paula Hammond and Governor Chris Gregoire chat at the Aug. 10, 2010, opening event for the Smarter Highways system on I-5 in Seattle. *WSDOT*

not only understands the engineering side of things, she understands the political side of things. And she has devoted her career to paving the way for women in professional careers. The tunnel wouldn't have happened without Paula's leadership, but it was really Governor Gregoire who pushed it through. Her persistence and skillset for problem solving are something else."

In the fall of 2011, when Ron Paananen, WSDOT's project manager for the $3.1 billion viaduct replacement project, departed for the private sector, Laird was handed full oversight for the biggest assignment of her career.

On Laird's watch, contracts were awarded, the southern mile of the viaduct was demolished and work began in Japan on construction of the world's largest tunnel-borer. The mammoth machine—57½ feet in diameter and more than 300 feet long—was dubbed "Bertha" in honor of Seattle's first female mayor, the redoubtable Bertha Knight Landes. Two schoolchildren won a WSDOT contest to come up with the best name. At the time, Laird conceded that "Bertha" might not be the prettiest name, but she said it conjured up something that was big, solid and had a "down-home" quality. She had no inkling that "Bertha" was going to conjure up big down-home trouble.

The delays and controversies that dogged the project for more than two years, including Bertha's litigious big breakdown, unfolded after Laird had moved on. She was named WSDOT's chief engineer in 2013 by the new secretary of transportation, Lynn Peterson, who was similarly dedicated to providing career opportunities for women.

The viaduct replacement project was back on track in 2017 when Laird interrupted her short stint as a retiree to answer Mayor Durkan's call to serve as interim director of the Seattle Department of Transportation. The job came with a mandate to help provide modal pathways during the next several years of intense citywide construction. Completion of the tunnel was just one phase of the transition. Viaduct demolition and waterfront construction would come next, as well as an expanded Convention Center, the major renovation of Key Arena, the City Center Street Car and several Sound Transit projects. Laird's mandate was to keep the "Move Seattle" levy projects moving.

"It was four intense months. I appreciated getting to work with the SDOT team and feeling like I could contribute to problem-solving, even in such a short

Linea, left, and other key players pose for a "Women in transportation" photo at the tunnel breakthrough event in 2017. The others, from left are state Representative Judy Clibborn; Patty Rubstello WSDOT's assistant secretary for Urban Mobility & Access; Paula Hammond, former Secretary of Transportation; Megan Cotton, WSDOT Tribal and Federal Relations Director, and Allison Camden, WSDOT Intergovernmental & Tribal Relations Director. *WSDOT*

timeframe. I learned that Jenny Durkan is intensely focused on making good decisions for the city while still maintaining a sense of humor. That's a tall order. I came away with the conclusion that she is an amazing leader."

It was time to retire—again.

Linea and Mike Laird, currently working on a bigger boat-shed, have three children—two daughters and a son. Daughter No. 1 is an accountant; Daughter No. 2 a nurse. Their brother is a mechanical engineer. "I have very independent and greatly balanced children," Laird says with pride. "My career required a lot of travel—and many days with long hours. My husband bore a lot of the brunt of the day-to-day stuff. That allowed me to have the career I had. It was incredibly fulfilling. I do miss being part of a great team and playing a role in supporting transportation. The future holds many opportunities, especially for women in STEM careers."

John C. Hughes
Legacy Washington

University of Washington

ANA MARI CAUCE

PRESIDENT WITH A CAUSE

Short of violence, University of Washington students tried almost everything to stop Ana Mari Cauce from taking over the American Ethnic Studies program in 1997. They staged sit-ins at Board of Regents meetings. They cursed at President Richard McCormick and threatened to occupy his office. They interrupted former Governor Dan Evans, the regents' president, again and again in an attempted filibuster. They issued demands.

A cadre of student leaders feared administrators were trying to kill the small department that focused on African American, Asian and Chicano studies. Popular faculty members were let go or passed over for promotion. Other teaching positions went unfilled. The dean of Arts and Sciences had not inspired confidence when he said classes on race, gender and ethnicity were essential, but "it is not essential that this requires the departmental programs such as now exist."

To students, Cauce, the dean's hand-picked new leader, was the manager of a hostile takeover, maybe worse. In any case, she was a psychologist moving into American Ethnic Studies, which traditionally focused on history, literature and political science. She had not taught in the field, students complained, and although Cuban-born, she was not one of the minorities the program studied. In the campus newspaper, *The Daily*, student leaders said she must've got the job through the "good old boy network."

Cauce was clueless to what awaited. *The Daily* ran a full front-page story about her, headlined "Under Fire." Editors superimposed a telescopic gun-sight on Cauce's forehead—unaware that her brother had been shot and killed by the Ku Klux Klan. On the first day of her new job, she

Cauce kept a copy of the student newspaper published when she started a controversial career-changing UW job. *Bob Young*

walked to her office down a hall plastered with copies of *The Daily*.

Her thoughts went to her mother. Cauce was the one who had delivered the news about her brother's murder. Her mother responded with a noise "not quite human."

Almost in slow motion, Cauce walked down the corridor with one thought enveloping her brain: "My mother…better…not…see this."

In a letter responding to *The Daily*, she said she did not want to be depicted as competing with the students' preferred candidate to lead the department, Professor Johnnella Butler. She expressed great respect for Butler, asked students to give her a year to prove herself, and ended by borrowing a metaphor from *The Daily*'s cover. She said it would be in everyone's interest to declare a temporary "ceasefire" in the emotional controversy.

Her entreaty was met with a volley from a graduate student who saw a veiled threat. If Cauce only wanted a temporary cease-fire, the student wrote in *The Daily*, why should students wait until she "desires to renew hostilities?" Paraphrasing the Scottish-American revolutionary John Paul Jones, the student concluded in all caps, "WE HAVE NOT YET BEGUN TO FIGHT."

A year later, students who had complained about Cauce gave her a "rookie of the year" plaque. The new boss had gone to every American Ethnic Studies class to talk to students and get their views. Dr. Butler was promoted to director of undergraduate studies. Connie So, a popular instructor whose contract had not been renewed, was rehired. At the end of Cauce's three-year term, an oversight committee gave her and the department favorable reviews.

The arc of Cauce's career changed. She had once seen herself as an "accidental administrator." She had disliked process, distrusted authority and disdained bureaucracy.

Two decades later, she was lauded as president of one of the world's top 10 universities led by women.

The UW's 33rd president has blazed trails to a rumba beat. She is the first Latina, first lesbian and first exile to hold the UW presidency. And she is an academic unicorn—the ultra-rare insider at a major university who climbed the ranks to the summit, in her case, all the way from assistant professor to top Dawg, overseeing three campuses, an $8 billion

"I was a geek before it was chic," says Cauce, here getting a tutorial from UW student Sukhdeep Singh during the national "Hour of Code" event. *Dennis Wise/University of Washington*

budget, 59,000 students, and 31,000 faculty and staff.

"Although I did not realize it at the time," she says of the American Ethnic Studies flap, "I had become hooked on administration—the ability to bring disparate groups to the table, the satisfaction of building a program or department, or helping one to change, the adrenaline rush that comes from decision making under pressure."

WHEN ANA MARI CAUCE (first name rhymes with "calamari," the other with "cow-say") was a young girl she dreamed of becoming a firefighter. Not for the red truck and all, but "only because of the Dalmatians." Once she got past that, she wanted to be a teacher. "School was always my refuge," she says. "No surprise, I was never one of those popular kids. I like to say I was a geek before it was chic. And so, books were what nurtured me."

There's a photo of her as a young school girl with a blissful smile, holding a basketball. That smile turned out to be a signature trait, unwavering through the decades. It's warm and strong, not quite bittersweet but with a hint of a deeper story behind it.

Cauce's family fled Cuba and settled in Florida when she was 3 years old. *Ana Mari Cauce*

Cauce's starts with the Cuban revolution in 1958. When Fidel Castro's rebels reached Havana, Cauce's parents feared for their lives. Her father, Vicente, was the country's minister of education. They left straight from a New Year's Eve party for the Chilean embassy, where the ambassador arranged for their safe passage out of Cuba. They eventually landed in Miami. Cauce, 3 years old, and her brother César, 5, soon boarded a Pan Am flight and joined them in Florida.

"He lifted me up and helped build the foundation that still grounds me," Cauce says about her father, who went from political elite in Cuba to facory-worker in Florida. *Ana Mari Cauce*

Despite her father's standing as a political elite in Cuba, he was just another exile in America. His first job was sweeping floors in a hotel. For many years, he worked in a shoe factory. Her mother, Ana, tried several factory jobs. The Cauces temporarily hosted so many relatives and friends arriving in the U.S. that it seemed Ana Mari or César was always sleeping on the couch.

Ana Mari, who quickly learned English, often translated for her parents. In her third-grade class, she was called on to translate for newly arrived Cuban immigrants, her first experience as a kind of teacher's assistant. While she and César felt like American kids, some things in the Cauce household still had a Cuban flavor, such as Thanksgiving, when they stuffed the turkey with beans and rice.

Ana Mari or her brother César (right) always seemed to be sleeping on the couch because her parents hosted so many Cuban exiles. *Ana Mari Cauce*

"I never felt deprived in any way, shape or form," Cauce says. Her parents shielded her from the reality of their sacrifices. Only when she applied for financial aid for college did she realize she was "poor" enough to qualify.

Back in the early 1960s, before food stamps as we know them, welfare meant surplus food. Her parents were too proud to take it, but her aunt and grandmother would bring it home. "And for a long time I hated peanut butter because that was welfare food," Cauce says.

Another enduring memory: To celebrate her brother graduating from eighth grade, the family went to a Howard Johnson's restaurant for dessert. "We had ice cream and they put sparklers and stuff in it so it was a big celebration," she says.

Her father left some money on the table.

She picked it up and took it home.

"And I very proudly gave it to my father and said, 'You forgot this.' He turned to my mom and said, 'We're raising a bunch of heathens,' or some equivalent of that. And I think back on the fact that we never went out to dinner."

Her father never stopped reminding her that education is one thing no one could ever take away from her. His own education "didn't translate in this country—into power, wealth, prestige, any of those kinds of things. But it made his life richer in so many different ways."

Cauce's brother graduated with honors from Duke University. She graduated from the University of Miami *summa cum laude*, the highest distinction. In 1979, she shoved off for Yale University to pursue advanced degrees in psychology. One Saturday night during her first semester she and friends were getting ready to play Monopoly when she got a call from her mother, who had heard something about a rally.

Cauce turned on the TV. News stations were running stories about what

Ana Mari had to tell her mother (left) about her brother's murder at an anti-KKK rally.
Ana Mari Cauce

became known as the "Greensboro Massacre."

César Vincente Cauce had become politically active at Duke. After receiving his bachelor's degree, he faced a decision: accept a full scholarship to graduate school, or, stay in North Carolina and join a union drive at Duke Hospital. He got a job as a data clerk at the hospital and dove into organizing. Friends described him as thoughtful, able to get along with all kinds of people, and "not at all like the bossy kind of men." A big man with a big bush of brick-red hair, he was a core leader of the hospital drive.

On November 3rd, 1979, he took part in an anti-Ku Klux Klan rally led by the Communist Workers Party. Billed as "Death to the Klan," the gathering of 40 to 50 protesters drew an angry response from Klansmen and Nazis, who filled nine vehicles in a caravan that rolled by the protesters.

Both sides shouted insults. Protesters banged on the Klan cars with fists or picket signs. A fight broke out with both sides wielding sticks from picket signs. A Klansman fired what appeared to be a warning shot into the air.

After 88 seconds of subsequent shooting, five protesters lay dead, including César Cauce, who was unarmed. He had been clubbed in the head with a stick, dropping him to his hands and knees. He was then shot in the neck and died on a patch of grass outside an apartment building.

Nazis and Klansmen claimed self-defense and were twice acquitted by all-white juries. A fact-finding commission created to reconcile lingering divisions in the Greensboro community, found that protesters used incendiary rhetoric and some fired guns (hitting no one) after the Klan shot first. But the Nazis and Klansmen were more responsible for the deaths, along with the Greensboro Police Department, which "showed a stunning lack of curiosity in planning for the safety of the event." Police commanders learned from an informant about the Klan's plans to disrupt the protest. But officers were directed away from the event, which was publicized enough that four TV news crews were on the scene. Officers stopped only one of the Klan cars from fleeing the scene after shots were fired.

In a snippet on TV, Ana Mari thought she saw her brother get shot. She called Greensboro police. Eventually, they confirmed that César, 25, was killed. It fell on her to inform her mother.

Afterwards, Cauce described herself as "flattened," too depressed to be angry.

FIVE YEARS LATER, Cauce was a newly minted doctor of psychology. Her mentor at Yale was Edmund W. Gordon, who had been mentored by W.E.B. Du Bois, acclaimed author and co-founder of the NAACP. Gordon's research focused on African American students who succeeded despite facing significant challenges. Gordon said Cauce was one of the best students he taught in his 60-year career. "Even in those early days Ana Mari was asking the hard-to-answer questions, and insisting on more than superficial and simplistic answers."

In 1999 Cauce received the Distinguished Teaching Award, the highest honor the UW gives faculty members for their work with students. *University of Washington*

Cauce landed a teaching job at the less-than-fabled University of Delaware, in the small city of Newark. She was on her way to Seattle two years later to become an assistant professor at the University of Washington.

Her research, funded by the likes of the National Institute of Mental Health, tended to focus on minority and homeless youth. Her practice as a clinical psychologist required her to watch video recordings of her meetings with clients. "It was a humbling and painful experience," she says. She learned that she came across as stronger than she really was, partly because she was raised in a big loud Cuban family and expressed herself boldly. She was reminded of an old joke: How do you quiet a Cuban? Tie their hands.

"So I will literally at times sit on my hands," she says, "because it's important for me to make sure I'm leaving room for others to speak and that I'm listening."

She became director of clinical training in the UW Department of Psychology, a post she held for seven years. She was about to go on sabbatical when she was asked to serve as chair of the embattled American Ethnic Studies program. She had reservations. But Edmund Gordon, her mentor, framed the decision as "why not you?" She had to do it, he said. She was the right person. It was a matter of duty.

Battle-tested by the demoralized department, its polarized faculty and tenacious students,* she began a steady ascent at Montlake. In roughly three-year tours of duty, she became director of the UW Honors Program, then chair of the Psychology Department. (One colleague called her a "chairapist" for her accessible

---

* In an editorial about their tactics hurting their cause, *The Daily* said American Ethnic Studies student leaders "made wild accusations and repeatedly played the race card."

style.) She moved up to executive vice provost, then dean of the College of Arts and Sciences. There was only one more stop before the summit. She was named provost, the university's second-in-command and top budget officer. Cauce joked that the provost's job is to trail behind the glad-handing president and say, "What he really means is 'No.' "

When President Michael Young, who was lured to Seattle from Utah, left the UW for Texas A&M, Cauce was elevated to interim president. After her appointment was announced at a Board of Regents meeting, staff, students and regents lined up for hugs. As a nationwide search was launched, the UW community surveyed the recent past and saw a series of outsiders who had bolted the president's office, or were asked to leave.

Cauce, on the other hand, bled purple. She had said the UW was her home, and as an exile, "home means a lot to me." She was not only a proven candidate, but one who just might supply a steady hand for years. And she was refreshingly collaborative and open. After telling a journalist about vacationing in Australia to help researchers count baby penguins, Cauce pulled up her sleeve to show a scar on her bicep. "That," she said proudly, "is a penguin bite."

She was not the first woman to serve as acting president. Phyllis Wise, a scientist and daughter of Chinese immigrants, preceded her. But Cauce would use her platform in a way that Wise, or no other UW president, had.

During a very personal speech in 2015, Cauce wiped away a tear while discussing her mother. *University of Washington*

JUST TWO MONTHS after becoming acting president, Cauce stepped to the microphone in the UW's Intellectual House, a longhouse-style facility created as a learning and gathering space for American Indian and Alaska Native students. It was April 16, 2015, Holocaust Remembrance Day.

Cauce's 37-minute speech was titled, "We the people: diversity, equity and difference at the UW."* She wrote it herself and practiced it on a hike with a UW staffer, tweaking the speech along the way. Several hundred in the audience waited with anticipation. A recent Black Lives Matter march through campus had been disrupted by someone shouting

---

* Diversity of UW's 2018 student population by percentage: Caucasian, 39; Asian, 22; international, 15; Latino, 8; Southeast Asian, 6; African American, 4; Filipino, 2; American Indian-Alaska Native, 1; Hawaiian-Pacific Islander, 1.

"apes" at those peacefully assembled. Rather than play it safe as some candidates for president might, Cauce leaned into the controversy.

And she made it personal, almost uncomfortably so.

"The fact I was interim (president) was not the moment to start being timid," she says. "I was also trying to decide, Is this a job I wanted?" At that point, she hadn't thrown her hat in the ring for the presidency. To some degree, she still wondered, "Can I be me? Are the things I care about, is that a good match for the presidency?"

The "apes" comment had gotten to her. It was a reminder that even in progressive Seattle "we often fall way short of our ideals." But before she opened up about her own life in a choked-up confessional, she took the audience down a provocative path.

Surveys showed that the current generation of college students thought they were color blind—to the point they didn't even know about differences in American ethnic cultures. But, Cauce asked, is this good? Who are we erasing when we go blind? What's being "whitewashed," so to speak?

She called the lack of knowledge about other cultures the makings of a Molotov cocktail. Racism was baked into our country's founding, she said, and consumed by generations of immigrants. She knew her family brought a Cuban strain of racism to America. Her aunt, charitable and religious, taught Cauce that her white skin was a gift so she should be extra kind to those who were darker. How, Cauce wondered, could she herself not have some racism lurking inside her?

We all need to be more aware of our prejudices, she said. When she met the woman, Susan Joslyn, who would become her longtime partner and wife, Cauce wanted to tell her mother. She expected her mother, a 4-foot-11-inch "Mack truck of persistence," to be unhappy. But she didn't anticipate what she said:

"Now both my children are dead."

Nothing could've been more hurtful, Cauce said.

Her mother later offered to sell her only valuable possession, her condo, to pay for "conversion" treatment, Cauce said, shrugging and smiling. Then she wiped away a tear.

But her mother changed. She opened her heart to Joslyn, a UW professor. And, after a massive stroke,

Cauce called UW alumni and champion Bill Gates Sr. (right) a "big man with an even bigger heart." *Ana Mari Cauce*

she died in Cauce's arms, mother and daughter proud of each other in the end.

"It's not just about bad people doing bad things," Cauce told the hushed audience. "It's about us. It's not about guilt. This is about change. This is about growth."

She challenged everyone in attendance to examine their own thoughts and feelings. She urged them to call out friends who tell racist or dumb-blonde jokes. And she encouraged them to learn about the pain and struggle of others.

WHEN REGENTS unanimously voted in October 2015 to appoint a new president, their decision was hardly a surprise.

Momentum for Cauce seemed to be building in the weeks and months beforehand. Katherine Long, veteran higher-education reporter for *The Seattle Times*, had written a story saying Cauce had widespread support on campus. Some even wondered why the UW was bothering with a nationwide search.

Sure, Cauce was informal, a bit unpolished and hardly the pale male candidate out of Central Casting. But her down-to-earth approachability was part of her appeal. She wrote on Facebook about the joys of mowing her lawn. She drove a Honda that friends said was often a mess inside. She wore sweat pants to the supermarket. "Whether she's posing with Husky mascot 'Dubs' or greeting Chinese President Xi Jinping during a formal ceremony at Microsoft, she always looks like she's having a good time," Long wrote.

While Cauce was likely to be picked as president from the minute Young decamped for Texas, Long said her emotional talk at the Intellectual House helped introduce her to a wider audience and "put her heart out there."

UW's 14th live mascot, Dubs II, an Alaskan Malamute, with the leader of the Husky pack. *Ana Mari Cauce*

One expert surprised at Cauce's appointment was Judith Block McLaughlin, a scholar of college presidential searches for three decades and chair of the Harvard Seminar for New Presidents. When asked to name an internal candidate promoted to president of a major American university, Block McLaughlin, came up empty. "Their warts are known…their enemies are right there on campus," she said.

As president, Cauce was more concerned about new toadies than old foes. "The further you rise the more people want to please you, so to speak. So you have to be very careful to make sure everyone doesn't just 'yes, yes' you."

As someone who believes you learn more from your critics than your supporters, Cauce wanted to encourage dissent among those who had her ear. "They're doing you no favors if they don't bring up the ifs, ands or buts to any particular direction that you're taking. I tell people: 'Come at me hard. This is the setting in which I want you to come at me hard because when we leave the room I want us to be on one page.' "

Cauce feels some ambivalence about all the "firsts" associated with her tenure. "On the one hand, you know, it makes me incredibly proud. And I recognize that it sends an important message to women coming after me.* On the other hand, there's a bit of, 'I'm not a woman president. I'm a president.'

"I want to be known for my accomplishments, not just that I accomplished them while being female."

Another one of her peeves is when people talk about someone like her overcoming her background. "I've overcome obstacles. My background is part of my strength. It's not something that I've overcome."

CAUCE'S STRENGTH was tested, when campus Republicans invited right-wing provocateur Milo Yiannopoulos to speak at the UW in January 2017, on the night of President Trump's inauguration festivities. Yiannopoulos was known for taking political incorrectness to the level of profane name-calling. He attacked specific college professors with insults and described "rape culture" on campuses as a myth. He was banned from Twitter for racism and misogyny. (He would later lose a book contract and editing job for endorsing sexual relations with boys as young as 13.)

Thousands of people asked Cauce to ban Yiannopoulos from speaking. An anti-fascism movement urged its members to shut Yiannopoulos down. Other schools, including New York University and Iowa State University, had canceled his scheduled talks for fears of violence between protesters.

While the leader of the UW's College Republicans said such retreats amounted to "babying students," some seemingly valid concerns were raised. Alysse Holt, a graduate student, said Yiannopoulos' college tour "really signals the renormalization of the particular brand of white supremacy and white nationalism that's being cloaked now within these broader conversations of free speech."

But the only exceptions to First Amendment rights involve what lawyers call "fighting words," or speech with a specific threat. Cauce stood her ground. "A university should—indeed it must—be a place where any policy or idea, even if offensive or outrageous, can be aired, discussed, examined and debated," Cauce wrote on her blog. "That's a cornerstone of our democratic system, and the University of Washington's commitment to this ideal is rock solid."

Conflict began brewing hours before Yiannopoulos' scheduled talk in Kane

---

* As of November 2018, 43 percent of UW faculty were women. New faculty hires from 2014-2015 through 2018-2019 averaged 49 percent women. Women accounted for 33 percent of UW professors and 53 percent of assistant professors.

The president met with angry students after a shooting on campus sparked by the appearance of right-wing provocateur Milo Yiannopoulos. *Katherine Long*

Hall. People started lining up in the afternoon. Clashes outside the hall started a couple hours later when anti-fascists and ticket-holders traded "nazi scum" and "white power" shouts.

Despite a large police presence—124 UW and Seattle officers were dispatched to the scene—tension escalated. Bricks were thrown at officers. Paint and pepper-spray doused others. Joshua Dukes, 34, an anti-fascist protester, took a bullet in the abdomen when he confronted a man using pepper spray. A Seattle couple, both 29, pleaded not guilty to assault charges, claiming self-defense. Police had initially suspected Marc Hokoana of the shooting. But his wife Elizabeth's attorney told prosecutors that she had fired at Dukes with a Glock handgun she had in a holster under her coat. (A King County Superior Court judge declared a mistrial in the case after jurors were deadlocked on a verdict. Prosecutors dismissed the case.)

In the aftermath of the shooting, Cauce was called "complicit," "collaborator," and "appeaser." "This blood is on your hands," said another message.

She held an impromptu meeting with protesters outside her office in Gerberding Hall. As the protesters, some wearing bandanas over their faces, shouted questions and accusations, Cauce tried to answer. She made it clear Yiannopoulos was "repulsive." (His talk to a UW audience of about 200 featured insults about women, the disabled, and the left, and repeated use of the "C-word.") She reminded the crowd that her brother was killed by white supremacists. She took responsibility for Dukes' serious injury.

Someone shouted that she wouldn't say she was sorry.

"I am truly sorry," she replied.

Another shout: "Are you sorry you invited a fascist to campus?"

Cauce is the rare insider who climbed the ranks to president of a major American university. "My background is part of my strength. It's not something that I've overcome," she says. *University of Washington*

"I didn't issue the invitation," Cauce said.

The shouting continued. "You enabled it." "You invited hate speech." "You invited violence."

Noting developments, such as President Trump's attacks on journalists as "enemy of the people," one newspaper columnist praised Cauce's commitment to free speech.

"Here's a Cuban immigrant whose brother died at the hands of right-wing nut-jobs, and she's the one standing up for the free-speech rights of right-wing nut jobs," wrote Danny Westneat of *The Seattle Times*. "Now that's spine. That's dedication to founding principles. That's America—at least as we imagine ourselves to be."

Two years later, Cauce remained convinced she made the right decision.

"Certainly I, you know, regret deeply whenever anyone on our campus is injured or hurt in any way. And so, I feel deeply, I feel awful about the young individual who was injured," she says. But there's a larger perspective to consider. "You know, at this moment in time, free speech seems to be a stand-in for allowing people with very disturbing views a position. But, we know that historically…by and large, free speech has been very empowering to disenfranchised groups. And so, we have to look at the long arc."

AS WITH THE ANGRY students in American Ethnic Studies, Cauce didn't blame those shouting at her outside Gerberding Hall, or get defensive with them. They weren't mad at *her*. They were mad at the *president*. And she knew as president she had to work with them if she was going to be successful. She couldn't personalize their gripes, sulk or lash out; nor could she generalize their behavior to all students.

As for admirers who wonder how she got to be president—and with a sense of inner peace—her advice is to say 'yes' a lot. Even if you're not sure you can do the job you're asked to take on. "But you say 'yes' and you figure it out as you go along. I think if you're going to wait until you're 100 percent sure, you might be waiting a long time."

Responsibility more than boldness has guided her. And chief among her responsibilities is to make the UW a place of excellence *and* access. About 30 percent of UW students are the first in their families to go to college. Many of those students are growing up in neighborhoods and schools increasingly segregated by income inequality. College is likely the most diverse environment they've experienced. By helping them understand differences in one another, and by helping them graduate, the university becomes an engine for social and economic mobility, a spark plug for empathy and equity.

"For me, it really is all about the work," she says, "not about the position."

She feels a sense of pride that women or immigrants or LGBT folks are inspired by her and think they can reach a position like hers. "But, it really isn't about aiming for the position. It's about the work. And you can do the work from a lot of different positions. And if it brings you here, that's fabulous."

Bob Young
Legacy Washington

"I fell in love with the logic, the elegance, and the fact it was useful," Mary-Claire King says about the first genetics course she took in graduate school. *University of Washington*

MARY-CLAIRE KING

"FOR HER, SCIENCE IS PERSONAL"

Mary-Claire King was pursuing a graduate degree in statistics at Berkeley when, on a lark, she took her first course in genetics. An avid puzzle-solver, King was enchanted. She sat up front for lectures by Curt Stern, who wrote a pioneering textbook on human genetics. The soft-spoken Stern would pose intricate story problems to his packed classes. Then he'd sort them out with elegant logic. It was human puzzles with purpose. She couldn't believe anything so important could be so much fun.

But life during wartime intervened. It was 1968, Vietnam's deadliest year for U.S. troops. The draft escalated. Protests roiled Berkeley. Governor Ronald Reagan, who had launched his political career by vowing to "clean up the mess" at the University of California, cracked down on dissident students.

The campus was shut down intermittently by conflict. King was looking to do something productive that summer when a little card posted on a bulletin board grabbed her imagination. The brainy consumer advocates known as Ralph Nader's Raiders were probing the tangle of money, politics and public land in a new project called "Who Owns California?" They were seeking a biologist, which King was not. Their posting stressed the job's long hours and low pay.

That's for me, she thought.

She researched the widespread use of pesticides for Nader and wrote about its harmful impact on farmworkers. She came to think of Delores Huerta, co-founder of the United Farm Workers union, as a hero. Huerta's slogan for the union, *Si se puede* ("Yes, we can."), could double as the motto of King's tenacious career as a superstar geneticist.

But at the time, King was very tempted to "bag this graduate career and go do politics." Nader had asked her to come to Washington, D.C., to help him put Congress under a microscope.

She sought out her informal adviser, Allan Wilson, a New Zealander with innovative ideas about evolution, who prowled the lecture stage "like a tiger." Researchers were intensely critical of one another in his almost gladiatorial lab, where you were only as good as today's experiments. But they were fiercely loyal to each other outside its walls. King called it "somewhere between a family and a kibbutz."

President Obama kidded King for saying about genetics, "I couldn't believe anything could be so much fun." *Michael Reynolds/EPA*

Working for Nader would be righteous, Wilson told her. He totally got where she was coming from. But he offered a caveat. Without an advanced degree she wouldn't be the one steering a science-based agenda in almost any organization. Sometimes credentials mattered.

She rethought Nader's pitch. She instead worked in Wilson's lab. Her Ph.D. thesis landed on the cover of the prestigious journal *Science,* akin to a songwriter's first hit making the cover of *Rolling Stone.*

Four decades later, President Obama draped a National Medal of Science around King, a University of Washington professor since 1995. Every "single American should be grateful for Mary-Claire King's path," the President said in a White House ceremony. At a time when many scientists were studying how environmental factors and viruses could cause cancer, she pursued a hunch that certain cancers were inherited. The self-described "stubborn" scientist plugged away at a marathoner's pace, her every step haunted by the loss of her childhood best friend to cancer.

"Seventeen years of work later, Mary-Claire discovered a single gene that predisposes women to breast cancer," Obama said. "And that discovery has empowered women and their doctors with science to better understand the choices that they make when it comes to their health and their future."

That's just a slice of King's panoramic story, which starts outside Chicago with math puzzles about baseball legend Ernie Banks. It later involves a coup d'etat in Chile, Argentina's Dirty War, and identifying victims of massacres ranging from El Salvadoran peasants to Russia's last czar and czarina. It reaches the Middle East, where she has worked on inherited hearing loss in Israeli *and* Palestinian children. It includes 13 honorary doctorates and comparisons to Marie Curie and Wayne Gretzky. And it's been fodder for a movie in which Helen

When presented with a prestigious Lasker Award, King was likened to hockey legend Wayne Gretzky, who said, "You miss 100 percent of the shots you don't take." *Bruce Bennett*

Hunt plays her on the big screen. King even uncorked a 12-minute excerpt of her own for a podcast called *The Moth*. The tale covers two fateful days in her life, starting with her husband leaving her for one of his graduate students. "He gave me a new vacuum cleaner to soften the blow," she deadpans. It ends with a cameo by Joe DiMaggio that will leave you beaming, if not howling.

Throughout her storied achievements, King has followed a belief that "you bring your whole self into the lab." She has been foremost a citizen-scientist, combining an activist's passion with clear-eyed objectivity. Or, as her brother Paul put it: "Mary-Claire's scientific interest is more an outcropping of her humanism than of a natural bent toward science."

PRESIDENT OBAMA feted King for her most renowned work. But King is the rare scientist with not one, but three "blue moon" discoveries to her credit.

When she won a Lasker Award, often called the "American Nobels," in 2014, presenter Marc Tessier-Lavigne likened her to Gretzky, who holds the National Hockey League record for most "hat tricks"—scoring three goals in a game. "Like the Great One himself," Tessier-Lavigne said, "Mary-Claire is in a league of her own." She made major impacts in at least three fields—evolutionary genetics, medical genetics and molecular forensics.

You're forgiven for not quite understanding what differentiates those fields. King and her peers operate in a league of *their* own, using state-of-the-art technology and terms most of us can't grasp to understand how vastly complicated recipes (genes) use the tiniest ingredients of life (building blocks of DNA) to produce blue eyes, or microscopic filaments of inner ear hair, or a defense against tumor cells.

Which is all the more striking because King was an undistinguished math major at Carleton College in Minnesota. The chairman of Carleton's math department didn't remember King as a standout undergraduate when he was asked to prepare remarks about her for an honorary degree she received in 1992.

She became fascinated by math as a young girl while playing story-puzzles with her father, a retired labor relations manager for Standard Oil. He was often bedridden in their suburban Chicago home with late-onset effects of the 1918 influenza epidemic. In the early days of television when there were few channels and programs, father and daughter would watch baseball games together and he'd ask questions such

King grew up in Wilmette, Illinois and attended New Trier Township High School, considered one of the best public schools in the country. Its alumni include former Boeing CEO James McNerney, actress Ann-Margaret and Nobel Prize-winning physicist Jack Steinberger.

as: How many hits does Cubs star Ernie Banks need in this game to lift his batting average to .280? Mary-Claire would mull over her dad's query and figure out she needed more information. He'd ask what she was missing. Well, she had learned batting average is number of hits divided by number of at-bats. So she'd say she needed his total number of at-bats.

In high school she had two women math teachers who were role models. But when she transferred to studying genetics at Berkeley she thought of herself as "totally clumsy" in the lab. Frustrated, she vented to Professor Wilson that she could never get her experiments to work.

The charismatic Kiwi told her there'd be no scientists if everyone quit when their experiments failed. He helped King design a project that combined her talent in statistics with his efforts to trace human evolution through genetics and

Allan Wilson, King's friend and adviser, died from leukemia at 56. *Jane Scherr*

molecular biology. Wilson asked her to compare the chemical properties of proteins from human and chimpanzee cells. Still insecure, she kept thinking her work was a disaster because she only found differences in about one out of 100 tests. "I was in total despair—my usual reaction to anything I tried to do in the lab," she recalled.

Wilson turned the prism.

"This is great," he said. "It shows how similar we are to chimps!"

King had revealed that humans and chimps are 99 percent identical at the genetic level. The two species were more than cousins, they were "almost genetic look-alikes."

The question then became: how to explain the obvious contrasts in anatomy and behavior?

King and Wilson proposed that the differences arose from a small number of mutations affecting how and

The April 1975 issue of *Science* touted King and Wilson's discovery that chimps and human are 99 percent identical at the genetic level.

when certain genes are expressed, thus altering specific features, such as the length of bones or the size of brains. In other words, distinctions between the two species were actually due to changes in the bits of genetic material that act something like traffic lights, regulating how and when genes carry out their tasks.

It was a bold theory and they became minor celebrities when King's thesis formed the basis for findings she and Wilson published in the April 1975 edition of *Science*. It also gave King a taste of the success that could come from swimming against the scientific tide.

But two years passed before King's thesis became the polished, peer-reviewed manuscript that made the cover of *Science*. During that time she and her then-husband, Rob Colwell, a zoologist, took off on a teaching project at the University of Chile in Santiago. Not long after the couple arrived, "all hell broke loose."

On September 11, 1973, the Chilean military overthrew the democratically elected President Salvador Allende. The U.S. Central Intelligence Agency had worked for years to foment a coup against Allende, a Marxist. He had nationalized Chilean industries, provoking a backlash from U.S. leaders who feared another Fidel Castro coming to power. Economic aid dried up. The World Bank was pressured to end all loans to Chile. The country was crippled by inflation, food shortages, and violence between the left and the right.

Under orders from General Augusto Pinochet, air force jets fired rockets into the palace which Allende vowed to defend to his death. As tanks and troops prepared to follow up the aerial assault, Allende reportedly placed his rifle under his chin and killed himself.

King had been away from Santiago during the attack but returned to see bodies in the streets and bodies in the Mapocho River that bisects the city. The university, a hotbed of political activity, was closed. Some of her Chilean friends went into hiding. King and her husband kept a low-profile. On Christmas day they returned to Berkeley.

King didn't have a job. "My mind and my soul were still churning over what was happening in Chile. I was very much at loose ends."

SHE SAW AN AD for a position at the University of California, San Francisco researching breast cancer, which she knew almost nothing about. She thought of the job as "just a place to land with the opportunity of doing something useful."

It was 1974. She was about to embark on an odyssey.

She began to meet surgeons who helped her understand the disease and its aggressiveness in some families. "They were older, they were without exception male, and they were wonderful to me. I was obviously no threat."

It dawned on her that young women in science—who were few and tended to exist on the margins—were pretty much ignored. That gave her a kind of freedom to "go after huge questions." And it gave her the freedom to fail.

She soon focused on the idea that there was a family component to breast cancer—and it was a key but overlooked risk. In 1866 French scientist Paul Broca documented 10 cases in his family over four generations. Broca didn't know why his family was afflicted because the natural laws of inheritance were not yet understood. In the 1920s British statistician Dr. Janet Lane-Claypon also reported evidence of a familial link.

When King returned from Chile, jobs in cancer research were abundant because President Nixon had declared a national "war on cancer." *Mary-Claire King*

But correlation isn't causation. And there wasn't a solid hypothesis about what caused familial clustering.

At the time, scientists believed cancer was acquired during one's life, not *in utero*. The disease grew out of damaging changes to one's genes, the thinking went, caused by viruses and environmental factors, such as chemicals or radiation. Breast cancer was common enough, scientists thought, that it wasn't surprising if it struck more than one member of a family.

King's instincts, coupled with the pattern-recognition skills she honed in puzzles and statistics, told her something different. In the back of her mind also loomed her childhood friend Debbie, who was in constant pain from what turned out to be a kidney cancer called Wilms' tumor. The cancer killed Debbie when she and King were both 13.

"I know for a fact that Mary-Claire never got over that," her mother Clarice recalled.

She was determined to find the deviant gene or genes that triggered hereditary cancer. First, though, she needed good data; she needed families ravaged by the disease. She heard about a large survey of breast cancer patients, and age-matched healthy subjects from the same neighborhoods, planned by the National Cancer Institute. The survey was mainly interested in whether the use of birth-control pills altered the risks of breast, ovarian or uterine cancer. (Men can get breast cancer, but the disease is about 100 times more common in women.)

King was able to get a few family history questions added to the survey, which would take years to complete. Meanwhile, her lab crafted and began running statistical models to determine if there was evidence of other reasons for breast cancer clustering besides genetics.

While immersed in studying other families, she started her own with the birth of her daughter Emily in 1975. King realized that living in Berkeley, where

"Science is also a very demanding child," King said, about juggling work and care for her daughter Emily. "It's not realistic to say one can drop out of science and drop back in." *Mary-Claire King*

Emily had child-care, and commuting across the bay to San Francisco every day was not a good long-term plan.

She applied for an assistant professor position in the epidemiology division at Berkeley. Her timing was exquisite. Affirmative action was being ushered in at Berkeley. Search committees for faculty posts had to include a woman or minority member. In King's case the female member was Cathy Schaefer, a student.

Weeks passed after King's interview. Finally, she was offered the job. Then she learned what really happened—the bulldoggish Schaefer had insisted that the epidemiology division needed a woman professor. She had "just got her teeth into it and wouldn't let go," the head of the search committee said.

After she accepted the job, the division chief told King she only got the post "because of all these new regulations."

Schaefer went on to earn a Ph.D. and become director of Kaiser Permanente's Research Program on Genes, Environment and Health. "She is responsible for my career," King said. "I am absolutely a child of affirmative action."

WHILE HER CANCER RESEARCH plodded along, hunting for families with a history of breast cancer and compelling evidence of a renegade gene, King took a sort of mini-sabbatical. She began commuting to Stanford University, where a mentor, Luca Cavalli-Sforza, was helping her gain expertise in molecular genetics. While at Stanford she also learned about grandmothers in Argentina trying to find children who disappeared during that country's military dictatorship.

In 1976, the military overthrew the government of Isabel Peron, the widow of populist President Juan Peron. The military junta coined the term "Dirty War" for its crackdown on fellow Argentines—which included throwing drugged prisoners into the ocean from airplanes. In one general's definition, the enemies were anyone whose ideas were "contrary to Western Christian civilization." During the military's reign, from 1976 to 1983, up to 30,000 Argentines were "disappeared."

About 30 percent of the disappeared, as they became known, were women. Some were killed in military assaults and their surviving children were taken by soldiers. Some were abducted with their young children. An estimated 3 percent of abductees were pregnant at the time of their capture or were impregnated by rape in prison. Those women were often kept alive until they'd given birth.

Grandmothers ("abuelas") of missing children began protesting every week in Argentina's capital. The government tried to marginalize the abuelas by calling them "las locas" or madwomen. Then one of the group's founders was kidnapped and murdered. But the women weren't cowed. *Abuelas de Plaza de Mayo*

The military and its allies thought they could reform the enemy's children to create "authentic Argentines" through adoption. Many of the disappeared children were given to military families. Others were handed to orphanages.

A group of courageous "abuelas" or grandmothers began to hold silent protests outside the presidential palace in Buenos Aires. And they began to collect tips about children who had been adopted by military families; some clues came from midwives and doctors who delivered babies in prison. Grandmothers started digging deeper; one even became a maid in a home where it was suspected a stolen child was being raised.

In 1984, the dictatorship had fallen. The grandmothers had already collected 145 case records of children who had been seen alive but whose parents had disappeared. King and others in Cavalli-Sforza's lab developed a blood test that could identify a genetic link between grandparents and grandchildren. In doing so, she was an innovator in the nascent field of molecular forensics.

Cavalli-Sforza asked King to go to Buenos Aires to put the blood-testing into practice. He said she was perfectly suited for the job. She knew Latin America. She had taught in Spanish. More important, she was the age of the grandmothers' missing daughters and Emily was the age of their children.

King developed a test based on maternal lines of heredity. With a sample from a granny, researchers could tell if a boy or girl was her grandchild without a trace of DNA from a missing parent. *Abuelas de Plaza de Mayo*

For King, the Dirty War echoed the Chilean coup. "It seemed that as an American I owed something back," she said.

Argentine reformers had set up a human rights commission to which King was a consultant. She helped create a national genetic database of families who lost children during the Dirty War that could be used to confirm the true identities of children. Courts ordered some suspected stolen children to be tested. Others volunteered after later learning they were adopted.

But King's blood tests had shortcomings. They needed samples from all four grandparents for bulletproof confirmation.

More puzzles to solve.

King and colleagues built a more powerful test based on maternal lines of heredity. They relied on analysis of DNA from mitochondria, a component in cells that passes from mother to child, creating a kind of genetic family crest. With a sample from granny, researchers could tell if a boy or girl was her grandchild without any remains or a trace of DNA from the missing mom.

It was the first application of mitochondrial DNA analysis. And in December 1984, Paula Logares became the first child reunited with her biological family based on King's genetic evidence.

Logares was 23 months old when she was kidnapped, along with her parents who were suspected radicals. She was raised by a police officer and his wife. A neighbor became suspicious when she heard the officer's wife shout at her husband that he had killed a little girl's parents and now expected her to care for the child. The neighbor snapped some photos of young Logares and got them to her maternal grandmother. After democracy was restored, and legal hurdles cleared, King's analysis showed with 99.98 percent certainty that Logares was related to her grandmother.

King's lab was soon asked to help the American military identify remains from as far back as World War II. And her lab began to identify victims of atrocities worldwide. Her efforts helped launch the United Nations forensic team.

At last count, 130 of the estimated 500 disappeared children in Argentina had been reunited with their true families.

In all the tributes heaped on King, one of her forensic feats has received little attention. She helped identify the mangled remains of Russia's last royal family, who were executed in 1918 by Bolshevik bullets, bayonets and rifle butts, then buried and chaotically reburied in a forest.

Misinformation and mystery had long

Paula Logares was "disappeared" along with her parents when she was 23 months old. Six years later she was the first of Argentina's missing children whose real identify was confirmed by King's tests. *Abuelas de Plaza de Mayo*

shrouded the deaths of the royal Romanov family and disposal of their corpses. After their murder in Yekaterinburg, a mining hub about 1,000 miles east of Moscow, Bolsheviks admitted to Czar Nicholas' death. But they claimed Czarina Alexandra and royal heir Alexei were alive and safe. Josef Stalin then banned discussion of the family, which only fueled questions and rumors and led to a string of royal impostors.

A pair of amateur sleuths found one of the burial sites but kept it secret until after the fall of the Soviet Union in 1991. Russians hired three teams of foreign scientists to analyze teeth and bones. The various scientists all concurred that the first discovered burial site contained Nicholas, Alexandra and three of their children. (Remains of the other two children would later be unearthed at another site.)

In the meantime, King had been contacted by surviving members of the Romanov family. King said she'd be glad to perform an analysis in the same way she did for relatives of kidnapped children in Argentina—at no cost to family members. "There's not going to be anything different about your family compared to any other family," she told the Romanovs. "No money changes hands."

Her findings were consistent with other scientists' conclusions. But she didn't publish her work. "I didn't send out a press release. I didn't talk about it. I said it was up to them to talk about it." When the family later went public, she felt free to disclose her role, though it's rarely been reported.

JUST AS KING HAD IMAGINED when she was smitten by Curt Stern's lectures, genetics was proving to be the greatest puzzle of all.

The search for reliable breast cancer data was long and painstaking. She had to collect a good number of large families in which a history of the disease was well-documented. Then she and her researchers had to determine whether these women were inheriting the same stretch of DNA on a particular chromosome.

The National Cancer Institute survey eventually collected details from 1,579 patients. And King received permission to contact women who said their mother or sister also had breast cancer. She had also found families on her own over the years, often referred to her by physicians. Other women with a family history contacted her after seeing an ABC-TV news

King's quest to find a breast cancer gene spanned 17 years as she painstakingly hunted for families ravaged by the disease, as well as compelling evidence of a renegade gene. *World Science Festival*

story about King in 1987 that had aired on 127 network affiliates around the country.

She and her lab researchers dove in with questions: Can we, using the large number of families, state genetic hypotheses based on the distribution of cancer in the families? Then can we test statistically whether those hypotheses fit the data better than other theories of clustering without a hereditary effect?

King applied statistical models to the 1,579 National Cancer Institute families. The results were striking. King's analysis, published in 1988, suggested that about 4 percent of the families carried a single gene that made them susceptible to breast cancer. The best way to validate her finding about familial clustering was to track down the gene.

New technology and processes were revolutionizing genetic analysis and King's small lab, with the help of young biochemist Jeff Hall, had begun implementing the advances. Scientists were now able to find "markers," or variations, in genetic material that could point them to a region of DNA, if not the precise location, where the culprit gene might be hiding.

Still the quarry remained elusive. King's team had narrowed their focus to 23 large families with 146 cases of invasive breast cancer. In each of the families the cancer struck three or more "first-degree" relatives: sisters, daughters, mothers, grandmothers or aunts. But the results were mixed. Some families showed convincing linkage to a genetic marker on the 17th of 23 human chromosomes. Other families did not fit that pattern.

King's researchers took the family trees, which look something like complex sentence diagrams, and rolled them out across lab benches and floors to further study.

One morning, King's colleague Beth Newman had a brainstorm: Let's look at this by age.

They stretched the family trees, or pedigrees, out in the halls of the Life Sciences Building, organized by average age of breast cancer diagnosis in the family. The pieces began to fall into place as more and more paper blanketed the halls. For each of the seven families in which women had been stricken before 50, the abnormal marker on Chromosome 17 proved a strong predictor of risk. "It was really clear that statistically there was something there," King said.

Once King and her researchers organized families by age of breast cancer diagnosis, they found an abnormal marker on the 17th of 23 human chromosomes that proved a strong predictor of risk. *University of Washington*

IN OCTOBER 1990 King stood backstage in Cincinnati's convention center ballroom. She had been a late addition to that night's meeting of the country's leading geneticists, so late that she wasn't on the printed agenda. Just weeks earlier, King's lab had made a breakthrough. King wanted to unveil the news in front of her peers, some of whom were deeply skeptical of her work.

She was nervous. While friends thought she remained cheerful, she had taken each new breast cancer death personally and stumbles on her long quest had sapped her confidence. Although she had been compared to "a terrier with a bone" in her dogged focus on a single gene, she had doubts. Earlier findings she published had not held up. She was not sure her hereditary theory was foolproof. That was one reason her research had digressed to forensics and other pursuits; she thought it was too risky to bet all her chips on the breast-cancer payoff.

Cavalli-Sforza, a mentor, comforted her backstage in Cincinnati. "Show them what you showed me," he said, giving her a friendly hug.

King stepped out of the wings and into the spotlight. Displaying charts, graphs and family trees on a large screen, she explained that her team looked closely at the 23 extended families. With a scary regularity that mimicked an inherited disease, not an acquired one, roughly half of the women in those families developed breast cancer at a rate far above the overall average for women.

More importantly, the cancer tended to hit these women before menopause, unlike most women who aren't diagnosed until after the age of 50. This was most likely a result of some inborn biological error, probably a mutated gene that deprived women of a tumor-suppressing defense mechanism and pushed them onto a premature path to cancer.

And King's lab found the error in a tiny region on Chromosome 17 that was consistently altered in DNA of women with cancer. The statistical link between this abnormal stretch of DNA and breast cancer was "many times stronger than any other association that King or anyone else had yet found." King thought she had located the gene. But she still wasn't 100 percent certain. Was it possible that her families were unique in some way she didn't see? There would be no popping Champagne yet. She said her discovery needed to be reproduced by another lab.

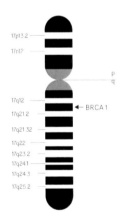

An illustration shows the location of the breast cancer gene on Chromosome 17, at "arm q" and "band 21."

A few months later King was on her way to London. Gilbert Lenoir, director of France's International Agency for Research on Cancer, was going to present a paper on inherited breast cancer. When Lenoir became interested in a breast cancer gene several years before, a colleague suggested he contact Henry Lynch, a doctor in Nebraska intrigued by familial cancer since the 1960s. Lynch had amassed records of dozens of families with breast cancer. But scientists had dismissed his evidence as anecdotal. Lenoir visited Lynch and plunged into the doctor's files. Lenoir was encouraged by the hidden treasure.

He was in the Cincinnati ballroom when King divulged her findings about Chromosome 17. The next day he called his French colleagues and directed them to look for the offending gene where King had pointed.

Just before Lenoir began his talk in England months later, he was coy with King. In a private aside, he asked her what she thought the chances were that she was right about Chromosome 17. She told him "fifty-fifty." Without a hint about his coming presentation, Lenoir said, "Maybe."

As the lights dimmed and Lenoir started showing slides of several family pedigrees, King thought he was offering a review of her data. She asked anxiously where his results were.

While friends thought she remained cheerful, stumbles on her long quest to find a breast cancer gene had eroded her confidence. *World Science Festival*

"Those are mine," he said.

He had applied King's methods to a set of families in France. His results were virtually identical to King's. Same markers, same age effect, but with different families.

"That," King said, "was when I believed the result was real."

Others agreed. Ellen Solomon, a top researcher who organized the London meeting, celebrated with both Lenoir and King over tea. "Lenoir's talk was very convincing," Solomon told Pulitzer Prize-winning journalist Michael Waldholz. "But, of course, Mary-Claire had gotten there first. It was a great, great moment for her."

King named the gene BRCA for breast cancer. It became BRCA1 when a similar tumor-suppressing gene with a defect was later detected on Chromosome 13 and named BRCA2. Both genes function like custodians, cleaning up mutations in other genes caused by ultraviolet radiation, tobacco smoke, or deterioration. Unfortunately, they are sometimes mutated themselves and can't repair damaged genes. Together, the two mutated genes account for about 5 percent of all breast cancers, and they increase a woman's lifetime risk of developing cancer dramatically.

King had found the neighborhood where BRCA1 resided on Chromosome 17. Now the race was on to pinpoint the exact street address amid a million subunits of DNA, a "task akin to searching for a car key dropped on the bottom on Lake Washington," wrote Paula Bock in *The Seattle Times*.[*]

Her lab did not win the high stakes competition to isolate, clone and patent the BRCA1 gene, which helped scientists understand how its mutations

---

[*] Francis Collins, another superstar geneticist, compared the hunt to searching all of Texas to locate a particular room in a single house in the Lone Star State.

triggered breast cancer, and how to craft diagnostic tests to look for the fugitive gene. Mark Skolnick, a Utah-based Berkeley alum, led a team of 44 colleagues from five institutions that won that prize, thought to be lucrative and glamorous. His company Myriad Genetics was awarded an exclusive patent on the gene.

But King didn't feel like a loser. Even though finding the gene "was her reason for getting up in the morning" and her "less-than-tender feelings" for Skolnick were known to colleagues, King told *The New York Times* his triumph was "lovely" and deserving of all the praise he might get.

She had pointed the way, moving science forward and changing thinking. In her view, Skolnick and Myriad cloned the gene first because "they had vastly more sophisticated equipment, so could move much more quickly through (analyzing) thousands of DNA fragments."

New puzzles awaited King, such as figuring out whether some mutations were associated more strongly with breast cancer, and others with ovarian cancer, which was also linked to BRCA1. And she felt a duty to do more.

ANOTHER REASON King didn't feel like a loser: she was being wooed by other institutions.

As her focus shifted from cloning BRCA to trying to use it for diagnosis and possible therapies, King wanted to get closer to surgeons and clinicians who saw cancer up close every day. Berkeley doesn't have a medical school and the drive to San Francisco, which does, had become intolerably gridlocked.

After more than a year of courtship by the University of Washington, King moved her lab north in 1995, along with a dozen researchers, all supported by federal grants or fellowships. King herself brought a lifetime grant from the American Cancer Society (via the Walt Disney family) to help defray research costs. Her new lab was just an indoor stroll from the UW's acclaimed medical center.

Calling Seattle the "Athens of genetics," King was impressed by its scientific luminaries such as Lee Hood, who then headed molecular biotechnology at the UW. But the most important factor in her move was Seattle's vibe. "I could've gone to many places," she says. "I came here because it was the minimal cultural move from Berkeley. I love Berkeley and I love Seattle."

Journalist Paula Bock captured the bustle of King's lab in 1998, as researchers—"who looked like a multicultural GAP ad"—removed teeth from packages postmarked Ethiopia and El Salvador, shattered them with a hammer, extracted DNA from their pulp, and then prepared tiny vials of genetic material for analysis in an oven-sized $100,000 instrument. When King was away on trips to raise money, receive an award, or help scientists on a distant continent, rock music bounced off the lab's beakers and pipettes.

On King's return, the stereo shut down. "It is replaced by the scientist's musical laughter, her chorus of questions, her hunger for results. At 52, King is a dynamic presence, mind leaping, hands gesturing, smile dimpling, pencil twiddling, tawny hair bobbing like a pony's mane as she nods excitedly and exclaims, "Really? That's WONDERFUL!"

By the time of Bock's story, King had begun collaborating with both an Israeli and a Palestinian scientist in the study of inherited deafness. And in four years the trio and their affiliated universities had identified four genes

King's UW lab researchers "looked like a multicultural GAP ad," wrote Paula Bock in *The Seattle Times*. "I had my own lab for 15 years before I had my first white, straight, male graduate student," King says. *World Science Festival*

associated with deafness. It was important to solve hearing loss, King said, but even more important to show "we can do this together for the sake of science and for the sake of peace."

King was back in the news in 2013 when Academy Award winner Helen Hunt played her in "Decoding Annie Parker," a movie that weaves the story of real-life breast-cancer patient Annie Parker with King's quest to find BRCA1. King wasn't consulted by the filmmakers or Hunt. "It will be my words with perfect hair," she predicted after learning about the movie from one of her students. *The Washington Post*'s review said the film didn't explore King's efforts "nearly as fully as they deserve," but it was rescued by a cast that included Samantha Morton, Rashida Jones and Aaron Paul. King deduced that Hunt watched video interviews to get her mannerisms down, such as the way her hands seem to be in perpetual motion when she talks, and her urgent efficiency that can seem chilly.

Describing King's movie character as "bordering on icy," *The New York Times* said "she is portrayed by Ms. Hunt with the simmering anger of someone so consumed by her quest that she has no room in her life for anything else." *Decoding Annie Parker*

Another Hollywood figure, Angelina Jolie, raised awareness of risk and treatment just as "Decoding Annie Parker" premiered at film festivals. Jolie

After testing positive for BRCA1 mutations and having a preventive double mastectomy, Angelina Jolie said her chances of developing breast cancer "dropped from 87 percent to under 5 percent." *PBS*

authored a column in *The New York Times* about the preventive double mastectomy she had after testing positive for BRCA1 mutations. While a harmful BRCA mutation is relatively rare, afflicting about one in 500 American women, it greatly increases risk for women like Jolie whose mother, aunt and grandmother died from breast or ovarian cancer. In the overall population, 1-in-12 women will have breast cancer by the age of 70. Among women with a BRCA1 mutation the risk rises to 6-in-10 women by age 70. The risk for a BRCA2 mutation is slightly less.

King praised Jolie's announcement as "really good, very clear, very accurate." Testing for BRCA mutations surged in what some called the "Angelina effect." But those tests cost $3,000, in part because Skolnick held exclusive rights to the genes.

With her UW colleague Tomas Walsh, King developed a one-time test in 2010 that could check for more than a dozen genes, in addition to BRCA1 and BRCA2, which scientists found to be implicated in breast cancer. Walsh and King did not seek an exclusive patent. But their test, called BROCA, could not be widely used because of Myriad's patent.

A month after Jolie's revelation, the U.S. Supreme Court ruled on an American Civil Liberties Union lawsuit challenging Myriad's patent. Unanimously, the justices said genes, as products of nature, couldn't be patented by companies. When called by Nina Totenberg of National Public Radio for reaction, King said she was "as high as a flag on the Fourth of July."

King's one-time test helped with earlier diagnosis of breast cancer and treatment through preventive surgery such as Jolie's. And her discovery of the BRCA1 gene later allowed for development of potential therapies that make it harder for some cancer cells to survive.

But curing inherited breast cancer remains an evasive goal. "To actually fix BRCA1 and 2 mutations, we would need new genetic engineering technologies that don't yet exist, or are not yet ready for human use," says Dr. George W. Sledge, Jr., chief scientific advisor to the Susan G. Komen Breast Cancer Foundation, and head of the oncology division at Stanford University School of Medicine. "We may get there, but we are a ways away."

THE UW IS A "fabulous place" to carry out her work, King says on an April morning in 2019. "There cannot be anyplace that's superior to this."

It's also a fine place for women in science, she says, on the Monday after a "depressing" story in *The New York Times* about sexism at the prestigious Salk Institute in California. "One of the great things about working here is that interactions are straightforward. Clearly that's not universal," she says at her tidy desk, below shelves lined by white binders full of family pedigrees.

Women account for a majority of her lab's roughly 20 researchers, who include surgeons, professors, post-doctoral fellows, and graduate students. "I had my own lab for 15 years before I had my first white, straight, male graduate student," she says.

While attitudes have changed, and "young men are very modern about this kind of stuff," women scientists still face a major challenge: their child-bearing years coincide with the time they need to bear down on building a career, publishing research and earning academic tenure.

"Science is also a very demanding child—you just can't walk away from either. That hasn't changed. It's not realistic to say one can drop out of science and drop back in." Until good, reliable, affordable child-care near work is widely available, the demands of a career in science are "always going to be an impediment for mothers."[*]

King says she "quite possibly" may have won the race to clone BRCA1 had she then been at the University of Washington which had superior technology to her lab at UC, Berkeley. *Newscom*

King once told *The New York Times* that she couldn't find time to excel in all three roles of young mother, young wife and young scientist—and wife was the one that suffered most. Then she still felt guilt as a single mother. When her daughter Emily was 6 or 7 she'd come to the lab and hang out in King's office with books and toys. Emily took to making posters that would go on the office door. When King asked why she made the posters, Emily said, "They are to keep people happy while they have to wait for you."

THE AMERICAN CANCER Society Professor of Genome Sciences and Medicine at UW, King hasn't slowed down as her career approaches the half-century mark.

Her UW lab continues to research breast and ovarian cancer with a focus on families whose genetic problems remain undetermined. Researchers in the King lab are also trying to sort out the genetics of schizophrenia, which occurs more frequently due to mutations that are acquired during life rather than inherited at birth.

---

[*] Asked in 2019 what she'd do if she weren't a scientist, King said: "I would open a daycare for the children of my lab where the kids would learn story problems while their parents do experiments."

King has long-running collaborations with both Palestinian and Israeli scientists, including Dr. Ephrat Levy-Lahad (left), saying it's important to show "we can do this together for the sake of science and for the sake of peace." *Judy Siegel-Itzkovich*

She keeps her passport at the ready. She's collaborating on breast cancer projects in South Africa and Mexico. And she's gone to Israel almost every year since 1995.

In addition to her work in the Middle East on inherited deafness, she's part of a team that established a modern lab to conduct genetic testing for women of Arab ancestry, which has led to characterizing cancer-causing mutations specific to that population. King and her colleagues also helped train Palestinian nurses and social workers in counseling for high-risk women. And she has teamed with Israeli scientists to publish research on the startling breast-cancer risk that Ashkenazi Jewish women face. In 2018, she received a $1 million Dan David Prize, administered by Tel Aviv University, for her career achievements.

She once imagined retiring to Berkeley at 80 and hosting "a salon for unrequited lefties." Maybe King, a fan of detective stories, might even find time to write that mystery novel she has all plotted out in her mind. "Needless to say," she smiles, "DNA is at the heart of that story."

But not now. She says she hopes never to retire. At 80 she expects to still be in her lab figuring out more about inherited susceptibility to breast cancer.

There are all those families waiting on her shelves. Someone's always waiting for her attention, for her to solve a human puzzle, no matter how long it may take.

Bob Young
Legacy Washington

Sharp declares war on "Big Oil."
Northwest Indian Fisheries Commission

FAWN SHARP

THE VOICE OF THE QUINAULTS

Fawn Sharp, fresh from a midday workout, seems remarkably calm for someone with so many plates spinning on broomsticks. As president of the Quinault Indian Nation, she oversees an array of enterprises, including timber management, seafood sales and a resort casino that just underwent a $25 million expansion. With 1,100 employees, the tribe is the largest employer in Grays Harbor County. Sharp was the first female president of the Affiliated Tribes of Northwest Indians. By a landslide vote in the fall of 2019, she was elected president of the National Congress of American Indians. She's a single mom with four lively kids. One just texted that he has an urgent need for an after-school pizza.

She looks up from her phone with a bemused mom smile. Work-life balance dictates a break from her plans to sue the rods out of ExxonMobil for damaging "the planet our Creator gave us." If only she could, she'd love to sue President Trump, too, for dismissing global warming as a "very expensive hoax." Sharp believes there is "irrefutable" evidence climate change is very real and very expensive. "Incalculable" is the word she uses. Her people are fighting for their livelihoods, she says. Maybe their very lives.

"The glaciers that feed the rivers and support the salmon that are integral to the Quinault culture and economy are disappearing," tribal scientists say. "Forests on tribal lands are changing, and invasive species threaten critical subsistence resources. Ocean acidification, hypoxia events, sea level rise, coastal erosion, tidal surge and

The Quinaults' ancestral village of Taholah is threatened by tsunamis and rising sea levels caused by global warming. *Quinault Indian Nation*

Sharp greets a canoe at Point Grenville near Taholah in 2013. More than 14,000 people came to watch 70 canoes from 60 tribes come ashore. *Northwest Indian Fisheries Commission*

increasing severity and intensity of storm events are now occurring with disturbing frequency." The residents of Taholah, the tribal village where the Quinault River flows into the Pacific, are perched atop a sliding tectonic plate that could trigger the mother of all tsunamis. The Tribal Council needs to move 700 people to higher ground. Meantime, "Broken Promises," a 2018 report by the U.S. Commission on Civil Rights, concludes that "due at least in part to the failure of the federal government adequately to address the wellbeing of Native Americans over the last two centuries, Native Americans continue to rank near the bottom of all Americans in health, education and employment outcomes." Sharp is tempted to say "Who's telling who?" In America, health care for prison inmates is funded at a higher level than tribal members. "The report the Civil Rights Commission issued in 2003 was called 'A Quiet Crisis.' It was a raging crisis back then," Sharp says, "and it's gotten worse. I pushed hard for them to update the report. This time we need to do something about it."

A FITNESS BUFF, she looks much younger than 49. Her eyes are a striking, almost golden blend of blue and brown. Her smile is disarmingly gentle for such a determined woman. She is now in her fifth term leading a nation thousands of years older than the United States of America. A few weeks after she was born, President Nixon delivered a landmark address rejecting congressional efforts to terminate the federal government's relationship with more than a hundred recognized tribes. "That would be no more appropriate than to terminate the citizenship rights of any other American," Nixon said, adding:

> The first Americans—the Indians—are the most deprived and most isolated minority group in our nation. On virtually every scale of measurement—employment, income, education, health—the condition of the Indian people ranks at the bottom. …From the time

of their first contact with European settlers, the American Indians have been oppressed and brutalized, deprived of their ancestral lands and denied the opportunity to control their own destiny. Even the Federal programs intended to meet their needs have frequently proved to be ineffective and demeaning. …We must make it clear that Indians can become independent of federal control without being cut off from federal concern and federal support.

"I tell people I was born in the eleventh hour, in the fifty-ninth minute of the Termination Era," Sharp says. "I truly think I was called by the Creator at this time."

She grew up around legendary tribal leaders. Her mother, Ann Masten, was a recording secretary for the Northwest Indian Fisheries Commission. "I traveled around with her when I was still in grade school," Sharp remembers. "It was my job to push the 'record' and 'play' buttons on the old-fashioned tape recorder." She met Billy Frank Jr., the charismatic Nisqually fishing-rights activist, when she was 4. "Other little girls treasured their Barbies. Billy was my hero." They cursed him, clubbed him, tear-gassed him and threw him in jail. "But he never gave up," Sharp says.

The Barbies, in any case, wouldn't have looked like her.

Sharp graduated from Gonzaga University at 20, received a law degree from the University of Washington, studied international human rights law at Oxford and was elected president of the Quinault Nation at 35 in 2006. She once worked for the CIA, too. We'll get to that later.

Sometimes when she looks at the photo she framed to commemorate her first meeting with President Obama she flashes

Sharp at The Billy Frank Jr. Pacific Salmon Summit in 2018. The summit, hosted by the Tulalip Tribes, is an effort to jump-start cooperation between the tribes and Washington state government to restore salmon populations. *Andy Bronson/The Herald*

back to being the "somewhat nerdy" bookworm who was elected class president in junior high—or the pint-size point guard "with fogged-up glasses," racing for a lay-in after stealing the ball. She also set a long-jump record at her grade school. Where did all those years go? "I have no idea," Sharp says with a shrug and a sigh. "Oftentimes I think about my journey and my responsibility to the 3,000 people of the Quinault Nation. And if the buck has to stop with me on every issue under the sun, so be it. Every single day I'm inspired by the idea that I'm the voice of the Quinaults—people who have existed since time began. I'm also the voice of Quinaults yet to be born and the voice of our ancestors. Holding public office means you have a sacred responsibility to honor the ones who spent their lifetimes and tremendous energy and resources to advance a nation."

Sharp's deep Christian faith gives her a sense of purpose and place. To her, "The Land of the Quinault" is sacred ground.

LIVINGSTON FARRAND, an Ivy League anthropologist who visited the Quinault Reservation in the summer of 1898, transcribed a remarkable collection of tribal traditions about the sky, the sea and the prized blueback salmon—about "How Eagle and Raven arranged things in the Early Days." Farrand wrote that the Quinaults reportedly had "a decidedly low degree of culture" until the whites established reservation schools and the natives took up "the so-called 'Shaker' religion." Whatever its perceived "absurdities," the blend of Christianity and shamanism promoted sobriety and dispelled indolence, Farrand wrote. He now detected "a marked advance in the cultural development of the group," despite the fact that most members of the tribe seemed to have forgotten the old customs.

Becoming "civilized," in other words, almost cost

INDIAN FISH TRAP ON QUINAULT RIVER, WASHINGTON.

Quinault men hauling in fish at a fish trap on the Quinault River. Engraving made in 1890. *University of Washington*

the Quinaults a decidedly rich culture of storytelling handed down for countless centuries around campfires as salmon sizzled on cedar planks. Smallpox, influenza, alcoholism and other diseases that arrived with the whites claimed many lives. The Quinaults almost lost their language, too.

The terrible irony of all this somehow escaped the anthropologist. Farrand counted himself fortunate in finding one person among "the older unregenerates"—a gifted storyteller named Bob Pope—who could relate how Raven took a fish scale from his nose and threw it into the river, saying: "If there are to be salmon here, then jump, and do not be angry if people catch you." The salmon jumped—"and ever since then Quinault salmon have been plentiful in the Quinault River."

"Ever since" ended 120 years later when the Quinault Nation's Department of Fisheries curtailed the 2018 commercial fishing season for the blueback, a unique population of sockeye salmon, after a total return of just 6,618 spawning fish. It was the third smallest return on record. The return was little better in 2019, so the commercial fishery was canceled once again. Annual runs once averaged nearly a quarter million fish. The blueback—one of the last largely undiluted wild salmon runs in the Northwest—are now a threatened, if not endangered, species. The decline, first noted in the 1950s, began accelerating 20 years ago. "The productivity of their prey, like plankton and krill, falls with ocean warming," tribal fisheries experts say. "Marine conditions for blueback returning in 2019 have been, on average, among the poorest in the past two decades."

Poaching is part of the problem, Sharp acknowledges. "That's nothing, however, compared to the impact of fossil fuels on an irreplaceable resource. It's time to hold oil companies accountable for their past record of denying climate change and their current obstruction of policies to reduce climate pollution. The devastation of our iconic blueback salmon has struck at the core of what it means to be Quinault. This incalculable loss jeopardizes the cultural identity of our people and our ability to support and nourish our families."

A week later, she was in Washington, D.C., to outline the crisis for members of Congress. A recent helicopter reconnaissance flight revealed the enormity of the disaster, Sharp said. Her heart sank when she saw how the entire Quinault ecosystem, 325 square miles, is being impacted by global warming, from the jagged peaks and rainforest valleys of the Olympic Mountains to Taholah and Queets, the coastal tribal villages. Anderson Glacier, once the source of the Quinault River, is mostly a memory. A nearby glacier is "nearly gone as well and the few remaining have dramatically receded in the last eight years," Sharp said, warning that the environmental and economic impacts "are going to become more frequent and more intense."

TWO OF SHARP'S MENTORS, Joe DeLaCruz and Guy McMinds, confronted a crisis the year she was a toddler. They changed the course of Quinault Nation history.

On the morning of September 11, 1971, DeLaCruz parked a pickup truck in the middle of the Chow Chow Bridge, a timber trestle suspended 30 feet above the Quinault River. With his warrior eyes and mane of jet-black hair, the tribe's 34-year-old business manager had a flair for the dramatic. Seattle TV crews captured his outrage two years earlier as he pointed to sacred rocks defaced with graffiti, beaches strewn with litter and clam beds disturbed by cars. Twenty-three miles of reservation beaches were being posted off-limits to non-Indians. Now he knelt defiantly beneath a hand-painted sign that predicted the "Battle of Chow Chow Bridge" would be a new best seller. All roads leading to tribal timberlands had been closed. The Quinaults were fed up with the incompetent paternalism of the Bureau of Indian Affairs. It had allowed logging companies to pay below-market rates for Indian timber and cause severe ecological damage to tribal lands.

Joe DeLaCruz, one of the most influential Native American leaders in U.S. history. *Larry Workman*

The reservation was now virtually "one big stump farm," DeLaCruz said. Gravel for logging roads had been scooped from salmon spawning grounds. Streams were clogged with silt and debris. Acre upon acre of "slash" residue from clearcutting created an extreme fire hazard and hampered reforestation—"all this, even though the BIA was responsible for enforcing the contracts it had made." DeLaCruz told reporters the 190,000-acre reservation was the most savagely logged area in the state. "We have 1,012 Indians living on the reservation. If we don't protect what we have, their own and their children's futures are at stake." The fundamental issue could be summed up with one word, DeLaCruz said: Sovereignty.

"For more than 50 years, our lands have been managed to meet the demand for short-term profit with no thought to the future," the Tribal Council wrote after the standoff at the Chow Chow Bridge. "Loggers were allowed to harvest our forests to meet the needs of men alone, and our land has paid a terrible price." The Quinaults set out to achieve "a degree of economic self-sufficiency and general well-being that is almost beyond imagination."

DeLaCruz and McMinds, a fisheries biologist first elected to the Tribal Council as a teenager, were the most charismatic of the college-educated young turks recruited by tribal elders to advance the cause of self-determination. Council President James "Jug" Jackson, the great-grandson of Chief Taholah, also respected the tribe's matriarchal tradition. Hannah Mason Saux Bowechop, Chief Taholah's granddaughter, was a charter member of the Taholah School Board in the 1920s and an influential member of the tribal business committee during its early years, as well as a Quinault language linguist. Helen Mitchell, Alice Chenois James, and

Pearl Capoeman-Baller, the first female president of the Quinault Indian Nation, poses with Sharp in 1996 when she became the Quinault Nation's lead attorney. *Quinault Indian Nation*

Blanche Ann Reed were among the bright and resourceful women who emerged as Quinault tribal leaders in the 1970s. Before long, they were joined by Pauline Kalama Capoeman, who would become the tribe's director of natural resources, and Pearl Capoeman-Baller, who in 1994 succeeded DeLaCruz, becoming the first female president of the Quinault Nation. One of their sisters in arms was Janet Renecker McCloud, a former Taholah resident who helped organize the first "fish-ins" on the Nisqually and Puyallup rivers in the 1960s as the Indians asserted their treaty rights. McCloud, a descendant of Chief Seattle, cranked out the movement's newsletter, *Survival News*, on a second-hand mimeograph machine.

When Fawn Sharp succeeded Capoeman-Baller in 2006 she became the ninth elected leader of the Quinault Nation in the past hundred years. In many ways, her female forebears are the Native American equivalent of the suffragists.[*]

FAWN RENA SHARP, who relished every volume of her grandmother's set of encyclopedias, was identified early on as a future tribal leader. Born in Aberdeen on May 20, 1970, she is a quarter Quinault, part Northern California Yurok, part Montana Kootenai and part Idaho Nez Perce. "Apparently my family has lineage to Chief Tendoy, a Lemhi Shoshone who was a broker of peace between the tribes in Idaho. So I might have some leadership blood in my veins," Sharp says. She's also almost 20 percent English and a smattering of German and French, according to her Ancestry.com DNA analysis.

Sharp graduated from the Lighthouse Christian Academy at Taholah and briefly attended a community college in the Seattle area before returning home to help care for her ailing grandfather. She coached girls' basketball and worked as a waitress to pay for tuition at Grays Harbor College, never imagining that one day she would become one of its trustees.

After receiving a degree in Criminal Justice from Gonzaga University, the 20-year-old was recruited by the CIA. "They specifically and explicitly mentioned

---

[*] Though Washington women won the right to vote in 1910, a decade before national suffrage, it wasn't until the Snyder Act of 1924 that Congress granted full citizenship to Native Americans born in the U.S. Some states suppressed their ability to vote for decades more.

they were going to campuses to recruit Native Americans who grew up on reservations because that was a testament to resilience and the ability to overcome barriers and obstacles," Sharp says. She remembers being simultaneously excited and apprehensive as she set out for Washington, D.C.

> When I got to there, it was quite a shock. I'd never been on my own in an apartment. I went to the grocery store and tried to have conversation. People were very rude. I remember getting on the bus, and the driver said, "Put your dollar in the [fare] box, kid—and sit down!" I remember sitting on the steps of the Lincoln Memorial just feeling completely invisible. I saw families. I saw a troop of Boy Scouts. Everybody was having a great time on a warm summer afternoon. I was sad about losing my grandfather, who had just passed away. I was homesick. I was wondering if this was a mistake. Nobody was talking to me. Finally I walked to the Museum of Natural History and discovered there was an elder doing basket weaving. She was surrounded by a group of 20 to 30 people, maybe more. She looked up—right at me, made eye contact and just smiled. It was as if I went from being absolutely invisible to being recognized by this incredible, beautiful woman who reminded me a lot of my grandmother. She just *recognized* me. Life was suddenly good. "I'm going to be OK," I said to myself. "I can do this."

Sharp worked in the agency's office of national security off and on for five years, conducting background investigations on potential CIA contractors. More than that she says she cannot say. "But I had firearms and fire safety training and I rappelled out of burning buildings, which was fun."

Next stop was UW law school. She graduated in 1995, worked in the tribal attorney general's office as the Quinault Nation's lead attorney and emerged as a bright new face in the 2006 race for Tribal Council president. Before long she was on the national stage, representing a new generation of Native American leaders. After she was elected to a third three-year term in 2012, dissidents charged that she was spending so much time away from Taholah—working on regional and national Native American projects, getting her picture taken with Obama—that the administration of the Quinault Indian Nation was "unstable." The recall attempt failed. She was re-elected president in 2015 and 2018.

In Indian country "tribal politics" has a whole different meaning. When Billy Frank Jr. and Joe DeLaCruz achieved international prominence in the 1970s, some early supporters charged that fame had gone to their heads. "I can relate to all that," Sharp says with a philosophical smile. Sometimes she still needs a place to go to find solace. There's a special tree along the South Shore of Lake Quinault. "The

Sharp, right, talks with President Obama at a meeting of tribal leaders in 2011. *White House*

root system is structured in a way that there's this seat that fits me just perfectly. Ever since I was a girl I could sit under that tree. Even on a rainy day, I'm protected by its branches. I return to my tree when I'm facing difficult challenges. It's been my life-long friend."

Sharp acknowledges that "internal tribal politics is highly charged—full of contention and long-standing, multi-generational family disputes—yet when it comes to actually making public policy, we adopt amazing policies that look seven generations out. I wouldn't even call this a job. For me it's truly a passion."

A voracious reader and internet surfer, Sharp is fascinated by the concept of Individual Development Accounts. IDAs are asset-building plans to help disadvantaged people save up to meet goals, such as attending college or vocational school, buying a car or first home. Boosted by matching funds from government agencies and nonprofits, IDAs are "compounding interest" that can change lives, Sharp says. Listen to her infectious enthusiasm:

> What if we were to add $5 an hour to our Youth Opportunity Program for every kid who works during the summer? One dollar would be dedicated to a retirement fund. And what if we were to create summer educational camp opportunities with the second dollar? Kids could go to Universal Studios to study filmmaking or spend time on a tall ship to learn about marine biology. They could go to Europe to learn about world history. One of the major barriers

to our students attending college, and *succeeding* in college, is the culture shock of leaving the reservation. We should have our kids going to regional camps when they're 10 or 12, to national camps at 13 to 15 and to international camps at 16 to 18. So by the time a Quinault kid graduates from high school they've had a world of new experiences. The third dollar would be for buying their first car. The fourth dollar might jump-start a small business. The Navajo Nation put together a youth business—a candy company—and won an SBA award. What a great idea! The kids at Quinault should learn about the private-sector economy as well as how their government works. We need to build business skill-sets. The fifth dollar would go toward a scholarship fund that would mature at 18 upon high school graduation. They could potentially save $20,000 with both their savings and the match. That's how you change lives.

She's working hard to find those "matching" funds. At the same time, she and the Tribal Council are working to attract outside investment. "I believe a healthy tribal economy is not just tribally-owned businesses, which we've done. We need to attract companies to locate here."

Another of her passions is instilling "the awareness of what it means to be a Quinault." Between intermarriage and mortality, there are no more full-blooded Quinaults, according to tribal records. Sharp's own multi-tribal/Caucasian heritage is typical. But there is an ancient common tongue: the Quinault language. The last of the elderly fluent speakers died in the 1990s, but the language lives on, thanks to prescient elders like the late Hannah Bowechop and Horton Capoeman. In the 1960s, Mrs. Bowechop—also an accomplished weaver and singer—helped university-trained linguists devise a 39-character Quinault alphabet and compile a 386-page dictionary. Augmented by recordings of Mrs. Bowechop and other fluent Quinault language speakers, this work is priceless. The process of reviving the language is ongoing, with school children and adults taking classes. Sharp is an avid student of her ancestral language. The Taholah School District's website features an audio-playback pronunciation guide to words and phrases. "Our language is an important cultural link to who we are," Sharp says. "It's our ancestors speaking to us." Thanks to a tribal endowment fund for graduate students, a Quinault, Cosette Terry-itewaste, recently earned a doctorate in linguistics from the University of Arizona.

THE COAST SALISH culture is steeped in reverence for elders. Sharp says she feels their presence every day. Sometimes it's as if Joe DeLaCruz, Guy McMinds and Billy Frank Jr. are speaking to her. Likewise the indelible spirit of Emmett Oliver, who in 1989 inspired a "Paddle to Seattle" as part of Washington's Centennial celebration. Oliver lived to be 102 and saw the Canoe Journey become an annual event involving

Sharp with Billy Frank Jr. in 2013. *Quinault Indian Nation*

paddlers from as far away as British Columbia. A different Native American nation hosts the event each year. "Emmett's legacy will last forever," Sharp says. "We have been canoe people for thousands of years, but that culture was lost on many of our people, especially our youth. …The physical and spiritual discipline required to participate in the Canoe Journey and the cultural sharing and traditional teachings that take place during the event have changed countless lives. …

"For me, our elders' lessons are timeless. Joe's charisma and vision elevated him to international prominence with the National Congress of American Indians and the World Council of Indigenous Peoples. Billy and Guy were founders of the Northwest Indian Fisheries Commission. Guy especially always understood the bigger picture. When I was in eighth grade, he told our class that water would be worth more than gold and clean air worth more than oil."

Chief Taholah wept bitter tears in 1855 when he signed the treaty that compelled the Quinault, Queets, Hoh and Quileute people to cede nearly a third of the Olympic Peninsula to the federal government. The Quinaults were luckier than many tribes across the continent, however, in that they retained 300 square miles of their ancestral lands and the right to fish in their "usual and accustomed" places, as they had done "at least since the close of the Pleistocene era, some 11,000 years ago." Masterful canoe-carvers and fishermen, the Quinaults were once whalers, like the Makahs to the north. They sold valuable whale oil, as well as meat and blubber, to other tribes and the whites. Salmon were so plentiful, however, that by 1890 the Quinaults had a thriving fish-selling enterprise. The blueback were especially prized. A century later, the landmark Boldt Decision in 1974 upheld the tribes' fishing rights, with lasting implications for every Washingtonian.

The oral histories collected by anthropologists—even the patronizing ones—leave no doubt that Fawn Sharp's people have always felt a spiritual connection to their forested coastal home. That the land is endangered is irrefutable. A massive earthquake along the Cascadia Subduction Zone could devastate the Northwest Coast, from Puget Sound to the Pacific, from the Strait of Juan de Fuca to the Columbia. The magnitude-9 earthquake that jolted northeastern Japan in 2011 generated a towering tidal wave that devoured everything in its path, including three-story buildings. At least 15,894 people died; more than 2,500 are still missing. Protective seawalls were breached by the first surge. Boats and vehicles were tossed about like Tonka toys; screaming people bobbed in the torrent. Taholah and Queets, already at sea level, would be wiped off the map in seconds. There's a legend among the Chimakum Indians along Hood Canal that they were a remnant of a Quileute band that fled the coast "because of a high tide that took four days to ebb." New scientific research authenticates the stories handed down for centuries by Olympic Peninsula tribes. Tsunamis swept away an ancient Klallam village near present-day Port Angeles every 200 to 500 years, according to a team of researchers from Portland State University, Western Washington University

Sharp with legendary tribal activist Ramona Bennett of the Puyallup Tribe in 2018. They helped launch a political action committee to advance public policies that protect the environment and human rights. *First American Project*

and the University of Rhode Island. The first of five occurred some 1,600 years ago. The waves could have been as high as 20 feet.

Scientists warn that the "Big One" is overdue, the last having occurred in 1700. Recorded by diarists in Japan, the Cascadia Subduction Zone mega-quake generated a mighty trans-Pacific tsunami. Evidence of what happened on the Northwest coast was first discovered by paleogeologist Brian Atwater in 1986. It's a "ghost forest" of dead cedars along the Copalis River some 20 miles south of Taholah. Jerry Thompson, who wrote *Cascadia's Fault,* a chilling book about the subduction zone, was amazed at what he saw when he accompanied Atwater to the site: "How could fully grown cedars several centuries old be standing in knee-deep salt water, their storm-battered trunks naked of bark, bleached gray by the sun and draped in moss and lichens, in the middle of a tidal marsh on Washington's west coast? Western red cedars don't grow in salt water."

The answer is that they *died* in salt water. The quake in 1700 abruptly lowered the land behind the beaches, turning a "forest meadow into a salt marsh." Atwater found the same evidence in other estuaries, all the way down to the Columbia. Each stream he studied "had the same signature of abrupt lowering of land and marshes and forests that had been at or above high-tide level" before the quake. He later learned that in the 1880s the Quinaults told white settlers there were once cedar groves along the mouth of the Hoquiam River. The river must have "eaten" them, the Indians said, because their bark was gone. "Hoquimts" was their word for "Hungry for wood."

"EXXONMOBIL" amounts to Fawn Sharp's word for "hungry for profits." She cites *Scientific American's* report that the industry giant was aware of climate change as far back as 1977, yet it obfuscated the risks. Sharp was hugely disappointed by the failure of a 2018 Washington state ballot measure to create the nation's first state fee on carbon emissions. Initiative 1631 advocated a tax of $15 per metric ton, beginning in 2020 and increasing by $2 annually until greenhouse gas reduction goals were met. Revenues from the carbon fee, estimated at a billion dollars a year by 2023, would have funded clean air, clean water and clean energy projects, including forest ecosystem restoration.

Sharp and Tyson Johnston, Vice President of the Quinault Indian Nation, at an oil train protest on Grays Harbor. *The Daily World*

A similar carbon tax proposal having been resoundingly defeated in 2016, Sharp and other tribal leaders set out to win over the electorate. Sharp teamed with Ramona Bennett, the formidable former chairwoman of the Puyallup Tribe; Estela Ortega, executive director of Seattle's El Centro de la Raza, and several other climate-change activists to launch the First American Project, a political action committee. The Inter-tribal and inter-racial group's goal is to revive the energy of the Northwest civil rights movement of the 1960s and 1970s. Sharp and her cohorts—dubbed "the road warriors"—visited 28 tribes in 10 days to rally the Native American vote. It wasn't enough. "Big Oil contributed most of the $31 million that was spent to defeat the initiative," Sharp says ruefully. "Frankly, I was depressed until my kids told me to keep fighting. That was all I needed to hear. I'm their voice and the voice of the children I hope they'll have some day." Billy Frank Jr. said it best, Sharp believes, when he observed that the challenge is colorblind: "We breathe the same air. We drink the same water. We are poisoned by the same pollution."

Last spring, when President Trump issued a pair of executive orders to "help American energy companies avoid unnecessary red tape" by making it easier for firms to build oil and gas pipelines and harder for state agencies to intervene, Sharp grew more resolute. The University of Washington Law School graduate believes tribes have the sovereign authority and legal standing to sue the fossil fuel industry for the collapse of their fisheries. "We're not getting the dollars to manage our fisheries; we're not getting the dollars to combat climate change," she told

Sharp's children on the beach near Taholah. *Fawn Sharp*

a meeting of the Affiliated Tribes of Northwest Indians earlier in the year—as if they needed reminding. The Boldt Decision and a follow-up ruling that mandated the removal of culverts injurious to salmon italicized the tribes' treaty rights. The fossil fuel industry's liability for damaging the fishery ecosystem is as clear as the state's, Sharp argues. "We will hold these large corporations accountable. … My new mission is to make Big Oil wish Initiative 1631 would've passed. We're going to take Big Oil down."

No one who knows her doubts she means it.

John C. Hughes
Legacy Washington

Cora Smith Eaton

The suffrage campaign in Washington reached new heights on July 30, 1909, when Dr. Cora Smith Eaton hoisted a "Votes for Women" pennant at the summit of Mount Rainier. Astute suffragists had planned a national women's suffrage conference in Seattle to coincide with the Alaska-Yukon-Pacific Exposition, a gala world's fair. For $40 apiece, suffragists were invited to join The Mountaineers club on a 21-day trek.

Dr. Eaton, an experienced climber, was the first woman to summit the East Peak of Mount Olympus in 1907, and she climbed Washington's six highest peaks. A founding member of the club, she created a long list of supplies for the female hikers to pack, including knickerbockers, smoked goggles, bee veils and cold cream. Eaton, a physician, provided medical advice to climbers. In the summer of 1909 she proudly attached the suffrage pennant to the A-Y-P flag and poked it in the glacier-capped summit. Washington women won the vote a year later.

Main photo: *Shanna Stevenson Collection*

Top: The A-Y-P flag to which the "Votes for Women" pennant was attached on Mount Rainier's summit. *Washington State Historical Society*

Bottom Left: As treasurer of the Washington Equal Suffrage Association, Cora Smith Eaton (right) played a significant role in Washington women gaining the right to vote. Pictured with key suffragists: Frances Maule Bjorkman, Jane Addams, and Emma Smith Devoe. *Washington State Historical Society*

Bottom Right: Eaton married Judson King and moved to Washington, D.C. In 1913, as the National Council of Women Voters congressional chair, she organized one of the first groups to meet with the newly inaugurated President Woodrow Wilson to push for national women's suffrage. *Shanna Stevenson Collection*

Dr. Cora Smith King, Treasurer, N. C. W. V., Leading the Delegations from Nine Suffrage States in Suffrage Parade in Washington, D. C.

Julia Butler Hansen

They called her "Mrs. Highways." Congresswoman Julia Butler Hansen, a Home Economics major, became a secretary in the Engineer's Office in tiny Wahkiakum County during the 1930s. Fascinated by transportation issues, she was the first woman to head the Roads & Bridges Committee of the Washington State House of Representatives; the first female chairman of the Western Interstate Highway Policy Committee and the first woman to head a congressional appropriations subcommittee. In the twilight of her legendary career she became the first woman to head the Washington State Transportation Commission. She was largely responsible for creating its predecessor, the State Highway Commission.

Never the token woman, she retired from Congress in 1974, undefeated in 41 consecutive elections. "No one ever represented her people better than Julia Butler Hansen," said U.S. Senator Warren G. Magnuson, her friend since their days as Young Democrats in the 1930s.

Main photo: Julia as chairwoman of the House Roads & Bridges Committee in the 1950s. *David Hansen Collection*

Top: Julia and her district aide, state Senator Bob Bailey, at the dedication of the Astoria-Megler Bridge in 1966. *David Hansen Collection*

Center: Julia with Congresswoman Catherine May, R-Wash., and Senator Maurine Neuberger, D-Ore., in the 1960s. *David Hansen Collection*

Center: Julia with U.S. Senators Magnuson and Jackson in the 1970s. *David Hansen Collection*

Bottom: Julia greets a constituent at the dedication of a fish protein concentrate plant in Aberdeen in 1971. *John Hughes*

Dorothy Bullitt

They called her "The Queen of KING." Dorothy Stimson Bullitt acquired Seattle's first TV station in 1949 when a few thousand viewers were jiggling rabbit-ear antennae. Over the next decade, she created one of the most admired broadcasting companies in America.

Dorothy Stimson came of age in the suffrage era as the adventurous daughter of a wealthy Seattle couple. In the 1930s, after losing her husband to cancer and her brother in a plane crash, she was thrust into the role of managing a large portfolio of downtown real estate. "I didn't even have a lawyer," she remembered. "Can you imagine?" Real estate was a clubby man's world, but the widowed Mrs. Bullitt proved to be a quick learner. As a self-taught broadcast executive, she was as concerned about quality as profits and succeeded on both counts. Her fearless passion for the First Amendment propelled KING Broadcasting's commitment to community service and investigative journalism.

Main photo: Dorothy Bullitt with a KING-TV camera in the 1940s. *KING Broadcasting Company Photograph Collection, University of Washington*

Top: Mrs. Bullitt with the KING-5 news copter in the shadow of the Space Needle. *KING-TV*

Middle: Mrs. Bullitt, right, gives visitors a tour of the fledgling station's equipment room. *KING Broadcasting Company Photograph Collection, University of Washington*

Bottom: Mrs. Bullitt with her longtime friend, U.S. Senator Warren Magnuson, D-Wash. *KING Broadcasting Company Photograph Collection, University of Washington*

Jean Enersen and Lori Matsukawa

Jean Enersen and Lori Matsukawa personified the high standards Dorothy Bullitt established for broadcast journalism. Enersen, the first and longest-tenured local TV female anchor in U.S. history, worked at KING-TV for 48 years, Matsukawa for 36. Enersen arrived in Seattle in 1968 and quickly made her mark as both a serious journalist and personable anchor. In local TV news circles, they called her "The Franchise."

Those were also the bankable attributes Matsukawa brought to the KING Broadcasting news team when she joined the station in 1983. A native of Hawaii, Matsukawa received the Lifetime Achievement Award from the Asian American Journalists Association in 2005.

"The first threat to our democracy is an effort to muzzle the press," Enersen wrote in a 2018 editorial. "Early in my career at KING 5, our founder Dorothy Bullitt sent a team to China. It was 1979. We were the first local TV station in the country to send a reporter to China after normalization of U.S.-China relations. Her orders to me were, 'Go out and find the truth.'"

Main photo: *King-TV*

Top: From left, Lori Matsukawa, Mike James, Tony Ventrella, Jean Enersen, Jeff Renner, and Don Porter share a laugh at the KING anchor desk. *KING-TV*

Middle: Jean Enersen and co-anchor Jim Harriott interview Mrs. Bullitt in 1973 at KING-TV's 25th anniversary event. *KING Broadcasting Company Photograph Collection, University of Washington*

Bottom: The station's "KING Mike" mascot was designed by Walt Disney. *KING-TV*

"KING MIKE"

Designed by Walt Disney

Carolyn Dimmick

Carolyn Dimmick, the first woman to serve on the Washington Supreme Court, was a novelty in 1953 when she passed the bar exam. "Pretty Blonde Water Skier Qualifies As Attorney" was the headline in the Seattle Post-Intelligencer. In 1981, her old boss, former King County prosecutor Charles O. Carroll, introduced her as "the prettiest justice on the Supreme Court." She shrugged off the sexism by making one thing abundantly clear: She was one of the brightest judges the court had ever seen.

Nearing 90, Judge Dimmick is a revered senior judge on the U.S. District Court and a role model for the Supreme Court's six female justices. That her career path is unremarkable by today's standards prompts this verdict: "That's progress."

Main photo: Dimmick is now a senior judge on the U.S. District Court in Seattle. *U.S. Courts*

Top: Dimmick with her husband, Cyrus A. Dimmick, and their children, Dana and Taylor, in the 1960s. *Dimmick Collection*

Bottom: Dimmick in 1981 as the first female member of the Washington Supreme Court. Back row (from left): Fred Dore, Floyd Hicks, William Williams, Dimmick; Front row (from left): Robert Utter, Hugh Rosellini, Robert Brachtenbach, Charles Stafford and James Dolliver. *Washington State Archives*

20 5• Mon. Sept. 21, 1963 Seattle Post-Intelligencer

Pretty Blonde Water Skier Qualifies As Attorney

3 Women Pass State Bar Tests

Carolyn Joyce Reaber, 23, blonde and beautiful Seattle water skier, will be sworn in as an attorney-at-law this Monday.

At least, she hopes to be, because as an assistant state attorney general she has a court case scheduled for trial in Goldendale on Tuesday.

Miss Reaber, daughter of Mr. and Mrs. Maurice C. Reaber, 808 W. 125th St., is one of three Seattle women graduated from the University of Washington Law School last June who learned over the week end that they had passed the state bar examinations.

P.-I. EMPLOYE—

Seattle-born Miss Reaber was a part-time employe in The Post-Intelligencer's circulation department from the time she was a sophomore at Lincoln High School until she became a University senior.

Miss Reaber said Sunday she became a lawyer because she doesn't like mathematics. She noticed no math courses in the law curriculum, so she took up the study, never intending to finish it.

"The first quarter they gave me a course in legal accounting," she said. "I almost died."

She liked law so well by this time, however, that she refused to quit till she got her degree.

After she completes her 1-year appointment as an assistant attorney general, begun last month, Miss Reaber hopes to enter private practice in Seattle. She hopes to specialize in admiralty law.

Last Friday, the day she waited for the bar examiners to announce whether she had passed or not, was the worst day in her life, Miss Reaber said, a lot worse than the day she went up Hell's Canyon Rapids on water skiis with a movie camera trained on her.

CAROLYN JOYCE REABER
New Lawyer Studies For First Case

Janet McCloud

Janet McCloud, a descendant of Chief Seattle, helped organize "fish-ins" on the Nisqually and Puyallup rivers in the 1960s as Northwest tribes asserted their treaty rights. When she was arrested for defying state game wardens, McCloud emerged from jail more determined than ever. Some called her "the Rosa Parks of the American Indian Movement."

McCloud and her husband, a Nisqually tribal fisherman, were founding members of the Survival of American Indian Association.

She cranked out its newsletter on a second-hand mimeograph machine. One day she said she was gazing at Mount Rainier, in all its white-robed majesty, when she "saw all the faces of the great chiefs" and heard a voice that sounded like Crazy Horse telling her not to be afraid. McCloud began "spreading the message of native spirituality and human rights worldwide."

The resilient activist who became known as "Yet-Si-Blue" — "the woman who talks" — died in 2003 at 69.

Top: Janet McCloud, Al Bridges (standing) and Jack McCloud on the Nisqually during a fish-in. *State Game Department/Washington State Archives*

Center: Janet McCloud and Tacoma NAACP attorney Jack Tanner (at her right), look on as Marlon Brando is interviewed by reporters during a fishing rights event on the Puyallup Reservation in 1964. *Seattle P-I Collection/MOHAI*

Bottom: Janet McCloud and her husband Don, both at left, with other Nisqually Indians who went to jail in 1964 to protest state fishing policies. The others, from left, are: Billy Frank Jr., Al Bridges, Herman Johns, Nugent Kautz and Jack McCloud. *Washington State Digital Archives*

Below: There were teepees on the lawn at the state Capitol in 1968 when Janet McCloud led a group of demonstrators to protest the restriction of Indian fishing rights and the jailing of Dick Gregory, civil rights activist. *Washington State Patrol Collection, Washington State Archives*

MICHELLE AKERS

Long before Alex Morgan and Megan Rapinoe became World Cup sheroes, Washington's Michelle Akers was a pioneering "goddess of soccer."

The sinewy girl with flowing curls was an All-American at Shorecrest High, which she led to a state championship in 1983. Later called "the Michael Jordan of soccer," Akers was just getting started.

She was the leading scorer in the first women's World Cup, won by the U.S. in 1991. Quiet and spiritual but fiercely competitive, she brought home a gold medal for the U.S. in the 1996 Olympics, despite battling chronic fatigue syndrome. She was an inspirational figure on the "99ers," the charismatic U.S. team that elevated women's sports with its 1999 World Cup victory before a record TV audience.

The first woman soccer star with an endorsement contract, Akers was FIFA's Female Player of the Century, jointly with China's Sun Wen. More than 30 surgeries drove her to retire. She now runs a farm for rescued horses. Akers, who had numerous concussions, helped launch a 2019 study of brain injuries that may be sustained by players heading balls. Goalies sometimes kick balls that drop from five-story heights.

Main photo: Akers was recovering in the locker room when the U.S. scored the winning goal in the 1999 World Cup. She ripped IV lines out of her arms to go celebrate with teammates. *Michelle Akers*

Top: Soccer legend Mia Hamm called Akers "a great athlete who's an even greater warrior."

Middle: Four Washingtonians helped win the first women's World Cup in 1991: (left to right) Lori Henry, Michelle Akers, Shannon Higgins and Amy Allmann, pictured in a Chinese hotel after their triumph. *Lori Henry*

Bottom: Her family couldn't afford a horse when Akers was a girl; she had to duct-tape her cleats together. She's run a farm for rescued horses since 2007. *Michelle Akers*

Melinda Gates

For years, Melinda Gates was a low-profile partner in the world's richest philanthropy, which has donated more than $45 billion for causes such as vaccinations in developing countries. But in 2012 she wanted the Bill & Melinda Gates Foundation to improve access to family planning for Asian and African women. As a Catholic, she struggled with the decision, but concluded contraceptives are the "greatest life-saving, poverty-ending, women-empowering innovation ever created."

She announced the foundation would increase its family planning spending to $1 billion by 2020. It was a milestone for Gates in her advocacy for gender equality. She unveiled a $170 million initiative in 2018 to improve economic opportunities for women in India, Kenya, Tanzania and Uganda. And her 2019 book, subtitled How Empowering Women Changes the World, emphasizes that the U.S. is the only industrialized country without a paid maternity leave law. "It's a better time in the world to be a woman than it has ever been," she told *The Chronicle of Philanthropy*. "Yet it's not getting better fast enough."

Main photo: *Melinda Gates*

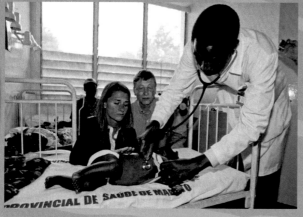

Top: Melinda and Bill first went to Africa to see animals, but were soon committed to helping children suffering from malaria, polio, and other diseases. *Melinda Gates*

Center: Women in India tell Gates they need contraceptives to space out their pregnancies, which is better for their health and their children's health. *Melinda Gates*

Bottom: Since Melinda French started at Microsoft in 1987 the percentage of computer science degrees going to women fell from 37 to 18 percent. *Melinda Gates*

Melissa Arnot Reid

Courtesy Melissa Arnot Reid

Almost a century after the suffrage pennant was planted atop Mount Rainier, Melissa Arnot was discovering her passion for ascending into thin air. Her parents put a premium on happiness, and Arnot found hers in climbing Rainier over 100 times as a guide. She went on to lead expeditions on some of the world's highest mountains. She has summited Mount Everest six times. The last of those treks was extraordinary.

In 2016, after seven years of training, Arnot reached her ultimate goal by becoming the first American woman to summit and descend Everest with no supplemental oxygen. Only six other women have completed the feat. Each breath at the extreme altitude has a third of the oxygen received at sea level. "The mountain doesn't care if you're male or female," she says. "It's going to give you the same challenges every day." Arnot has earned a reputation as America's best high-altitude female climber. Now married with a daughter of her own, Melissa Arnot Reid lives in the Methow Valley and mentors young female climbers and guides.

Top: Arnot didn't even tell her sponsor, Eddie Bauer, she was climbing Everest without oxygen because she didn't want to be distracted from her challenge. *Tyler Reid*

Middle: After her friend and Sherpa, Chhewang Nima (center), was killed in a 2010 avalanche, Arnot co-founded The Juniper Fund to support Nepalese families who lose a member on an expedition. *Melissa Arnot Reid*

Bottom: Arnot guided protégé, Maddie Miller, on a record breaking 50 Peaks Challenge, climbing each state's highest peak in 41 days. "I'm trying to teach these girls that the hard work is what you're proud of," Arnot said. "It's not all records and summits." *Microsoft*

ADDRESS CONFIDENTIALITY PROGRAM

State Senator Nita Rinehart was holding a "town hall" meeting in her northeast Seattle district when a woman in the audience stood up to speak. The woman said she couldn't risk voting for Rinehart, or anyone else. If she registered, her address would become a public record. That could allow the person who had been abusing her to track her.

Rinehart never got the women's name. But she spurred the 1991 creation of Washington's first-in-the-nation plan to protect victims of domestic violence. Called the Address Confidentiality Program, it's another example of Washington leading the way on women's issues. Some 39 other states have adopted similar strategies. Washington's ACP has expanded to include victims of stalking, sexual abuse and trafficking, as well as criminal justice employees threatened or harassed because of their work.

The program works like this: Because everyday necessities, such as a driver's license, create public records, the state provides those who want confidentiality with a "substitute address" in Olympia. They might reside anywhere in the state, but an abuser can't tell that from public records. Mail to ACP participants goes to the Olympia address. State workers then forward it to a participant's confidential location.

Address confidentiality is not a panacea, says Mary Pontarolo, former executive director of Olympia's SafePlace. The fact that ACP serves 4,700 Washingtonians shows how pervasive problems remain. But as part of an overall safety plan it helps survivors, she says.

DEAR ABBY

Victims of domestic violence live without fear in Washington

STATE OF WASHINGTON

DEAR ABBY: Because you have devoted so many columns to domestic violence, I thought you might like to know about the Address Confidential Program in Washington state.

Established by the Legislature in 1991, this innovative victims' assistance program is administered by the office of the secretary of state. The goal is to assist domestic violence victims who have permanently relocated to avoid further victimization by keeping their actual locations confidential.

Clients are referred to the program by police departments, community-based victims' assistance programs, and the Washington State Coalition Against Domestic Violence. Most of these victims are fleeing for their lives; if found, they may be killed. The program helps victims re-establish their lives by providing a substitute address that is accepted by state and local agencies. Participants use the substitute addresses for driver's licenses, marriage licenses and voter registration forms. There is a mail-forwarding service that enables them to keep their actual addresses confidential.

The Address Confidentiality Program is now in its fifth year of operation. Help is offered to men, women and children — but women involved in the program far outnumber men. Of the 1,061 participants enrolled, 469 are women, 9 are men and the remainder are children. Of the nine men enrolled in the program, eight reside with women who are victims of domestic violence.

**RALPH MUNRO,
SECRETARY OF STATE,**

DEAR MR. MUNRO: Thank you not only for sharing the news that such a compassionate program is available to the citizens of Washington state, but also for providing some figures on the ratio of women to men who are victims of domestic violence. Other states could learn from your farsighted legislators.

BIBLIOGRAPHY

JOSEPHINE CORLISS PRESTON

Andrews, Mildred Tanner, *Woman's Place, A Guide to Seattle and King County History*, Gemil Press, Seattle, 1994

Blair, Karen, *Preston, Josephine Corliss (1873-1958)*, HistoryLink.org Essay 9706, 3-27-2011

Bjorkman, Frances M. and **Porritt, Annie G.,** (editors), *The Blue Book, Woman Suffrage: History, Arguments and Results*, National Woman Suffrage Publishing Co. Inc., New York, 1917

Bragg, L.E., *More Than Petticoats, Remarkable Washington Women*, A Twodot Book, Falcon Publishing, Helena, Montana, 1998

Edwards, G. Thomas, *Sowing Good Seeds*, Oregon Historical Society Press, 1990

Ellis, Richard J., *Democratic Delusions, The Initiative Process in America*, University Press of Kansas, 2002

Ficken, Robert E., *Washington Territory*, WSU Press, Pullman, 2002

Goodwin, Doris Kearns, *The Bully Pulpit*, Simon & Schuster, New York, 2013

Lyman, W.D., *Lyman's History of Old Walla Walla County, Vol. 1*, The S.J. Clarke Publishing Co., Chicago, 1918

Mead, Rebecca J., *How the Vote Was Won*, New York University Press, New York, 2004

Morris, Edmund, *Colonel Roosevelt*, Random House, New York, 2010

Newell, Gordon, *Rogues, Buffoons & Statesmen*, Hangman Press, Seattle, 1975

Ross-Nazzal, Jennifer M., *Winning the West for Women,* University of Washington Press, Seattle, 2011

Rude, Gary Gordon, *Josephine Corliss Preston: A Study of Educational Leadership*, Ed.D. dissertation, Seattle University, 1985, Washington State Library

Scott, George W., *Governors of Washington*, Civitas Press, Seattle, 2012
         (editor) *Turning Points in Washington's Public Life*, Civitas Press, Seattle, 2011

Stevenson, Shanna, *Women's Votes, Women's Voices, The Campaign for Equal Rights in Washington*, Washington State Historical Society, Tacoma, 2009

Weiss, Elaine, *The Woman's Hour*, Viking, New York, 2018

ELSIE PARRISH

Rogers St. Johns, Adela, *Some Are Born Great*, Doubleday, Garden City, New York, 1974

Schwartz, Bernard, *A History of the Supreme Court*, Oxford University Press, 1993

Daniels, Roger, *Franklin D. Roosevelt: The Road to the New Deal, 1882-1939*, University of Illinois, 2015

Sheldon, Charles H., *The Washington high bench: a biographical history of the State Supreme Court, 1889-1991*, Washington State University Press, 1992

Irons, Peter, *A People's History of the Supreme Court*, Viking Penguin, 1999

STEPHANIE COONTZ

Coontz, Stephanie, *The Way We Really Are: Coming to Terms With America's Changing Families*, Basic Books, New York 1998
 Marriage, a History: How Love Conquered Marriage, Penguin Books, New York, 2006
 A Strange Stirring: The Feminine Mystique and American Women at the Dawn of the 1960s, Basic Books, New York, 2012
 The Way We Never Were: American Families and the Nostalgia Trap, Basic Books, New York, 2016
Crowley, Walt, *Rites of Passage: A Memoir of the Sixties in Seattle*, University of Washington Press, Seattle, 1995
Matt, Susan J., *Homesickness: An American History*, Oxford University Press, Oxford, United Kingdom, 2011

CHRIS GREGOIRE

McCann, Michael W. , *Rights at Work, Pay Equity Reform and the Politics of Legal Mobilization*, University of Chicago Press, 1994
Hoerr, John, *We Can't Eat Prestige: The Women Who Organized Harvard*, Temple University Press, Philadelphia, 2001
Hughes, John C., *Booth Who?*, Washington State Legacy Project, Olympia, 2010
Remick, Helen, "Comparable Worth in Washington State," *Comparable Worth, Pay Equity and Public Policy*, (editors Rita Mae Kelly and Jane Bayes) Greenwood Press, New York, 1988
 "Major Issues in a priori Applications," *Comparable Worth and Wage Discrimination: Technical Possibilities and Political Realities*, Temple University Press, Philadelphia, 1984

ANA MARI CAUCE

Sternberg, Robert J., Davis, Elizabeth, Mason, April C., Smith, Robert V., Vitter, Jeffrey S., Wheatly, Michele (editors), *Academic Leadership in Higher Education: From the Top Down and the Bottom Up*, Rowman & Littlefield, Lanham, Maryland, 2015
Bermanzohn, Sally, *Through Survivors' Eyes: From the Sixties to the Greensboro Massacre*, Vanderbilt University Press, 2003
Wheaton, Elizabeth, *Codename Greenkil: The 1979 Greensboro Killings*, University of Georgia Press, 2009

MARY-CLAIRE KING

Yount, Lisa, *An A to Z of Women in Science and Math*, Facts on File, New York, 2008
Bass, Thomas, *Reinventing the Future: Conversations with the World's Leading Scientists*, Addison-Wesley, Boston, 1993
Waldholz, Michael, *Curing Cancer: Solving One of the Great Medical Mysteries of Our Time*, Simon & Schuster, New York, 1997

Entine, Jon, *Abraham's Children: Race, Identity and the DNA of the Chosen People*, Grand Central Publishing, New York, 2007

FAWN SHARP

Capoeman, Pauline K. (editor), *Land of the Quinault*, Quinault Indian Nation, Taholah, Wash., 1990
Farrand, Livingston, *Traditions of the Quinault Indians*, Memoirs of the American Museum of Natural History, Volume IV, 1902, facsimile reproduction 1973, The Shorey Book Store, Seattle
Hughes, John C., *Slade Gorton, A Half Century in Politics*, The Washington State Heritage Center, Office of the Secretary of State, Thomson-Shore, 2011
Ruby, Robert H., and Brown, John A., *Indians of the Pacific Northwest*, University of Oklahoma Press, Norman, Okla., 1981
Shale, Warren (director), *Portrait of Our Land, A Quinault Tribal Forestry Perspective*, Quinault Tribal Council, Taholah, Wash., 1978
Thompson, Jerry, *Cascadia's Fault*, Counterpoint, Berkeley, Calif., 2011
Van Syckle, Edwin, *The River Pioneers, Early Days on Grays Harbor*, Pacific Search Press, Seattle, 1982
Workman, Larry J., *Land of Trees*, Quinault Indian Nation, Taholah, Wash., 1997

SOURCE NOTES

JOSEPHINE CORLISS PRESTON

CHAPTER 1:

JCP Childhood reminiscences, "a teacher" and "so lonesome," from "Famous Educator Once Lived in Fergus Falls," *Fergus Falls Daily Journal*, 5-29-1929, p. 1

Fully certified and high marks, 1891 teacher certification examinations, Otter Tail County Historical Society Archives

Barbed-wire fence quip, Gary Wigdahl, Otter Tail County historian, to author, 10-23-2018

"alacrity, clarity and confidence," "The Rise of Women in Washington's Politics," George W. Scott, *Turning Points*, p. 181

speculation on cabinet appointment, "Noted Educator May Be First Woman In Cabinet," *The Seattle Star*, 3-2-1920

elected NEA president; 6,000 attended convention, "Mrs. Preston Elected President of N.E.A.," *Washington Standard*, 7-11-1919

elected vice chairman of GOP Women's Division, "Republicans Honor Mrs. Preston," *Washington Standard*, 11-14-1919

"a personal friend," of Carrie Chapman Catt, "Advises Women Not to Nag Governor," *Washington Standard*, 11-7-1919, p. 4

Preston arranges Olympia luncheon, "Don't Nag the Poor Man Says Mrs. Carrie C. Catt," *Morning Olympian*, 11-5-1919

"An act to prevent discrimination," House Journal, 36th Day, 2-17-1919

Graduation statistics, Josephine Corliss Preston profile, Carol J. Lind, Washington State Historical Society, http://www.washingtonhistory.org/research/whc/ElectedWomen/preston/

jaunty hat trimmed in red, clipping in JCP scrapbook, p. 143, Washington State Library

Washington State History course for sixth graders, "Will Teach State History," *The Dispatch*, 8-25-1927

"quick to realize her wrath," *Josephine Corliss Preston: A Study of Educational Leadership*, p. 10, Washington State Library

called her "The Duchess," Josephine Corliss Preston profile, Lind

Corliss and Kinney family histories, Otter Tail Historical Society archives and Ancestry.com

"big in stature" and "possessed of great resolution," "An Old Settler Taken Off Before His Time," *Fergus Falls Weekly Journal,* 10-3-1889, p. 5

"home training" prized "self-reliance," quoted in "E.E. Corliss Goes To His Long Home," *Wheelock's Weekly*, 7-26-1917, p. 1

William Corliss achievements, "Death of W. M. Corliss," *Fergus Falls Advocate,* 11-18-1871

E.E. Corliss engineered bill to move county seat, "E.E. Corliss Memorial," *Fergus Falls Weekly Journal,* December, 1917, p. 7

Moved into town, built "handsome" house, "An Old Settler Taken Off Before His Time"

"shun all excitement," "An Old Settler Taken Off Before His Time"

"one of the longest ever seen," John Wesley Corliss funeral, *Battle Lake Review*, 10-3-1889, p. 1

Mother matron at Umatilla Indian School, "Mrs. Corliss… Dies," *Seattle Daily Times*, 2-20-1933

"wishes her daughter to return," Scrambler news squibs, *Fergus Falls Daily Journal*, 7-23-1891

$30-per-month teaching position, *Lyman's History of Old Walla Walla County, Vol. 1*

Railroad arrives at Waitsburg, *Waitsburg—Thumbnail History*, Michael J. Paulus Jr., HistoryLink. org. Essay 9862, 8-12-2011

"conscientious" teacher, "Josephine Corliss Preston: Avant-Garde Educator," Zola Burnap Irwin, Washington State Library

CHAPTER 2:

"follow in the footsteps" and "lovely and lovable," quoted in "Hymeneal Knot," *Waitsburg Times*, 7-21-1893, p. 4

"disregarded the solemnity," Walla Walla County Clerk's Archives, Microfilm 4906

bequeathed JCP $1,000, "Will Distribute Preston Estate," *The Spokesman-Review*, Spokane, 2-28-1916, p. 8

annual salary $2,500, 1913 *Legislative Manual* quoting Washington State Constitution, Washington State Library

"a prominent teacher" appointed deputy, "Put Woman On Ticket," *Tacoma Daily Ledger*, 1-27-1904; "Myers Gets Deputy," *Walla Walla Evening Statesman*, 1-9-1904

salary $75 per month, "Put Woman On Ticket"

"to honor fair womanhood," "Put Woman On Ticket"

"all white females over 18," Washington Territorial Legislature, *Journal of the House*, Territory of Washington, 1st Session, Olympia, 1854

"a voice in granting liquor licenses," *Women's Votes, Women's Voices*, p. 6

"all white American citizens twenty-one years of age," *Women's Votes, Women's Voices*

speaking for the "silenced and unrepresented," document reproduced in *Women's Votes, Women's Voices*, p. 14

"an odd looking lot," quoted in *Washington Territory*, p. 189

"If they can reform politics," *Washington Territory*

clarifying "his" meant "her" as well, *Women's Votes, Women's Voices*, p. 25

"male" hand-written, document reproduced in *Women's Votes, Women's Voices*, p. 25

"judicial jujitsu," Justice Gerry Alexander to author, 10-31-2018

"weakened the cause of suffrage," "The Fight for Washington Women's Suffrage," Shanna Stevenson, Women's History Consortium essay, Washington State Historical Society, http://www. washingtonhistory.org/research/whc/milestones/suffrage/; *Women's Votes Women's Voices*, p. 31

"eloquent and exhaustive," Proceedings of the Constitutional Convention, 8-12-1889, Washington State Archives

"Give woman the right to vote," Proceedings of the Constitutional Convention

"To attempt ...is as impossible," quoted in *Washington Territory*, p. 189

School Suffrage Act becomes law, *Women's Votes, Women's Voices*, p. 31, and HistoryLink.org., http://www.historylink.org/File/469

"Had state constitutions allowed," *Democratic Delusions*, p. 191

CHAPTER 3:

"As Uncle Jasper would say," *Colfax Gazette*, 12-4-1908, p. 1

"The time is inevitable," quoted in *The Blue Book,* p. 212

Clapp's friendship with John W. Corliss, referenced in *Josephine Corliss Preston: A Study of Educational Leadership*, p. 40

Account of DeVoe speech at Whitman, "Tells Why Women Should Get Ballot," *Walla Walla Evening Statesman*, 12-14-1908, p. 1; Josephine Corliss Preston scrapbooks

Background on DeVoe/Hutton dispute, *How the Vote Was Won*, pp. 107-112

African American population 1910, 1910 Census analysis, John Caldbick, HistoryLink.org Essay 9444, 6-6-2010

Nettie J. Asberry, *More Than Petticoats, Remarkable Washington Women*, L.E. Bragg, pp. 120-122

Appeal to women of Scandinavian descent, *Winning the West for Women,* p. 120

"while her foot soldiers canvassed," *Winning the West for Women*, p. 134

"stunningly decisive victory," *Women's Votes, Women's Voices*, p. 61

"a reformer on the right," quoted in *Governors of Washington*, p. 44

"keenly interested in rural areas," *Josephine Corliss Preston: Avant-Garde Educator*

"It takes trouble to get things started," quoted in *Josephine Corliss Preston: Avant-Garde Educator,* and "Magazine Tells of Mrs. J.C. Preston," *Morning Olympian*, 7-1-1916

"Always be good natured and cheerful," quoted in *Women's Votes, Women's Voices*, p. 44

"As early as 1904," "Talking Points, The Debate about Teachers' Cottages and Women's Place in Education, 1905-1920," Lynette L. Felbert, *Pacific Northwest Quarterly*, Volume 103, Issue 1, Winter 2011-12

ensuring the moral propriety, "Talking Points"

The story of Miss Cassandra Messegee, quoted in *Josephine Corliss Preston: Avant-Garde Educator*, Washington State Library, Olympia; photo is here: https://books.google.com/books?id=MkA_AAAAYAAJ&pg=PP1#v=onepage&q&f=false

"Know Your City Congress," "Children Learn of City," *Spokesman-Review*, 3-8-1910

JCP granted 48 hours of credit, JCP matriculation records, 2-23-1909, Whitman College Archives

Charles W. Corliss activities, "Charles W. Corliss," *History of Seattle*, pp. 1064-67

John H. Corliss activities, "J.H. Corliss, M.D.," *Washington West of the Cascades,* Vol II, pp. 657-658

"an ardent supporter of public education," "Dr. J.H. Corliss, Beloved Pioneer, Dies," *Puyallup Valley News*, 4-19-1961, p. 1

CHAPTER 4:

"wisdom, integrity and efficiency," quoted in *Josephine Corliss Preston: A Study of Educational Leadership*, p. 18

Burrows elected WEA president, "Victory for Friends of Dewey's Assistant," *Seattle Times*, 12-29-1911; "Burrows May Head State School Teachers," *Seattle Times*, 12-28-1911

Endorsements noted, same sources

Showalter opposed to Josephine, noted in *Josephine Corliss Preston: Avant-Garde Educator*

History of "normal" schools, "State Normal School at Cheney Opens," Jim Kershner, HistoryLink.org Essay 8246, 8-13-2007

"vastly more about education," quoted from letter from Dr. Penrose to JCP, 1-21-1931, Whitman College Archives

"the best teachers," "Good Roads Congress To Be Held In Tacoma," *Seattle Daily Times*, 12-23-1912

"it was far more important," "Good Roads Congress To Be Held In Tacoma"

"in interest of harmony," "J.M. Layhue withdraws in interest of harmony," *Seattle Daily Times*, 2-14-1912

"promises to be a pretty one," "State Capital Political Talk," *Tacoma Ledger*, 2-11-1912

Mary A. Monroe background, "Woman is seeking state office," *Seattle Daily Times*, 8-24-1912

Eldridge Wheeler background, "National Delegate," *Aberdeen Herald*, 2-15-1912

"a workman for the people," "Socialist Candidate for State Superintendent," *The Commonwealth*, Everett, Wash., 7-12-1912

experienced principal and teacher, "Socialist Candidate for State Superintendent"

Sylvester's earlier candidacies, "Socialist Candidate for State Superintendent"

"make short work of bloody capitalism," Socialist platform, *The Commonwealth*, 8-7-1913, p. 4

Sylvester shares platform with Maley, "Great Socialist Demonstration" advertisement, *Seattle Star,* 11-2-1912

"woman against woman," "Woman Against Woman," *The Town Crier*, Seattle, 10-19-1912, p. 6

"bring out the feminine vote," "Woman Against Woman"
"numerous well-known," "Woman Against Woman"

CHAPTER 5:

1.3 million women of voting age, *The Woman Citizen's Library*, Vol. 7, 1913, National Archives
"fathead" with "the brains of a guinea pig," quoted in "Remembering the 1912 Presidential Election," Jesse Greenspan, History.com, https://www.history.com/news/remembering-the-1912-presidential-election
"vociferous protests," quoted in *Rogues, Buffoons & Statesmen*, p. 246
"If girls were horses," quoted in *Rogues, Buffoons & Statesmen*
$1.57 for a nine-hour day, *Rogues, Buffoons & Statesmen*
"a matter of natural right alone," *Colonel Roosevelt*, p. 222
"arguably the most famous woman in America," *Colonel Roosevelt*, p. 221
"waving a great banner," quoted in *The Suffragents*, p. 107
"In most cases," quoted in *The Bully Pulpit*, p. 721
"We Stand at Armageddon," Theodore Roosevelt to Progressive Party Convention, Chicago, 8-6-1912, transcript National Archives
Addams betrayed non-partisan stance, *The Suffragents*, p. 107
African Americans excluded, *The Suffragents*
"electoral college vote women could effect," "The Rise of Political Woman in the Election of 1912," Joe Freeman, 2003 https://www.jofreeman.com/polhistory/1912.htm
Washington population doubled and women of voting age analysis, 1910 U.S. Census; *Historical Statistics of the U.S.*, Millennial Edition, Vol. 1, Population, pp. 1-366-336; "With women voting, Washington voters favor," HistoryLink.org Essay 5589, David Wilma and Kit Oldham; also *The Woman Citizen's Library*, Vol. 7, 1913, National Archives
"the thinking men of our country," quoted in *The Suffragents*, p. 114
"not within the purview," *The Woman's Hour*, p. 79
"If I could be sure," quoted in "President Taft Receives Mixed Greetings," David Dismore, Feminist Daily Newswire, 4-14-2014
"acted wisely," quoted in "The Rise of Women in Washington's Politics," *Turning Points*, p. 159
T.R. addresses 2,000 women, "Bull Moose Leader Praises Spokane," *Spokane Daily Chronicle*, 9-9-1912, p. 1
T.R. won't discuss "dead folks," "Colonel Tells It to Spokane," *Walla Walla Union-Bulletin*, AP, 9-10-1912, p. 1
"The argument that participation," "Colonel Tells It to Spokane"
Beach enters race, "Beach Will Run for Superintendent," *Morning Olympian*, 8-22-12
"old-time prophets" perplexed, "All Washington State Uncertain," M.M. Mattison, *The Oregonian*, 8-9-1912, p.1
"Nobody knows," "All Washington State Uncertain"
"three-to-one" Republican state," "All Washington State Uncertain"
"it seems generally admitted," "All Washington State Uncertain"
"a campaign of hustle," "Win? Of Course We Will Win," *Walla Walla Union-Bulletin*, 9-18-12
"not especially gallant," Editorials, *Seattle Times*, 11-3-1912
a lot of "joshing" and "among a flock of the fair sex," "Beach to Run Among Flock of Fair Sex," *Morning Olympian*, 9-13-1912
"a chance to split their votes," "Beach to Run Among Flock"
"a plurality of not less than 20,000," "Rupp Predicts Victory," *Walla Walla Union-Bulletin*, 11-14-1912, p. 1
"Women of all ages," "Walla Walla Out In Force," *Walla Walla Union*, 11-6-1912
"had occasion to hunt a hiding place," "Walla Walla Out In Force"

"cheering wildly," "Walla Walla Out In Force"
"Many a staunch Republican," "Walla Walla Out In Force"
"despite his lingering doubts" "The Rise of Women in Washington's Politics," *Turning Points*, p. 159

CHAPTER 6:

"more saloons than doctors and dentists," *Rogues, Buffoons & Statesmen*, p. 253.
"more Democrats than the capital city had ever seen," *Rogues, Buffoons & Statesmen*, p. 257
"willing to spend money and innovate," *Governors of Washington*, p. 48
"His transparent sincerity," *Governors of Washington*, p. 48
"poor and needy" rural districts, *Josephine Corliss Preston: A Study of Educational Leadership*, p. 5
"oversight" of **"delinquent and deficient children,"** "Mrs. Preston Here Today," *North Yakima Herald*, 4-8-1916
Statistics on children in state and expenditures, *Josephine Corliss Preston: A Study of Educational Leadership*, p. 5
Staffing levels at OSPI, *Josephine Corliss Preston: A Study of Educational Leadership*, p. 4
Annual operating budgets, *Josephine Corliss Preston: A Study of Educational Leadership*, p. 5
Attorney general's ruling on cottages, "Talking Points," pp. 26-27
"a comfortable place to live," never go **"a-begging,"** "Homes for Teachers is New Slogan," *Morning Olympian*, 3-5-1915, p. 1
"I nearly fainted with surprise," quoted in *Teachers' Cottages in Washington*, OSPI Bulletin No. 27, 1915, p. 15, Washington State Library
"A good evening lecture," quoted in *Teachers' Cottages in Washington*, p. 20
 "inestimable," and **"neither can work effectively,"** *Parent-Teacher Associations of Washington*, OSPI Bulletin 31, 1915, Washington State Library
"generally served at the whim," *Josephine Corliss Preston: A Study of Educational Leadership*, p. 37
"It is your duty …to revoke," quoted in *Josephine Corliss Preston,* p. 37
"The 20th century is demanding," "Give Libraries to Rural Districts," *Tacoma Ledger*, 7-7-1914, p. 4
nearly 10,000 congratulatory letters, "Eighth Grade Graduates," Washington Standard, 6-1-1920
"She endeared herself," *Historical Development and Outlook of Education Since 1900*, Council of Chief State School Officers, NEA, 1969, Washington State Library
JCP on dangers of dancing, *Josephine Corliss Preston.* p. 98

CHAPTER 7:

"very exacting in her demands," "Rumpus In State House Given Airing," *Morning Olympian*, 6-20-15, p. 1; "Official Statement," JCP scrapbooks, Washington State Library
"on account of incompetency," **"rumpus" died down,** "Rumpus In State House Given Airing," "Official Statement"
"abuse of women subordinates," "Calls Mrs. Preston 'Entirely Unfit,' " *Washington Standard*, 6-2-1916, p. 1
"a public calamity," "Calls Mrs. Preston 'Entirely Unfit' "
"nothing but the most courteous," "Issue Statement in Defense of Employer," *Seattle Daily Times*, 6-4-16, p. 30
"malicious and willfully misleading," "Charges Made Against Mrs. Preston Are Branded False," *Morning Olympian*, 6-4-1916, p. 1
"The fact that she was …a widow," "Official Statement," JCP scrapbooks, Washington State Library
"there has never been a time in the history," "Official Statement," JCP scrapbooks, Washington State Library

"The main trouble with Mrs. Preston," Editorial, *North Yakima Republic*, 3-29-1916
"a few of the second grade," quoted in *Josephine Corliss Preston: A Study of Educational Leadership*, p. 101
"try to forget" about brewery, quoted in *Josephine Corliss Preston: A Study of Educational Leadership*, p. 21
"knowing that you have very little to do," quoted in *Josephine Corliss Preston: A Study of Educational Leadership*, p. 107
illness result of "over work," "State Official Is Ill In City," *American reveille,* Bellingham, JCP scrapbooks
Reception at Whitney estate, "Mrs. Preston at Hughes Function," *Olympia Daily Recorder*, 7-8-1916
ranked first in "efficiency," "State is First in School Efficiency," *The Aberdeen Daily World*, 1916, JCP scrapbooks
Preston meets Maude Kimball Butler, "New School Dedicated," *Columbia River Sun*, Cathlamet, JCP Scrapbooks
Background on 1916 opponents, "King County Schoolman For Superintendent," *Colville Examiner*, 9-2-1916; "Ellensburg Woman Seeks State Office," *Seattle Daily Times*, 8-27-1916; "Morgan Wants To Be School Head," *Seattle Daily Times*, 6-11-1916; Centralia-Chehalis City Directory, 1916-17
Morgan crippled in stage accident, *Territorial/ State Superintendents*, OSPI pamphlet, p. 6, Washington State Library
1916 election results, https://www.sos.wa.gov/elections/results_search.aspx
"certificates increased from 563 to 5,000," *Historical Development and Outlook* of Education Since 1900

CHAPTER 8:

"the fundamental issue," A Patriotic Bulletin No. 32, published by the authority of JCP, 1918, p. 6, Washington State Library
"At a given hour in the morning," *A Patriotic Bulletin,* p. 64
"this great war crisis," quoted in *Josephine Corliss Preston,* p. 23
"pro-German inclinations" "Washington State Council of Defense," "Minute Women of Washington," Shanna Stevenson, Washington State Historical Society, http://www.washingtonhistory.org/research/whc/milestones/aftersuffrage/minutewomen/postww1/
"I feel it is your duty," quoted in *Josephine Corliss Preston: A Study of Educational Leadership*, pp. 44-45
"unholy, unrighteous" war, "Carr Says Opposed to War Ways," *Olympia Daily Recorder*, 2-2-1918; "Teacher's Remarks Bring Dismissal," *Tacoma Daily Ledger*, 2-13-1918
"But if I did make such a statement," "Carr Says Opposed to War Ways," "Teacher's Remarks Bring Dismissal"
"detrimental to the interests of the government." "Carr Says Opposed to War Ways," "Teacher's Remarks Bring Dismissal"
expressed contempt for Red Cross, "Revoke His License," *Olympia Daily Recorder*, 7-18-1918

CHAPTER 9:

"If the task is performed as well," "State Superintendent to Ask Legislature to Pass Equal Pay For Women Law," *Morning Olympian*, 12-24-1918
1919 omnibus package, "New State Laws Make For Better Education," *Seattle Daily Times*, 3-24-1919
"She pushed through," *Historical Development and Outlook of Education Since 1900*, pp. 1325-26
Catt and Preston call on governor, "Don't Nag the Poor Man Says Mrs. Carrie C. Catt," *Morning Olympian*, 11-5-1919
"can't reach a man by nagging" and other quotes from Olympia speech, "Don't Nag the Poor Man"
"gladsomely greeted," "Don't Nag the Poor Man"
"secret compact," "Secret Compact Between Hart and Howell Bared," *Morning Olympian*, 1-7-1920
"already carrying an overdraft," "Urge Governor Not to Invoke Special Session," *Olympia Daily*

Recorder, 2-16-1920

"the whole thing" and "temporary executive capacity," "Secret Compact"

"their argument being," "Has Governor Hart Been 'Passing the Buck' on Special Session Proposal?" *Morning Olympian*, 1-7-1920

"surely will lead the way again," "Has Governor Hart Been 'Passing the Buck?' "

women **"of all classes" and "in a position of blame,"** "Gov. Hart Says Women Against Extra Session," *Morning Olympian*, 2-20-1920

"Whatever Washington does," "Praise Woman Suffrage," *Seattle Star*, 2-11-1920

"emergency funds," *Rogues, Buffoons & Statesmen*, p. 298

"The governor was horrified" and "plaintive telegram," *Rogues, Buffoons & Statesmen*, p. 299

"I am sure you will join me," *Rogues, Buffoons & Statesmen*, p. 299

"He didn't get very far" and "leaving in droves," *Rogues, Buffoons & Statesmen*, p. 299

The women of our grandmothers' time," Vote for Suffrage at Olympia Is Unanimous," *Seattle Daily Times*, 3-23-20

"prove to the world the greatness," "Suffrage Amendment Ratified Unanimously, *Washington Standard*, 3-23-1920, p. 1

"20-10" law doubled state aid, "Olympia Session Ratifies Suffrage," *Oregonian*, 3-23-20; *Rogues, Buffoons & Statesmen*, pp. 299-300

"worked it through most cleverly," recalled in *Bellingham Herald*, 11-23-1943, p. 2

"true equalization could never be achieved," *Historical Development and Outlook of Education Since 1900*

Details on three 1920 opponents, "Everett Woman's Bonnet in Ring," *Tacoma Daily Ledger*, 3-28-1920; "Lizzie Jones," *Labor Journal*, Everett, 8-20-1920; "Catherine Montgomery For State Supt. Of Schools," *Washington Standard*, Olympia, 10-12-1920; "Alfa Salmon Ventzke," *Labor Journal*, 10-22-1920

"woman warfare," "Mrs. Jones Here After Place Mrs. Preston Now Has," *Olympia Daily Recorder*, 6-18-1920, p. 1

"If anything or anybody stands in the way," "Mrs. Jones Here"

"no other Western woman" better known, "Mrs. Josephine Preston, State School Leader, Dies," *Seattle Post-Intelligencer*, 12-13-1958

"Farmer-Labor Party emerges," "The Emergence of the Farmer-Labor Party in Washington Politics, 1919-20," Hamilton Cravens, *PNQ*, Vol. 57, No. 4, October 1966

Washington ranked first in the nation, *Historical Development and Outlook of Education Since 1900*, p. 1326

CHAPTER 10:

"hard blue eyes," "The Battle That Almost Ended the University of Washington," David M. Buerge, *Seattle Weekly*, first published 2-25-1987, *http://www.seattleweekly.com/news/the-battle-that-almost-ended-the-university-of-washington/*

teacher salaries $16.6 million, *Josephine Corliss Preston: A Study of Educational Leadership*, p. 6

Teachers average $1,459 per year, *Josephine Corliss Preston*

"Can we wonder why our children go wrong?" "What This State Thinks," quoting *The Tacoma News-Tribune*, *Seattle Daily Times*, 9-2-1928

"The embryo citizen we start out," "What This State Thinks"

egged on by president of Washington State College, "The Battle That Almost Ended"

resented Suzzallo salary, "The Battle That Almost Ended"

Duncan Dunn's role, "The Battle That Almost Ended"

proposed to abolish the boards of regents, "The Battle That Almost Ended"

"The proposal was met with outrage," "The Battle That Almost Ended"

Hartley ousts Rupp; McKee resigns, "Regents Turn to Courts," *Tacoma Daily News*, 5-7-1926, p.1; "Two Independent Regents Resign In Protest," *Seattle Daily Times*, 10-5-1926

"I deeply appreciate," "Students Cheer For Suzzallo," *Seattle Daily Times*, 10-5-1926

Recall indictment details, "Decision On Charges Is Due Tuesday," *Tacoma Daily Ledger*, 10-19-1926; "Editorial: Hartley Starts His Own Recall," *Seattle Daily Times*, 5-6-1926, p. 1

"The purpose of the bill was to give further state support," quoted in *Josephine Corliss Preston*, p. 6

"expected to be the beneficiary," "Showalter Plans to Oppose Mrs. Preston," *Seattle Daily Times*, 3-18-1928, p. 1

"a state school system recognized nationally" and **"through devious methods,"** "State School Leader Files," *Morning Olympian*, 8-5-1928, p. 1

"out of sympathy," "Hartley candidates for six elective state offices," *Bellingham Herald*, 4-16-1928, p. 1

allegedly opposes junior college movement, "Mrs. Preston for Junior Colleges," *Tacoma Daily Ledger*, 8-29-1928

"a definite plan for financing," "Mrs. Preston for Junior Colleges"

"incidental expenses," "State Head of Schools Witness at Washington," *Seattle Daily Times*, 10-24-1928, p. 1

"political attacks," "State Head of Schools Witness"

"thinly veiled propaganda," quoted in *Rogues, Buffoons and Statesmen*, pp. 339-340

controversy "ridiculous," "State Head of Schools Witness"

Times endorsement of Preston, "Right Now!" *Seattle Daily Times*, 9-10-1928, p. 1

Showalter and Preston campaign expenditures, "Hartley Nomination Cost Him $2,735," *Seattle Daily Times*, 9-21-1928

"The published inference," "Right Now!" *Seattle Daily Times*, 10-22-1928, p. 1

"already had exonerated her," "Right Now!"

pamphlet approved by a Normal School president, "State Head of Schools Witness"

"pleasure" for him to see the UW budget cut, *Governors of Washington*, p. 60

one of the top five states, "Mrs. Preston Gives Report," *Tacoma Daily Ledger*, 1-18-1929

Hartley orders state printer to omit, "Two Parting Shots," *Bellingham Herald*, 1-17-1929

Preston's farewell remarks, "Retiring Director Plans Schooling," *Morning Olympian*, 1-13-1929

Washington schools best in nation, quoted in "Mrs. Josephine Preston, State School Leader, Dies," *Seattle Post-Intelligencer*, 12-13-1958

CHAPTER 11:

"Memory Lodge" summer home, "Reunited After 60 Years," *Washington Standard*, Olympia, 8-24-1917; "For Rent—Summer Cottages," *Tacoma Daily Ledger*, 2-22-1925; "Enjoy Picnic Party At Lodge on Vashon," *Morning Olympian*, 8-18-1927

Added a new wing for mother, "Visits daughters," *Tacoma Daily Ledger*, 12-29-1929, p. 32

addresses University Women in New York, "Former State School Head Speaks in East," *Seattle Daily Times*, 3-5-1929

Nurses bedridden mother, "Mrs. Preston's Mother Dies," *Seattle Daily Times*, 2-20-1933

"orchids quivering on luxurious furs," "Lunching at the Olympic," Virginia Boren, *Seattle Daily Times*, 11-7-1933

"a writer's club over on the island," "Lunching at the Olympic"

Reeves banquet details, "Speeches Outshine Gowns at Affair for Mrs. Reeves, *Morning Olympian*, 3-9-1938

Preston's obituary, "Mrs. Preston, Ex-School Official, Dies," *Seattle Times*, 12-12-1958, p. 45

Bequeathed her assets, *Preston, Josephine Corliss (1873-1958)*, Karen Blair, HistoryLink.org Essay 9706, 3-27-2011

Mabel Seagrave

hunchback "nearest to an able-bodied man," "Back From France With Medal," *The Seattle Daily Times*, 4-10-1919, p. 9

awarded Medaille D'Honneur, *The Wellesley Alumnae Quarterly*, 1912, pp. 72-73, Mabel Seagrave Papers, University of Washington,

"labored as a superwoman," quoted in "Back From France With Medal," *The Seattle Daily Times*, 4-10-1919, p. 9

"Stunt Nights" at Women's University Club, "City's 'best-kept secret' is out," Jack Broom, *The Seattle Times*, 10-2-2013

Suffrage Association sponsors hospital, "American Women Physicians in World War I, American Medical Women's Association, https://www.amwa-doc.org/service-in-the-war/

Denny backs voting rights for "all white females over 18," Territorial Assembly transcript, Washington State Library

"it was plainly up to me to 'carry on,' " quoted in "Hospital Units For Americans," *Richmond Times-Dispatch*, 7-21-1918, p. 1

"A fine thing for suffrage," quoted in *The Woman Citizen*, 5-4-1918, p. 449, 450

"unusual wounds," quoted in *Votes for Women: A Portrait of Persistence*, Kate Clarke Lemay, Susan Goodier, Lisa Tetrault, Martha S. Jones, Princeton University Press, 2019, p. 76

Just to see such cavities opened up, quoted in *Votes for Women: A Portrait of Persistence, and The Woman Citizen*, 7-6-1918, p. 114

sent 78 women physicians to Europe, "American Women Physicians in World War I," American Medical Women's Association, https://www.amwa-doc.org/service-in-the-war/

"Not a man in the outfit," quoted in "Back From France With Medal"

"We had to do all our own heavy work," quoted in "Back From France With Medal"

"turned her hand to any and all tasks," quoted in "Back From France With Medal"

"Sometimes she was an undertaker," quoted in "Back From France With Medal"

at "evacuation" hospital, "Back From France With Medal"

"sleepy little village," "How the News Came to One Village of France," Marion R. Parsons in *The Mountaineer*, 1911, pp. 74-75

"her strength was marvelous," quoted in "Back From France With Medal"

"more deadly than war" statistics, *More Deadly Than War*, Kenneth C. Davis, Henry Holt and Company, New York, 2018, p. 6; "Have American forgotten the history of this deadly flu?" PBS News Hour, 11-16-2018, www.pbs.org/newshour/nation/have-americans-forgotten-the-history-of-this-deadly-flu

Trump's grandfather and FDR stricken, *More Deadly Than War*, p. 69, 29

Details of Armistice celebration, "How the News Came to One Village of France," Marion R. Parsons in *The Mountaineer* (Seattle), *Vol. 11*, December 1918, pp. 74-75,

Seagrave family details, "Mabel Seagrave, M.D.," *History of Seattle*, Vol. III, S.J. Clarke Publishing Co., Chicago, 1916, pp. 721-722

"notably kind and devoted" "Mabel Seagrave, M.D."

"making no pretension," "A.A. Seagraves," [sic] *The Seattle Republican*, 2-24-1902

"There was a splendid run down 17th Avenue, "Friends of the Saddle," *Daily Intelligencer*, 9-9-1900

"the honors were divided," "Friends of the Saddle"

co-valedictorian and warmly applauded, "Great Crush For Seats," *Seattle Daily Times*, 1-13-1901, p. 4

Details of 1902 Wellesley Field Day, "Field Day," *College News*, 11-12-1902, Vol. 2, No. 6, p. 1

Withdraws after stepmother's death, *College News*, 1-13-1904, Vol. 3, No. 13, page 2

Roosevelt rally details, "The Republican Rally," *College News*, 11-2-1904, p. 1

Seagrave's Johns Hopkins admission records, The Alan Mason Chesney Medical Archives, The

Johns Hopkins Medical Institutions, Baltimore, Md.
"considered too frivolous," About Johns Hopkins Medicine, "Women—or the Female Factor," https://www.hopkinsmedicine.org/about/history/history6.html
Only six other women in Class of 1911, https://medicalarchives.jhmi.edu:8443/garrett/graduates.htm
2.6 percent of all medical school graduates in 1910, *Restoring The Balance, Women Physicians and the Profession of Medicine, 1850-1995*, Ellen S, More, p. 07
Seagrave admitted to American College of Surgeons, "Club To Honor Dr. Seagrave," *Seattle Daily Times*, 10-29-1928
"Women physicians all too accustomed," "Women Physicians Face Extra Challenges," Lisa Esposito, 5-11-2018, https://health.usnews.com/health-care/articles/2018-05-11/women-physicians-face-extra-challenges
offered her $1,000, "Ask Seattle Girl To Practice in New York," *Seattle Daily Times*, 7-9-1910
"hundreds of thoroughly educated professional women," "Suffragettes Use Cuts To Nail Argument," *The Seattle Sunday Times*, 1-31-1909
"the vote of the lowest class," "Suffragettes Use Cuts To Nail Argument"
Members of Medical Women's Club of Seattle, "Seattle Women Physicians Plan Organization of State Society," *Seattle Daily Times*, 3-16-1920
"Women who did become physicians," *Restoring The Balance, Women Physicians and the Profession of Medicine, 1850-1995*, Ellen S, More, p. 07
Seagrave's changing styles of dress, "Seattle Society Dons Its Best For Wedding," *Seattle Daily Times*, 6-27-1935
"Dr. Mabel" to her friends, "In Memoriam," *Seattle Medical Bulletin*, 12-2-1935
Lectures on infant care, "Delivers Lecture on Baby's Care," *Seattle Daily Times*, 10-7-1914
Warns against over-prescription of morphine, "State Prison Association To Assemble," *Seattle Daily Times*, 3-27-1920
"having trial marriages," *Causes Underlying Sex Delinquency in Young Girls*, read before the State Conference of Social Agencies at Bellingham, Wash., 6-14-1926, http://hearth.library.cornell.edu/cgi/t/text/pageviewer-idx?c=hearth;rgn=full%20text;idno=4732756_858_009;view=image;seq=11
"The ease with which," *Causes Underlying Sex Delinquency*
Women's University Club building dedication, "College Women Dedicate Home," *Seattle Daily Times*, 10-22-1922
"Tried to go on living at my old home," and details of 1929 trip, Seagrave to *Johns Hopkins Alumni Bulletin*, 1930
Seagrave Guild formed, "Guild Dinner For Fun, Not Funds, *Seattle Times*, 10-30-1962, p. 23
Dies of cerebral hemorrhage, United Press, *Bellingham Herald*, 11-11-1935
"she had worked to alleviate," "Dr. Mabel Seagrave Calls Last 'Good-bye,' Cynthia Grey, Mabel Seagrave Papers, University of Washington, and "Dr. Seagrave Dies While At Dinner, *Seattle Daily Times*, 11-11-1935
Seagrave death certificate, Washington State Board of Health, #4002, Mabel Seagrave Papers, University of Washington
"She was a woman of fortitude," *King County Medical Bulletin*, 12-2-1935
Details of will, "Dr. Seagrave Leaves Estate of $15,000," *Seattle Daily Times*, 11-14-1935
"always putting some youngster through college," Mabel Seagrave Papers, University of Washington

ELSIE PARRISH

a block from the Cascadian, Dr. Helen J. Knowles to author 10-29-2018

pink in the fragrant blush, William E. Leuchtenburg, "The Case Of The Chambermaid And The Nine Old Men," *American Heritage* magazine, December 1986 , Volume 38, Issue 1

Washington was the fourth state, Knowles email to author, 1-31-2018

minimum wage of $14.50, Gerry L. Alexander, "Did This Washington Case Cause the Famous 'Switch in Time That Saved Nine?'" *Washington State Bar News*, December 2010, p. 22

stood at a stubborn 24 percent, Knowles to author

she couldn't afford to pay him, Alexander, "Did This Washington Case..." p. 22

"I took what they gave me," Alexander, "Did This Washington Case..." p. 23

seemingly frozen in a 19th century view, Leuchtenburg, "The Case Of The Chambermaid..."

admitted he only pretended to pay, Jonathan Grossman, "Fair Labor Standards Act of 1938: Maximum Struggle for a Minimum Wage," U.S. Department of Labor, originally published in *Monthly Labor Review*, June 1978

"The sacred right of liberty to contract...," Leuchtenburg, "The Case Of The Chambermaid..."

the court had also swatted down a dozen, Bernard Schwartz, *A History of the Supreme Court*, Oxford University Press, 1993, p. 234

"After slaughtering practically every New Deal...," Leuchtenburg, "The Case Of The..."

"minimum pay law Joan D'Arc...," Dr. Helen J. Knowles, "Omak's Minimum Pay Law Joan D'Arc," *Journal of Supreme Court History*, 12-20-2012

"ordinary Washington citizen benefited millions...," Alexander, "Did This Washington Case..."

"Not only did it give...," Alexander, "Did This Washington Case..."

Parrish "detonated" a revolution, Leuchtenburg, "The Case Of The..."

Her victory was even greater, Adela Rogers St. Johns, *Some Are Born Great*, Doubleday, Garden City, New York, 1974

Roberts only recently learned, Barbara K. Roberts to author, 11-9-2018

She was born, State of California, *California Death Index 1940-1997*, Department of Health Services, accessed via Ancestry.com, 7-17-2019

"one of the most deplorable...," "Killed By Thresher," *Wichita Eagle* (no byline), 7-20-1900, p. 2

"With almost superhuman strength...," "Killed By Thresher," *Wichita Eagle*

Elsie's oldest brother drowned, Knowles to author

So did the Lee family, whom the Murrays knew, Knowles email to author, 1-31-2019

Why both ended up living near, U.S. Census, 1920

Their 8-year old son died, U.S. Presbyterian Church Records, 1701-1970 via ancestry.com

Neppel became Moses Lake, Jim Kershner, "Moses Lake – Thumbnail History," *HistoryLink.org*, 11-4-2007

Elsie divorced Roy, finally unable to tolerate, Knowles email to author, 1-31-2019

Wenatchee was somewhat insulated from the Depression, Laura Arksey, "Wenatchee – Thumbnail History," *HistoryLink.org*, 7-10-2008

started working at 22 and ½ cents, Dr. Helen J. Knowles, "Omak's Minimum Pay Law Joan D'Arc," *Journal of Supreme Court History*, 12-20-2012

who listed orchard work, Marriage Certificate No. 7796, *Chelan County, State of Washington*, 7-28-1934

She worked a full shift, Supreme Court of Washington, *Parrish v. West Coast Hotel*, 185 Wash. 581, 4-2-1936

The Cascadian was part of a growing chain, Knowles to author

An imposing mix of Art Moderne and Beaux Art, Knowles, "Omak's Minimum Pay Law Joan D'Arc"

Innovations such as air conditioning, Knowles to author

The 1911 Triangle Shirtwaist Factory fire, Leah Sprague, "Her Life: the Woman behind the New Deal," *Frances Perkins Center*, 6-1-2014, accessed via http://francesperkinscenter.org/life-new/
Factory owners had locked some doors, "The worst day I ever saw," The Triangle Shirtwaist Factory, *Occupational Health & Safety Administration*, U.S. Department of Labor, undated, accessed via https://www.osha.gov/oas/trianglefactoryfire.html
Forty-seven workers, Sprague, "Her Life…"
New York's most lethal workplace tragedy, "The worst day I ever saw," *OSHA*
Alice Lord had organized, Lorraine McConaghy, "True grit: Alice Lord demanded respect for working women – and won," *Crosscut.com*, 9-2-2016
But it was Croake, a doctor, Phil Dougherty, "Croake, Nena Jolidon (1865-1934), *HistoryLink.org*, 11-24-2010
poverty was the "parentage of prostitution," Joseph Tripp, "Toward an Efficient and Moral Society: Washington State Minimum Wage Law, 1913-1925," *Pacific Northwest Quarterly*, Volume 66, July 1976, p. 98
women accounted for just 4 percent, Joseph Tripp, "Toward an Efficient and Moral Society," *Pacific Northwest Quarterly*, p. 101
"an unprecedented number of women flocked," Tripp, *Pacific Northwest Quarterly*, p. 102
"look like a mangy kitten," Tripp, p. 99
Instead they overwhelmingly supported, "Piper Bill Passes," *The Seattle Times*, no byline, 3-13-1913
"emissaries of His Satanic Majesty," Joseph Tripp, *Pacific Northwest Quarterly*, p. 103
In early 2014 the commission, Tripp, *Pacific Northwest Quarterly*, p. 104
Increased the minimum to $13.20, Tripp, *Pacific Northwest Quarterly*, p. 104
"decidedly hostile treatment…," Knowles, "Omak's Minimum Pay Law Joan D'Arc"
Starting with the so-called Lochner case, Knowles, "Omak's Minimum Pay…"
tossed a rock that would start a judicial avalanche, Roger Daniels, *Franklin D. Roosevelt: The Road to the New Deal, 1882-1939*, University of Illinois, 2015, p. 329
(Washington's community property law did not), Gerry L. Alexander to author 10-31-2018
Conner's motive for taking on, Knowles to author
Conner wrote in his journal, Alexander to author
"I would be false to myself…," C.B. Conner, unpublished memoir, page 192 given to Gerry L. Alexander by John Conner
who relied on the *Adkins* precedent, Alexander, "Did This Washington Case…"
Her case "reaches into every home where…," Supreme Court of Washington, *Parrish v. West Coast Hotel*, 185 Wash. 581, 4-2-1936
The Cascadian's lawyer, Fred Crollard, Knowles, "Omak's Minimum Pay Law Joan D'Arc,"
Millard had worked in railroad yards, Charles H. Sheldon, *The Washington high bench: a biographical history of the State Supreme Court, 1889-1991*, Washington State University Press, 1992
"I don't consider cases as much as a judge…," Sheldon, *The Washington high bench…*
"are prone to accept pretty much…," Supreme Court of Washington, *Parrish v. West Coast Hotel*
"they are peculiarly subject to the overreaching…," Supreme Court of Washington, *Parrish v. West Coast Hotel*
"The same Constitution applies to both," Alexander to author
"Well, the judge replied…," Leuchtenburg, "The Case Of The Chambermaid…"
known as the "four horsemen," Alexander, "Did This Washington Case…" p. 24
"the most curmudgeonly person…," Alexander, "Did This Washington Case…" p. 24
McReynold was so anti-Semitic, Ruth Bader Ginsburg, "Remarks for Touro Synagogue Celebration of the 350th Anniversary of Jews in America," 8-22-2004
Their average age was 74, Alexander, "Did This Washington Case…" p. 25
A trio of reliable liberals, Alexander, "Did This Washington Case…" p. 25

"They were also in the philosophical sense...," Alexander, "Did This Washington Case..." p. 25

The conservative justices rejected farm debt relief, Bernard Schwartz, *A History of the Supreme Court*, Oxford University Press, 1993, p. 232

"government by judiciary...," Bernard Schwartz, *A History of the Supreme Court*, p. 231

seemed to blow taps, Leuchtenburg, "The Case Of The Chambermaid..."

"among the most unpopular ever rendered...," Jonathan Grossman, "Fair Labor Standards Act of 1938: Maximum Struggle for a Minimum Wage..."

It came at a time when populist movements, Peter Beinart, "Will the Left Go Too Far?" *The Atlantic*, December 2018

Newspaper editorials pilloried the court's, Knowles to author

Even foes of FDR's said the court, Grossman, "Fair Standards Act of 1938..."

The Dred Scott decision "upheld a slave's status..." Richard Bernstein, "The Case of Order v. Disorder in the Court," *The New York Times*, 5-10-1995

"After the court decision, business looked...," Leuchtenburg, "The Case of The Chambermaid..."

"My goodness...," Associated Press, "Hotel Chambermaid Surprised By Interest Caused By Suit," *Morning Olympian*, 11-17-1936

"the welfare of the whole state...," Supreme Court of Washington, *Parrish v. West Coast Hotel*

Conner even wrote a letter, Knowles to author

Because the Supreme Court was the most aged, Leuchtenburg, "The Case of The..."

On that Monday morning, Leuchtenburg, "The Case of The..."

Chief Justice Hughes was known for leading, Schwartz, *A History of the Supreme Court,* p. 227

There was the "importance of the question," Peter Irons, *A People's History of the Supreme Court*, Viking Penguin, 1999, p. 316

"The Constitution does not speak...," Associated Press, "Tribunal Approves New Deal Measures," *The Seattle Times*, 3-30-1937

"What can be closer to...," Associated Press, "Tribunal Approves New Deal Measures,"

"the dogmatism of upper-class ladies...," Leuchtenburg, "The Case of The..."

"market and states had found the crisis...," Schwartz, *A History of the Supreme Court*, p. 233

It marked a whole new role for government, Schwartz, A History... p. 234

the realigned Supreme Court found no problem, Leuchtenburg, "The Case of The..."

Perkins would see all of her New Deal priorities, Sprague, "Her Life...," *Frances Perkins Center*

In their closed-door conference on December 19, Knowles to author

"It is too facile to state...," Schwartz, *A History of the Supreme Court*, p. 234

Evidence supports Chief Justice Hughes' later, Schwartz, *A History of the Supreme Court*, p. 235

"To him, the law was neither an *is*...," Schwartz, *A History of the Supreme Court*, p. 230

"Justice is not be to be taken by storm," Dahlia Lithwick, "The Irony of Modern Feminism's Obsession With Ruth Bader Ginsburg, *The Atlantic*, January/February 2019

"Judges are like everyone else...," Alexander to author

The newspaper called him a "pioneer attorney," "Conner Rites Tuesday," *Wenatchee Daily World*, 5-26-1941, p. 12

In 2018, it had the highest minimum wage, U.S. Department of Labor, "Minimum Wages by state," updated 1-1-2019, accessed via https://www.dol.gov/whd/minwage/america.htm

"launched a thousand law review articles," Knowles, "Omak's Minimum Pay Law Joan D'Arc"

"Other than one distant cousin," Bill Murray email to author, 11-11-2018

"Hers was a female and legal story," Barbara Roberts interview with author

Debbie Stewart, a great granddaughter, Debbie Stewart to author, 12-3-2018

Parrish came to the door, Adela Rogers St. John, *Some Are Born Great*, Doubleday, Garden City, NY, 1974, p. 187

"I had to do it," Adela Rogers St. John, *Some Are Born Great.* p. 187

"the women of Lib and let Lib do not know the name," Rogers St. John, p. 185
"There is no evidence…," Helen J. Knowles, *Making Minimum Wage: Elsie Parrish vs. The West Coast Hotel Company,* (excerpted) under contract with University of Oklahoma Press
"But that is beside the point," Knowles email to author, 10-25-2018

STEPHANIE COONTZ

Waiting was a flurry of messages, Stephanie Coontz email to author, 4-15-2019
The court's 5-4 opinion cited Coontz, U.S. Supreme Court, Obergefell v. Hodges, 14-556, Opinion of the Court, June 26, 2015
"Like national," Danny Westneat, "Evergreen prof guided highest court," *The Seattle Times*, 7-1-2015
Rates of poverty, child abuse, Stephanie Coontz, "The Way We Never Were," *The New Republic*, 3-29-2016
Quayle made coast-to-coast news, Jacey Fortin, "That Time 'Murphy Brown' and Dan Quayle Topped the Front Page," *The New York Times*, 1-26-2018. (The front page of the New York *Daily News* screamed, "Quayle to Murphy Brown: YOU TRAMP!")
telling Oprah, Lisa Pemberton, "Q&A: Evergreen historian Stephanie Coontz talks about the Supreme Court's gay marriage ruling," *The Olympian*, 7-5-2015
"It's Plato's Republic with electricity," interview with author, 2-28-2019
She sees Trump supporters, Stephanie Coontz, "The Nostalgia Trap," *Harvard Business Review*, 4-10-2018
"Some of them can be won over," interview with author, 2-28-2019
Protests she led in the 1960s, John Hinterberger, "Petite Co-ed Doesn't Look Like a Revolutionary," *The Seattle Times*, 11-30-1969
"I believed strongly," interview with author
"perhaps the best-known radical woman," Richard W. Larsen, "Radical in a straight world," *The Seattle Times*, 11-2-1970
She was a 108-pound "charmer," Larsen, "Radical in a straight world," 11-2-1970
Coontz started making news in 1968, no byline, "Members of Peace Group Expelled From Fort Lewis," *The Seattle Times*, 10-26-1968
"My dad was a big supporter," interview with author
Used the G.I. bill, interview with author
Was an "ambitious, independent" student, Lee Swedberg and Patricia Coontz, "Oral history interview transcript with Pat Coontz," Eastern Washington University Libraries, Archives & Special Collections, 1982
"It was as if someone had sucked," "Oral history interview transcript with Pat Coontz," 1982
Friedan's radical idea, Stephanie Coontz, *A Strange Stirring: The Feminine Mystique and American Women at the Dawn of the 1960s*, Basic Books, New York, 2012
Her activism had been partly driven, interview with author
librarians in Seattle and Ephrata were fired, Louise S. Robbins, "After Brave Words, Silence: American Librarianship Responds to Cold War Loyalty Programs, 1947-1957," *Libraries & Culture*, Vol. 30, No. 4, pp. 345-365, University of Texas Press, 1995
Police were grabbing students, "Oral history interview transcript with Pat Coontz," 1982
"One conscientious reporter," Gene Marine, "The Students Strike at California," *The Nation*, 12-3-1964

Coontz initially went limp, Stephanie Coontz email to author 3-15-2019

inducting 2 million American men, U.S. Selective Service System, "Induction Statistics," https://www.sss.gov/About/History-And-Records/Induction-Statistics

She was part of a group, no byline, "Members of Peace Group Expelled From Fort Lewis," *The Seattle Times*, 10-26-1968

Costumed as a cigar-chomping general, no byline, "'Free Army' Group Tries to Cross Lake A la Washington But Fails," United Press International, *Sacramento Bee*, 7-14-1969

"the dark-eyed girl with the clear voice," John Hinterberger, "Petite Co-ed Doesn't Look Like a Revolutionary," *The Seattle Times*, 11-30-1969

didn't speak in the "strung-out," Hinterberger, "Petite Co-ed…"

"I never used the word 'pig,'" interview with author

She condemned bomb-throwing, "Petite Co-ed…"

But it didn't do black people much good, "Petite Co-ed…"

"Here we have a 25-year-old woman," Daryl M. Hogan, "Times Readers Have Their Say" (letter to editor), *The Seattle Times*, 12-7-1969

TV reporter Don McGaffin, interview with author

"I always thought," interview with author

Coontz led thousands of students, Walt Crowley, *Rites of Passage: A Memoir of the Sixties in Seattle*, University of Washington Press, Seattle, 1995, pp. 59, 159, 161, 173

"dressed like radical students or hangers-on," Stephanie Coontz email to author 3-15-2019

She was kept overnight, no byline, "Three Men Beat Miss Coontz," *The Seattle Times*, 5-12-1970

urging a 100 percent tax on war profits, Larsen, "Radical in a straight world," 11-2-1970

One headline captured the election, no byline, "Minor parties remain minor," *The Seattle Times*, 11-4-1970

"Ex-war resister gets Evergreen faculty post," no byline, *The Seattle Times*, 1-3-1975

"Although Evergreen didn't have disciplines," interview with author

editor for the publishing arm, no byline, "Ex-war resister gets Evergreen faculty post," 1-3-1975

She wasn't thrilled about what she found, interview with author

"Suddenly, it was like," interview with author

"So thank god for Evergreen," interview with author

"Neither they, nor the liberals," interview with author

She set out to write. interview with author

"fuel in the sound-bite fires," Eden Ross Lipson, "Domestic Solutions," *The New York Times* Book Review, 9-24-1997

Instead Mary Ann Gwinn produced, Mary Ann Gwinn, "Don't Leave It to the Cleavers: Scholar Debunks Family Myths," *The Seattle Times*, 10-9-1982

When she didn't hear creative solutions, Kathleen Merryman, "Facts of Life for a Whole Nation," *Tacoma News Tribune*, 5-28-1997

layered with "pragmatic optimism," Eden Ross Lipson, "Domestic Solutions"

Government supported families in the 1950s, Merryman, "Facts of Life for a Whole Nation"

Even if families were to return to 1950s, Merryman, "Facts of Life for a Whole Nation"

It was absurd, "Facts of Life for a Whole Nation"

Coontz saw child care, parental leave, "Facts of Life for a Whole Nation"

"She's no chatty pop-prof," Kimberly Marlowe Hartnett, "'Marriage, a History:' for better and for worse," *The Seattle Times*, 5-27-2005

from cave dwellers to computer programmers, Judith Warner, "Enduring Union," *The Washington Post*, 6-26-2005

"What's Love Got to Do With It?" Stephanie Coontz, "The Secret History of Marriage," (video)

Decode DC, 4-18-2015, https://www.youtube.com/watch?v=87p9_Y5Bb98

"marriage was considered too important," Ellen Goodman, "Score one for Cupid," *The New York Times*, 5-15-2005

"Marriage had as much to do with getting," Kimberly Marlowe Hartnett, "'Marriage, a History:' for better and for worse"

But then heterosexuals began to change it, Ellen Goodman, "Score one for Cupid"

The Supreme Court embraced Coontz's logic, Danny Westneat, "Evergreen prof guided highest court," *The Seattle Times*, 7-1-2015

But when she read his decision, email to author, 3-7-2019

"For thousands of years," Stephanie Coontz, "The Way We Never Were," *The New Republic*, 3-29-2016

In Washington state, husbands could use, Jonathan Kaminsky, "Proposal would remove marital exception for rape," *Associated Press*, 1-29-2013

"still stuck in the basement," Stephanie Coontz, "Women have come a long way, but still have far to go," *Courier Journal* (Louisville, Kentucky), 3-16-2014

Gender equity had stalled, Stephanie Coontz, "Why Gender Equity Stalled," *The New York Times*, 2-16-2013

Progress had slowed so much, American Association of University Women, "The Simple Truth about the Gender Pay Gap," accessed via https://www.aauw.org/research/the-simple-truth-about-the-gender-pay-gap/

The lack of family-friendly, Coontz, "Women have come a long way..." *Courier Journal*, 3-16-2014

"On average, when a woman leaves," Coontz, "Women have come a long way..."

"Studies show that employers," Coontz, "Women have come..."

"So your discrimination against men," interview with author, 2-28-2019

If women were paid the same as men, Coontz, "Women have come..."

Of 193 countries, Jessica Deahl, "Countries Around The World Beat The U.S. On Paid Parental Leave, *National Public Radio*, 10-6-2016

"Again, this is where we recruit men," interview with author

Norway has implemented, interview with author

"I want society to tell people," Bill O'Reilly, "State of Disunion," The O'Reilly Factor, *Fox News*, 5-23-2005

Coontz, a single mom, Kathleen Merryman, "Facts of Life for a Whole Nation," *Tacoma News Tribune*, 5-28-1997

A 17th-century Swiss doctor, Stephanie Coontz, "The Nostalgia Trap," *Harvard Business Review*, 4-10-2018

Union Army doctors reported 5,000 serious cases, Susan J. Matt, "Home, Sweet Home," *The New York Times*, 4-19-2-12

"This kind of nostalgia," Coontz, "The Nostalgia Trap," 4-10-2018

"start to identify," Coontz, "The Nostalgia Trap"

"And when people get scared," Interview with author, 2-28-2019

Trump supporters appear to idealize, interview with author

For roughly three decades, Coontz, "The Nostalgia Trap"

But this prosperity was an exception, Stephanie Coontz, "Taking the Nostalgia of Trump Supporters Seriously," *Berggruen Insights*, 7-26-2016

CEO salaries soared, John Kruzel, "Do CEOs make 300 times the average worker, as Joe Kennedy said?" *Politifact*, 1-31-2018

Between 1980 and 2007, Coontz, "The Nostalgia Trap"

"Irish indentured servants," interview with author

"I see this as a huge obstacle," interview with author

"Would you EFFIN' name," interview with author

"So I don't think it helps," interview with author
"When he was working," interview with author
"Too often they've just been kept," interview with author
NBC asked her to weigh-in, Stephanie Coontz, "Kellyanne and George Conway: A modern marriage in the age of Trump? Or a couple in crisis?" NBCnews.com, 3-21-2019, https://www.nbcnews.com/think/opinion/kellyanne-george-conway-political-marriage-age-trump-or-couple-crisis-ncna985911
'60s radical-turned-*Ladies Home Journal* marriage consultant, Stephanie Coontz, "About Stephanie," https://www.stephaniecoontz.com/about.htm
"I don't feel comfortable," interview with author
O'Reilly, meanwhile left Fox, Emily Steel and Michael F. Schmidt, "Bill O'Reilly Is Forced Out at Fox News," *The New York Times*, 4-19-2017
"There are two things," interview with author

PIONEERS IN PAY EQUITY

A few days after flinging her Husky mortarboard, Chris Gregoire interview with author, 1-14-2019
"There was nothing about this case," Chris Gregoire interview with Sharon Boswell, Women's History Consortium, 6-26-2014
"The union was very strategic," Gregoire interview with Women's History Consortium
"the most unique case" Gregoire ever handled, Gregoire interview 6-26-2014
on which she was a leader in negotiating for 46 states, James Tierney, "The Tobacco Settlement: 20 Years Later," *StateAG.org*, accessed via https://www.stateag.org/initiatives/the-tobacco-settlement#gregoire
"On this one, I had constant mixed emotions," Gregoire to author 1-14-2019
Following an elaborate survey of 2,700 jobs, Diana Stone, "Comparable Worth in the Wake of AFSCME v. State of Washington," *Berkeley Journal of Gender, Justice & Law*, September 1985
"I had been a clerk-typist," Gregoire interview 6-26-2014
It is one of seven states, Kate Nielson email to author, 12-5-2018, and "AAUW Policy Guide to Equal Pay in the States," via https://www.aauw.org/resource/state-equal-pay-laws/
Comparable worth was born, Shelby Scates, "'Comparable' is a mighty word," *Seattle Post-Intelligencer*, 12-4-1983
In his talk, he accused, Scates, "'Comparable' is a mighty word," 12-4-1983
In Olympia, Goodman's boss, Scates, "'Comparable' is a mighty word"
"permeates through the private sector," Helen Remick, "Comparable Worth in Washington State," *Comparable Worth, Pay Equity and Public Policy*, (editors Rita Mae Kelly and Jane Bayes) Greenwood Press, New York, 1988, p. 225
The Washington Women's Council, Remick, "Comparable Worth in Washington State," p. 226
Elected officials earned less than managers, Helen Remick, "Beyond Equal Pay for Equal Work: Comparable Worth in the State of Washington," Paper prepared for the Conference on Equal Pay and Equal Opportunity Policy for Women in Europe, Canada, and the United States, Wellesley College, May 1978, p. 4, 5
"then we must move to reverse this inequity," Diana Stone, "Comparable Worth in the Wake of AFSCME v. State of Washington," *Berkeley Journal of Gender, Justice & Law*, September 1985
The governor paid consultant Norman Willis, Helen Remick, "Comparable Worth in Washington State," p. 226

"sex seemed to be the only" factor, Associated Press, "Washington State in Court on Women's Pay," *The New York Times*, 9-1-1983

"According to the Old Testament," Barbara Reskin, "Shortchanged: The Pay Gap and What to Do about It," unpublished presentation to League of Women Voters, 2016

Helen Remick moved to Washington, Remick interview with author, 12-3-2018

"I thought I had gone to heaven," Remick interview with Sharon Boswell, Women's History Consortium, 5-26-2014

She had faced discrimination, Remick to Women's History Consortium, 5-26-2014

The Seattle-King County chapter…was as brash, Remick interview 5-26-2014

Remick was comfortable with computers, Remick to author 12-3-2018

The female-dominated position of Secretary III, Helen Remick, "Beyond Equal Pay for Equal Work: Comparable Worth in the State of Washington," p. 11

Because the state had more than 4,000 job titles, Helen Remick, "Comparable Worth in Washington State," *Comparable Worth, Pay Equity and Public Policy*, p. 224

Washington was the first employer to use, Remick, "Comparable Worth in Washington State," p. 226

"Before the comparable worth study," Remick, email to author, 12-11-2018

While the terms "comparable worth" and "pay equity," Michael W. McCann, *Rights at Work, Pay Equity Reform and the Politics of Legal Mobilization*, University of Chicago Press, Chicago, 1994, p. 4

Along the way she would get to know, Remick to author 12-3-2018

Belcher was an administrative secretary, Jennifer Belcher to author 11-8-2018

She played a pivotal role, Jennifer Belcher to Sharon Boswell, Women's History Consortium 4-23-2014

"You couldn't be a woman in work," Belcher to Women's History Consortium, 4-23-2014

Belcher's mentor was Jo Garceau, Belcher to author 11-8-2018

"I got to sit in on executive pay issues," Belcher to author

She recalls that near the end of Evans' 12 years in office, Belcher to author

Evans included $7 million, Helen Remick, "Comparable Worth in Washington State," p. 226

"It was a tough place to be," Belcher to author

"apples with pumpkins and a can of worms," Helen Remick, "Major Issues in *a priori* Applications," *Comparable Worth and Wage Discrimination: Technical Possibilities and Political Realities*, Temple University Press, Philadelphia, 1984, p. 104

"The ultimate irony," Doug Underwood, "Evans tells court of state pay disparity for men and women," *The Seattle Times*, 8-31-1983

"the cost of perpetuating unfairness," Diana Stone, "Comparable Worth in the Wake of AFSCME v. State of Washington," *Berkeley Journal of Gender, Justice & Law*, September 1985

Newman had won groundbreaking anti-discrimination, Michael W. McCann, *Rights at Work, Pay Equity Reform and the Politics of Legal Mobilization*, University of Chicago Press, Chicago, 1994, p. 50

Newman modeled his arguments, McCann, *Rights at Work*, p. 61

He had gone to work for AFSCME, McCann, *Rights at Work*, p. 62

More than half of its 1 million members, John Hoerr, *We Can't Eat Prestige: The Women Who Organized Harvard*, Temple University Press, Philadelphia, 2001, p. 188

A committee on sex discrimination was created, Johanna Russ, "Pay Equity and the Public Employee," Walter P. Reuther Library, Archives of Labor and Urban Affairs, Wayne State University, 1-27-2014

Schut later explained that he had started, Randy Brooks, "Norm Schut interview transcript," *The History of Council 28, Community History Project, University of Washington at Tacoma*, 1-28-1992, via https://digitalcollections.lib.washington.edu/digital/collection/tacomacomm/id/65

"We needed something we could sell, Randy Brooks, "Norm Schut interview transcript," 1-28-1992

Progress had been slowed in the 1970s, Joseph Hower, "With Janus, the Supreme Court guts the modern labor movement," *The Washington Post*, 6-27-2018

Schut also faced resistance from Jerry Wurf, Randy Brooks, "Norm Schut interview transcript," 1-28-1992

Just as that deadline passed, Equal Employment Opportunity Commission, "Clarence Thomas, Eighth Chairman of the EEOC, May 6, 1982 – March 8, 1990," accessed via https://www.eeoc.gov/eeoc/history/35th/bios/clarencethomas.html

Thomas would prove dismissive, Robert Pear, "Equal pay is not needed for jobs of comparable worth," *The New York Times*, 6-18-1985

By that time, more than 100 state employees, Bill Dietrich, "Many state employees received welfare even before pay lag," *The Seattle Times*, 10-6-1982

Helen Castrilli, a medical secretary at Western State Hospital, Elizabeth Whitney, "Equal pay for different work: fair or Looney Tunes?" *St. Petersburg Times*, 4-14-1985

Castrilli studied business, Carol Kleiman, "A Secretary And A Sense of Self-Worth," *Chicago Tribune*, 6-16-1985

"I wanted to stay home," Carol Kleiman, "A Secretary and a Sense of Self-Worth," *Chicago Tribune*, 6-16-1985

Castrilli, in a quiet but firm voice, Kleiman, *Chicago Tribune*, 6-16-1985

"Through the union, I've learned," Kleiman, *Chicago Tribune*, 6-16-1985

"It's a revolution," Kleiman, *Chicago Tribune*, 6-16-1985

Belcher had spent a good part of the previous year, Belcher to author, 11-8-2018

"He came to the conclusion," Gregoire to author

"I scored high on the test," Gregoire interview with Women's History Consortium, 6-26-2014

"You've got trouble," Gregoire interview with John C. Hughes, *Legacy Washington*, 3-25-2009

"A huge number of things went through my mind," Gregoire to author

And as she later realized, Gregoire to author

What's more, the state's good intentions, Diana Stone, "Comparable Worth in the Wake of AFSCME v. State of Washington"

Studying "a unique and novel theory," Stone, "Comparable Worth in the Wake of AFSCME v. State of Washington"

"At trial we were very clear that attributing points," Gregoire to Women's History Consortium

who had served in a segregated Army unit, Paul Andrews, "'The Court of First Resort'—Judge Jack Tanner Champions Underdogs and Fields Criticism," *The Seattle Times*, 2-2-1986

a former Northwest-area president of the NAACP, Paul Andrews, "'The Court of First Resort,'" *The Seattle Times*, 2-2-1986

In the end, Gregoire said, the decision, Doug Underwood, "Evans tells court of state pay disparity for men and women," *The Seattle Times*, 8-31-1983

Tanner said that comparable worth was a reasonable, Helen Remick, "Major Issues in *a priori* Applications," p. 106

"We were dead on arrival," Gregoire to author

"In my opinion," Gregoire later said, Gregoire to Women's History Consortium

"And the judge was unmerciful in the barbs," Doug Underwood, "Comparable-worth obstacles are money, Tanner record," *The Seattle Times*, 11-21-1983

Tanner ruled that the state was guilty, United Press International, "State found guilty of sex bias on pay," *The Seattle Times*, 9-16-1983

Tanner rejected the state's claim…crushing burden, Jo Freeman, "Real, False Dilemmas," *Democratic Left*, Sept.-Oct. 1984

"When the state lost at trial," Gregoire to Women's History Consortium

"In fact, appeal is always on everybody's mind," Underwood, *The Seattle Times*, 11-21-1983

***The New York Times'* first edition of 1984,** Tamar Lewin, "A New Push to Raise Women's Pay," *The New York Times*, 1-1-1984

And it was fast becoming a partisan issue, Tamar Lewin, "A New Push to Raise Women's Pay"

"provided a new rallying point," Lewin, "A New Push..."

"ERA through the back door," Jo Freeman, "Real, False Dilemmas," *Democratic Left*, Sept.-Oct. 1984

Schafly herself sounded an alarm, Freeman, "Real, False Dilemmas"

"Let's be blunt," Eric Pryne, "Evans, Schafly exchange barbs," *The Seattle Times*, 7-25-1985

Evans' face remained straight, Eric Pryne, "Evans, Schafly exchange barbs"

And about those 'commissars,' Pryne, "Evans, Schafly..."

"Comparable worth did not come out of the cosmos," Ross Anderson, "Rights chief, Evans clash on comparable worth," *The Seattle Times*, 3-5-1985

"which of course brings all kinds of emotions to the fore," Gregoire to author

"The 9th Circuit not only granted us," Gregoire interview with Women's History Consortium

President Reagan called it "cockamamie," Jay Mathews, "Comparable Worth Rule Overturned," *The Washington Post*, 9-5-1985

"middle-class, white women's reparations," Associated Press, "Washington State Settle Dispute Over Pay Equity," *The New York Times*, 1-2-1986

In Congress, Republicans lambasted, Jack Anderson, "Congress debates comparable worth," *The Olympian*, 9-3-1985

Their decision was seen as "a signal...," Robert Pear, "Equal pay is not needed for jobs of comparable worth," *The New York Times*, 6-18-1985

"Those who used to be in the middle," Bob Partlow, "Even proponents agree comparable worth losing some of the allure," *The Olympian*, 4-7-1985

"You tell me how to set up a system," Tamar Lewin, "A New Push to Raise Women's Pay"

There are "general characteristics of fruit..." Brad Rind and Paul Herrick, "Comparable Worth, Making the case for skepticism," *The Seattle Times*, 6-10-1984

"And we had it on the record," George Masten to author, 1-25-2019

"We have to drop the law suits," Booth Gardner for Governor press release, 9-29-1984

"with the unwillingness of governors," Associated Press, "Comparable-worth settlement still target," *The Seattle Times*, 4-4-1985

Gardner held a press conference, Peter Perl, "'Comparable-Worth' Settlement Sought," *The Washington Post*, 8-14-1985

He also said he hired a trio, Walter Hatch, "Gardner Names Comparable Worth Negotiators," *The Seattle Times*, 8-13-1985

"We wanted the governor to hire," Walter Hatch, "Gardner Names Comparable Worth Negotiators"

Negotiations....were to start, Peter Perl, "'Comparable-Worth' Settlement Sought," *The Washington Post*, 8-14-1985

But he'd take input, and no more, George Masten to author 1-25-2019

"I'll admit I had blinders on," Masten to author

"You had to stay on message," Gary Moore to author 1-25-2019

"Feminists groaned," Walter Hatch, Elouise Schumacher and Joni Balter, "Pay ruling won't end dispute – comparable-worth edict overturned, but union will appeal to high court," *The Seattle Times*, 9-5-1985

"Neither law nor logic deems the free market," *AFSCME, et al v. State of Washington*, U.S. Court of Appeals for the Ninth Circuit, 770 F. 2d 1401, 9-4-1985

"does not obligate it," *AFSCME, et al v. State of Washington*, U.S. Court of Appeals for the Ninth Circuit, 9-4-1985

"we reject a rule," *AFSCME, et al v. State of Washington*, 9-4-1985

"You've got to be kidding," Hatch, Schumacher and Balter, *The Seattle Times*, 9-5-1985

Eikenberry "got calls saying it was wrong," Gregoire to Women's History Consortium, 6-26-2014

"That was a surprise that we won outright," Gregoire to Women's History Consortium

It had not been in the state's interest, Gregoire to author 1-14-2019

What's more, Gregoire wanted to raise women's pay, Gregoire to author

"the decision we have today is the ultimate," Hatch, Schumacher and Balter, *The Seattle Times*, 9-5-1985

"He wanted his trial," Masten to author, 1-25-2019

He called AFSCME national President Gerald McEntee, Masten to author

"I'm delighted with the result," Jay Mathews, "Comparable Worth Rule Overturned," *The Washington Post*, 9-5-1985

"It really devalues the union's position," George Ramos and Dan Morain, "Equal-Pay Decision Overturned: Comparable Worth Not Covered by Law, Appeal Court Says," *Los Angeles Times*, 9-5-1985

"I was suspicious of Chris at first," Becky Bogard to author, 1-18-2019

"And we drank a bottle," Bogard to author, 1-18-2019

"more open and honest she became," Gregoire to author

"we will settle, and we will do it right," Gregoire to Women's History Consortium, 6-26-2014

"To Ken's credit," Gregoire to author

She and Agid, Gregoire to author

Bogard, who served as treasurer, Bogard to author

The negotiating teams celebrated with Champagne, Greoire to author

A *Chicago Tribune* headline, James Warren, "A Major Victory for 'Comparable Worth'," *Chicago Tribune*, 1-1-1986

On the other hand, a *Los Angeles Times* story, Sara Fritz, "'Comparable Worth' Case Settled OKd: Union and Washington State Agree to Terms Distributing $482 million to 34,000 Workers," *Los Angeles Times*, 1-1-1986

"tears of rage," Walter Hatch, "Angry tears punctuate wage-raise deliberation," *The Seattle Times*, 1-18-1986

"particularly with business leaders opposing it," Neil Modie, "Pay-equity bill sails through the Senate," *Seattle Post-Intelligencer*, 1-21-1986

Boeing lobbyists "worked franctically," Walter Hatch, "Angry tears punctuate wage-raise deliberation," *The Seattle Times*, 1-18-1986

"I didn't expect Boeing to break their pick," Hatch, *The Seattle Times*, 1-18-1985

Left him a "nervous wreck," Neil Modie, "Pay-equity bill sails through the Senate," *Seattle Post-Intelligencer*, 1-21-1986

Lee accused Hayner, Modie, *Post-Intelligencer*, 1-21-1986

Hayner denied the charge, Hatch, *The Seattle Times*, 1-18-1985

When the vote was called, United Press International, "How they voted," *Seattle Post-Intelligencer*, 1-21-1986

"Sure it feeds the ego," Elizabeth Pulliam, "Ironies tint comparable-worth reforms," *The Seattle Times,* 5-4-1986

"Gregoire did take flak," Helen Remick email to author, 12-12-2018

"We were negotiating with the governor," George Masten to author 1-25-2019

"in the management-only caucuses during negotiations," Mark Brown to author 1-25-2019

"She likes the finality, I think," Jennifer Belcher to author, 12-26-2019

Gardner was impressed by Gregoire's team, John C. Hughes, *Booth Who?*, Washington State Legacy Project, Olympia, 2010, p. 125

***The Olympian* asked,** Bob Partlow, "The attorney general: Governor in waiting?" *The Olympian*, 4-23-1995

she "wouldn't have been governor," John C. Hughes, *Booth Who?*, Washington State Legacy Project, Olympia, 2010, p. 125

Gregoire agreed, Hughes, *Booth Who?*, p. 125

The agreement required the state, U.S. General Accounting Office, "Comparable Worth in Washington State," *GAO/GGD-92-87BR*, July 1, 1992, p. 17

That line was plotted, Helen Remick to author, 12-3-2018

Well over half of the jobs had moved up, GAO, "Comparable Worth in Washington State," p. 3

After compounding the expense, GAO, "Comparable Worth in Washington State," p. 4

By 1989, an estimated $450 million, Michael W. McCann, *Rights at Work*, The University of Chicago Press, 1994, p. 42

McCann's research showed a steep spike, McCann, *Rights at Work*, p. 59

"the biggest bang," McCann, p. 54

Women said they gained confidence, McCann, pp. 230, 231

"It all of a sudden looked like the issue," McCann, p. 57

A Massachusetts special committee, McCann, p. 58

The U.S. Chamber of Commerce and the Business Roundtable, McCann to author, 1-2-2019

Reagan and allies began employing a new tool, McCann to author, 1-2-2019

"discrimination is all right if everyone does it," Michael W. McCann, "Money, Sex, and Power: Gender Discrimination and the Thwarted Legacy of the 1964 Civil Rights Act," *Denver University Law Review*, Vol. 91: 4, 2015, p. 796

Seen as "the death of pay equity claims," McCann, "Money, Sex, and Power," 2015, p. 797

By 2002, progress had slowed, American Association of University Women, "The Simple Truth about the Gender Pay Gap," accessed via https://www.aauw.org/research/the-simple-truth-about-the-gender-pay-gap/

"That sounds pretty optimistic," Remick to author 12-3-2018

Women were earning a majority, National Equal Pay Task Force, "Fifty Years After The Equal Pay Act," The Obama White House, June 2013, p. 20

In 1960, roughly 15 percent of managers, National Equal Pay Task Force, 2013, p. 6

Almost one-quarter of women earned, Task Force, p. 17

The narrowing gap had as much to do, Task Force, p. 17

"Women with less education," Task Force, p. 16

"even after controlling for the effects of specialty," Task Force, p. 29

over half of all women, Task Force, p. 6

Historical "patterns of exclusion," Task Force p. 26

Discrimination, they concluded, Task Force, p. 17

corporations such as Allstate Insurance, Task Force, pp. 18, 19, 22

The law allows employees to talk about their earnings, Agueda Pacheco-Flores, "Women are struggling to catch up with men's pay; what's the gap look like here?," *The Seattle Times*, 10-24-2018

The new law defines it as, Laura Turczanski, Mike Reiss, "Washington's New Pay Equity Law Creates More Stringent Requirement for Employers," *Davis Wright Tremaine LLP*, 4-11-2018

Washington goes further than California, Erin Connell, Jessica R. L. James, "Washington State Overhauls Equal Pay Laws After Seventy Five Years," *Orrick Equal Pay Pulse*, 3-29-2018

 All the more reason, Remick says, Helen Remick email to author 12-11-2018

"that would be inconsistent," *Scope of bargaining*, RCW 41.80.020, subsection 4

Another state law requires that job classifications, author interview with Franklin Plaistowe, assistant director, state Human Resources, Karen Durant, section chief, Enterprise Classification, Compensation & HR Analytics, Marisa McKay, manager, Classification & Compensation, Angie Hogenson, HR Analytics and Initiatives manager, 3-11-2019

"So the fight moves on," Chris Gregoire to author, 1-14-2019

TRISH MILLINES DZIKO

"We've been lucky," Carey Goldberg, "Microsoft millionaires give back," *The New York Times*, 7-6-1997

"It's become a multi-billion dollar," Trish Millines Dziko interview with author, 4-18-2019

A survey, Battalia Winston, "The State of Diversity in Nonprofit and Foundation Leadership," 6-7-2017 http://www.battaliawinston.com/the-diversity-gap-in-the-nonprofit-sector/

"They don't look like me," Dziko interview with author 4-18-2019

Served some 19,000 students, "About us: Our history," *Technology Access Foundation*, accessed 5-14-2019 via https://techaccess.org/about-us/

"We are the product of," interview with author

"Sometimes I feel the pressure," interview with author

"That comes directly from my mother," interview with author

Pat Millines was born, *Asbury Park Press*, "Mrs. Patricia Millines (obituary)," 5-14-1975

renowned for launching Bruce Springsteen's career, Jessica Glenza, "New Jersey town made famous by Springsteen at centre of gentrification row," *The Guardian*, 6-17-2018

Springsteen's E Street Band is named, Chris Jordan, "Bruce Springsteen: How the E Street Band got its name," *Asbury Park Press*, 2-20-2017

cleaned the homes of two, interview with author

Millines would pocket cab fare, Richard Seven, "No Time For Talk," *The Seattle Times*, 1-23-2000

"I knew I was adopted," interview with author

She also took in troubled relatives, Richard Seven, "No Time For Talk," *The Seattle Times*, 1-23-2000

"Well, as a black woman," interview with author

"None of our parents had gone to college," interview with author

"Another one of my genius moments," interview with author

At Asbury Park High, Jessah Foulk, "Trish Millines Dziko oral history interview," *Museum of History and Industry*, 8-8-2002

"kind of geeky," Jessah Foulk, "Trish Millines Dziko oral history interview," *Museum of History and Industry*, 8-8-2002

Her teachers got her into the honors track, Jessah Foulk, "Trish Millines Dziko oral history interview," *Museum of History and Industry*, 8-8-2002

When it came to sports, "Camp Zehnder Opens," *Asbury Park Press*, 6-25-1968

Seven years later the newspaper, "Pat Millines, the only senior on the Asbury Park team..." *Asbury Park Press*, 3-10-1975

"It was the sport you played," interview with author

she emulated New York Knicks' guard, interview with author

She was Asbury Park's high-scorer, "Asbury captures girls title," *Newark Star-Ledger*, 3-9-1975

But she really loved, interview with author

who was bedridden with cancer, Richard Seven, "No Time For Talk," *The Seattle Times*, 1-23-2000

Pat Millines died a month before, *Asbury Park Press*, "Mrs. Patricia Millines (obituary)," 5-14-1975

Her will stipulated, Richard Seven, "No Time For Talk," *The Seattle Times*, 1-23-2000

"I think if I had done anything different," interview with author

She wanted to major in electrical engineering, Jessah Foulk, "Trish Millines Dziko oral history interview," *Museum of History and Industry*, 8-8-2002

"She was an athlete when she enrolled," Richard Seven, *The Seattle Times*

She was drafted, Jessah Foulk, *Museum of History and Industry*, 8-8-2002

After graduation, Jessah Foulk, *Museum of History and Industry*

"I'm kind of sorry that I learned, Jessah Foulk, *Museum of History and Industry*

She bought a motorcycle, Jessah Foulk, *Museum of History and Industry*

"You were like, you know, a god," Jessah Foulk, *Museum of History and Industry*

"really good programmer," Jessah Foulk, *Museum of History and Industry*

you want a little more, Jessah Foulk, *Museum of History and Industry*

Trish also lettered, (footnote) "Former Monmouth Student-Athlete Trish Millines Dziko to receive NCAA Silver Anniversary Award," *Northeast Conference* press release, 12-4-2003

She bought a small motor home, Jessah Foulk, *Museum of History and Industry*

"It's not a time I'm particularly proud of," Trish Millines Dziko interview with author

thought it was the greatest place, Jessah Foulk, *Museum of History and Industry*

"I like that we can go out as a family," Jessah Foulk, *Museum of History and Industry*

She figured she'd work for Boeing, Jessah Foulk, *Museum of History and Industry*

Men tended to think hardware, Clive Thompson, "The Secret History of Women in Coding," *The New York Times Magazine*, 2-13-2019

"In contrast, programming it seemed," Clive Thompson, "The Secret History of Women in Coding," *The New York Times Magazine*, 2-13-2019

And computers didn't see gender, Clive Thompson, *The New York Times Magazine*, 2-13-2019

By 1960, the proportion of women, Clive Thompson, *The New York Times Magazine*

By the 1983-84 academic year, Clive Thompson, *The New York Times Magazine*

favored a new type, Clive Thompson, *The New York Times Magazine*

From where the first home computers, Clive Thompson, *The New York Times Magazine*

"did not seem to be correlated with coding talent," Clive Thompson, *The New York Times Magazine*

That's where women really felt they hit a wall, Clive Thompson, *The New York Times Magazine*

she came to dislike, Jessah Foulk, *Museum of History and Industry*

"And I'm like, well," Jessah Foulk, *Museum of History and Industry*

"We didn't have any lives," Jessah Foulk, *Museum of History and Industry*

"That was a cool project," interview with author

On top of that, she was going, interview with author

"BAM was created totally out of necessity," Jessah Foulk, *Museum of History and Industry*

Only about 40 African Americans, Jessah Foulk, *Museum of History and Industry*

"I really, really, really wanted to pursue," Jessah Foulk, *Museum of History and Industry*

Her mission was to flood, Jessah Foulk, *Museum of History and Industry*

"You have to get people to really think," Richard Seven, "No Time For Talk," *The Seattle Times*, 1-23-2000

There was a reservoir of talent, Jessah Foulk, *Museum of History and Industry*

On a winter day in 1996, Trish Millines Dziko email to author, 5-24-2019

lack of opportunities for kids of color, Richard Seven, *The Seattle Times*

"mired in a racially divided past," David Ruben & Angela J. Krum, "Parenting Leaders," *Parenting*, March 1999

rose by a factor of 250, Carey Goldberg, "Microsoft millionaires give back," *The New York Times*, 7-6-1997

after the conversation in the park, Trish Millines Dziko email to author, 5-24-2019

"It seemed to happen overnight," Richard Seven, *The Seattle Times*

The William H. Gates Foundation gave $444,000, Seven, *The Seattle Times*

In its first year, 27 out of 32 students, David Ruben & Angela J. Krum, "Parenting Leaders," *Parenting*, March 1999

23 were hired for paid summer internships, Seven, The Seattle Times

Trish and Jill dressed in new outfits, Trish Millines Dziko, "Finally Legal," *Women For One*, 12-11-2013

they chose "Dziko," interview with author

After Washington adopted its marriage equity law, Trish Millines Dziko, "Finally Legal," *Women For One*, 12-11-2013

They rounded up some close friends, Trish Millines Dziko, "Finally Legal," *Women For One*

Dziko and foundation staff realized the limitations, "Our History," *Technology Access Foundation*

The foundation hoped to provide at least $1.5 million, Linda Shaw, "Tech Foundation aims to open schools," *The Seattle Times*, 9-27-2006

only 27 percent of Rainier Beach 10th graders, "Don't miss opportunity at Rainier Beach High (editorial)," *The Seattle Times*, 11-26-2006

"the first African American, at least locally," Nina Shapiro, "Schooling the District," *Seattle Weekly*, 2-12-2007

Dziko faced community opposition, Cara Solomon, "Technology-academy proposal provokes anger at high school, *The Seattle Times*, 11-12-2006

"weren't really sure where she comes from, Nina Shapiro, "Schooling the District," *Seattle Weekly*, 2-12-2007

PTSA president led a walkout, Cara Solomon, "Technology-academy proposal provokes anger at high school, *The Seattle Times*, 11-12-2006

"It was all politics," interview with author

There was nothing fundamentally wrong, Carla Santorno interview with author, 5-29-2019

"I liked what I heard," Linda Shaw, "Foundation, Federal Way district plan science, tech school," *The Seattle Times*, 6-27-2007

rejected three times by Washington, Linda Shaw, "As voters weigh charter schools again, Federal Way's public TAF Academy offers lessons it has learned," *The Seattle Times*, 10-11-2012

TAF's academy would be the first, Linda Shaw, "Foundation, Federal Way district plan science, tech school," *The Seattle Times*, 6-27-2007

a deal was signed to bring the TAF Academy, Emily Heffter, "Federal Way takes tech-school idea that Seattle rejected," *The Seattle Times*, 11-14-2007

opened in 2008, Linda Shaw, "Renton may get second TAF school next fall," *The Seattle Times*, 10-11-2010

"to get it open," Trish Dziko, "Beyond the Blue Badge (podcast)," Paul Shoemaker (host), *Microsoft Alumni Network*, 3-13-2019

"You're never a prophet," interview with author

Plans were hatched, Linda Shaw, "Renton may get second TAF school next fall," *The Seattle Times*, 10-11-2010

Bill Gates gave $3 million, Valerie Strauss, "21 wealthy donors had decisive impact on charter law in Washington state," *The Washington Post*, 1-30-2014

They have more latitude, Linda Shaw, "As voters weigh charter schools again, Federal Way's public TAF Academy offers lessons it has learned," *The Seattle Times*, 10-11-2012

Teachers at a charter school, Linda Shaw, "As voters weigh charter schools again, Federal Way's public TAF Academy offers lessons it has learned," *The Seattle Times*, 10-11-2012

Dziko says she's agnostic, "Beyond the Blue Badge (podcast)," Paul Shoemaker (host), *Microsoft Alumni Network*

The "reality is that most charter schools," Linda Shaw, "As voters weigh charter schools again, Federal Way's public TAF Academy offers lessons it has learned," *The Seattle Times*, 10-11-2012

Teachers at a charter school, Linda Shaw, "As voters weigh charter schools again, Federal Way's public TAF Academy offers lessons it has learned," *The Seattle Times*, 10-11-2012

After TAF's success in the Federal Way district, Carla Santorno interview with author, 5-29-2019

82 percent of its students, "School Transformation, Pilot Schools," *Technology Access Foundation*, via https://techaccess.org/school-transformation/#1462491034349-64e400c2-c460

"I was always very impressed," Santorno interview with author, 5-29-2019

"Trish learns and adapts," Josh Garcia interview with author, 5-29-2019

Principal Arron Wilkins embraced the idea, Debbie Cafazzo, "Tacoma's Boze Elementary School embraces hands-on learning," *The News Tribune*, 11-11-2015

The overarching goal, Debbie Cafazzo, "Tacoma's Boze Elementary School embraces hands-on learning," *The News Tribune*, 11-11-2015

Debra Hendrix, a fourth-grade teacher, Debbie Cafazzo, *The News Tribune*, 11-11-2015

They studied tectonic plates, tsunamis, volcanology, Debbie Cafazzo, *The News Tribune*

Third-graders wanted, Debbie Cafazzo, *The News Tribune*

Sixth graders were given a hypothetical, Trish Millines Dziko interview with author, 4-18-2019

"TAF is about kids driving our learning," Debbie Cafazzo, *The News Tribune*

TAF petitioned the district, Trish Millines Dziko interview with author

With a woman's false accusation, Alice Randall, "Why Are We Still Teaching 'To Kill a Mockingbird' in Schools?" *NBC News*, 10-19-2017

College readiness starts in kindergarten, interview with author

"just in a fun way," interview with author

"I like that because that's how I grew up," interview with author

It hopes to transform, interview with author

Totem Middle School was feeling squeezed, Heidi Jacobs, "Federal Way Public Schools' TAF Academy to move to Saghalie Middle School," *Federal Way Mirror*, 6-3-2016

It couldn't add more classrooms, interview with author

number of students from 300 to 700, interview with author

Students who started at TAF, "TAF Academy, They Did It! TAF@Saghalie graduates its first senior class," *Technology Access Foundation*, via https://techaccess.org/taf-saghalie-graduates-first-senior-class/

"I think our partnership with public education," Trish Dziko, Beyond the Blue Badge (podcast), Paul Shoemaker (host), *Microsoft Alumni Network*, 3-13-2019

A 2017 survey of 4,000 people, Sean Thomas-Breitfeld, Frances Kunreuther, "Race to Lead: Confronting the Nonprofit Racial Leadership Gap," *Building Movement Project*, 2017

But those doing the recruiting and hiring, Ben Paynter, "5 Charts That Illustrate The Racial Bias In The Nonprofit World," *Fast Company*, 6-5-2017

"So that's the kind of stuff," interview with author

"For what? For what?" interview with author

She didn't take a salary at TAF, interview with author

"Then I think," interview with author

"Generational change is my legacy," Trish Dziko, "Beyond the Blue Badge (podcast)," Paul Shoemaker (host), *Microsoft Alumni Network*, 3-13-2019

MARY FAIRHURST

"a sense of being at peace," Debra L. Stephens to author, 5-21-2019

"Pretty Blonde Water Skier Qualifies As Attorney," *Seattle Post-Intelligencer*, 9-21-1953

"Woman Wields the Gavel," quoted in *Carolyn Dimmick: A judge for all seasons*, John C. Hughes, Legacy Washington, 2009, https://www.sos.wa.gov/legacy/stories/carolyn-dimmick/

"the prettiest justice," quoted in *Carolyn Dimmick: A judge for all seasons*

"Which do you prefer?" James Dolliver quoted in *The Washington High Bench*, Charles H. Sheldon, WSU Press, Pullman, 1992, p. 115

"That's progress," quoted in "Women's Advances in Law Careers are 'So Heartening,' " United States Courts online profile, 3-8-2018, https://www.uscourts.gov/news/2018/03/08/judge-carolyn-dimmick-womens-advances-law-careers-are-so-heartening

"and a little Yankee," "Gonzalez sworn in," Brad Shannon, the *Olympian*, 1-10-2012

sister surrendered new mittens, "Terminal cancer can't shake," Rebecca Nappi, *The Spokesman-Review*, 2-12-201

Running as a "blue-collar attorney," "Usually quiet, Supreme Court races heating up," Paul Queary, AP, *The Daily World*, Aberdeen, 10-24-2002

"The timing was impeccable," Charles W. Johnson quoted in *The Washington High Bench*, p. 230

"I knew Justice Madsen would be elected," Alexander to author, 6-26-2019

"I actually got listened to," Barbara Madsen to author, 6-7-2019

"the animals around the watering hole," Stephens to author, 5-21-2019

"But the reality is," Stephens to author, 5-21-2019

"essential to the survival of the human race," Madsen quoted in "Washington Court Upholds Ban on Gay Marriage," Adam Liptak, *The New York Times*, 7-26-2006

"There is no rational basis," Fairhurst quoted in "Washington Court Upholds Ban on Gay Marriage"

"Mary is the peacemaker," Madsen to author, 6-7-2019

Her **"fortitude and faith tell us a lot,"** Alexander to author, 6-26-2019

"time is precious," State of the Judiciary speech, TVW, https://www.youtube.com/watch?v=b4yIC653SA8

"I don't see it as a death sentence," Fairhurst quoted in "I'm alive for a reason," KING5 News, 2-1-2019, https://www.king5.com/article/news/politics/im-alive-for-a-reason-washington-chief-justice-reacts-to-3rd-colon-cancer-diagnosis/281-d6804fc7-aa4d-42ff-8c1f-86e3e680875c

Fairhurst announces retirement, Rachel La Corte, AP, and Drew Mikkelsen, KING-5 News, 10-3-2019

LINEA LAIRD

"people at SDOT couldn't believe Linea," Doug MacDonald to author, May 2019

"Linea Laird cannot be shined," MacDonald to author

"Woman named highway engineer," story by Travis Baker, *Kitsap Sun*, 2-1-1993

WSDOT statistics on female engineers, email from Holly Sage, WSDOT HR, 5-6-2019

only 14 percent composed of women, "The State of Women in Civil Engineering," Anabella Tourkaman, ASCE News, 4-11-2018

Women in construction trades, "Share of Women Working in Construction Trades in 2018," Institute for Women's Policy Research, https://iwpr.org/share-of-women-working-in-construction-trades-in-2018-is-the-highest-in-20-years/

"She's not my wife," John Conrad to author, May 2019

"Residents had long dreamed," "Lacey V. Murrow and his 'Upstanding Bridges,' " Craig Holstine, *Columbia* magazine, Spring 2017, Vol. 31, No. 1, p. 15-16

Bone letter to Murrow, quoted in "Lacey V. Murrow," p. 15

"the biggest celebration," "Lacey V. Murrow," p. 18

Description of bridge collapse, "Lacey V. Murrow," p. 19

"a wide variety of sealife," "Bridge builder taking measures to avoid 'Galloping Gertie' remains," *Kitsap Sun*, 2-21-2000

"smartest person you've never heard of," MacDonald to author, May 2019

"One of the things I came to appreciate," Amy Arnis to author, May 2019

"intricately involved," "Q&A with Linea Laird," Greg Lamm, *Puget Sound Business Journal*, 4-24-2012

"cram into downtown streets," "Tunnel + tolls = traffic trouble," Mike Lindblom, *The Seattle Times*, 6-28-2012

"Bertha" might not be the prettiest name, "The Tradition of Naming Tunneling Machines," Derek Wang, KUOW, 4-3-2013

ANA MARI CAUCE

They staged sit-ins, Roberto Sanchez, "Ethnic-Studies Appointee Protested," *The Seattle Times*, 7-19-1997

They cursed, Karen Gaudette, "Tension high at most recent AES meeting," *The Daily*, 6-25-1997

They interrupted, William Lutz, "Regents back Cauce despite student protests," *The Daily*, 7-23-1997

attempted filibuster, Staff editorial, "So Good," *The Daily*, 10-22-1997

They issued demands, (no byline) "ESSA Demands and Administration Responses," 7-23-1997

"it is not essential," Staff Editorial, "No Rubber Stamp," *The Daily*, 7-16-1997

manager of a hostile takeover, Theresa N. Duque, "No cease-fire in AES," (Letters to the Editor), *The Daily*, 7-16-1997

she was not one of the minorities, Dale Bernardini, "ESSA students courageous," *The Daily* (Letters to the Editor), 7-23-1997

"good-old-boy-network," Parissh Knox and Melissa Lin, "Butler's Qualifications" (Letters to the Editor), *The Daily*, 7-2-1997

full front-page story, Matt Keyes, "Under Fire, AES: A Department Divided," *The Daily*, 6-25-1997

Cauce was clueless, Ana Mari Cauce, *Academic Leadership in Higher Education: From the Top Down and the Bottom Up*, edited by Robert J. Sternberg, Elizabeth Davis, April C. Mason, Robert V. Smith, Jeffrey S. Vitter, Michele Wheatly, Rowman & Littlefield, Lanham, Maryland, 2015, p. 80

On the first day of her new job, Ana Mari Cauce, *Academic Leadership in Higher Education: From the Top Down and the Bottom Up*, edited by Robert J. Sternberg, *et al,* p. 80

"not quite human," Ana Mari Cauce, "We the people: diversity, equity and difference at the UW," (text), 4-16-2015, video at https://www.youtube.com/watch?v=9uWxEJhehjM&t=1560s

"My mother…better…not," Ana Mari Cauce, interview with author, 3-1-2019

In a letter responding, Ana Mari Cauce, "AES chair responds," (Letter to the Editor), *The Daily*, 7-9-1997

"WE HAVE NOT YET BEGUN TO FIGHT," Theresa N. Duque, "No cease-fire in AES," (Letters to the Editor), *The Daily*, 7-16-2019

gave her a "rookie of the year," Cauce interview with author, 3-1-2019

The new boss had gone to every American, Ana Mari Cauce, *Academic Leadership in Higher Education: From the Top Down and the Bottom Up,* edited by Robert J. Sternberg, *et al,* p. 80

At the end of Cauce's three-year term, Cauce, *Academic Leadership in Higher Education: From the Top Down and the Bottom Up,* p. 81

"accidental administrator," Cauce, *Academic Leadership in Higher Education,* p. 79

She disliked process, Cauce, *Academic Leadership in Higher Education,* p. 79

she was lauded, Ellie Bothwell, "World's top 10 universities led by women 2016," *Times Higher Education*, 8-17-2016

ultra-rare insider, Katherine Long, "Supporters of Cauce say look no further for UW's next leader," *The Seattle Times*, 9-27-2015

overseeing three campuses, "Fast Facts 2019," University of Washington Office of Planning and Budgeting

"Although I did not realize it at the time," Cauce, *Academic Leadership in Higher Education,* p. 81

"only because of the Dalmatians," interview with author 3-1-2019

"School was always my refuge," interview with author

They left straight, Ana Mari Cauce email to author, 5-20-2019

They fled to the Chilean embassy, Cauce, "Citizen Story Project," Seattle City Club, 6-25-2016

soon boarded a Pan Am flight, Cauce, "Citizen Story Project," Seattle City Club

His first job in the U.S., Cauce, "Citizen Story Project"

In her third grade class, Cauce, "Citizen Story Project"

"I never felt deprived," interview with author

Only when she applied for college, Cauce, "Citizen Story Project"

"And for a long time I hated peanut butter," interview with author

"We had ice cream," interview with author

"didn't translate in this country," interview with author

Cauce's brother graduated with honors, Sally Bermanzohn, *Through Survivors' Eyes: From the Sixties to the Greensboro Massacre*, Vanderbilt University Press, 2003, p. 161

She graduated from University of Miami, Ana Mari Cauce, Curriculum vitae

One Saturday night, Gabriel Spitzer, "How the President of UW Was Shaped by Her Brother's Murder at the Hands of the Klan," KNKX, 5-26-2018

accept a full scholarship, Sally Bermanzohn, *Through Survivors' Eyes: From the Sixties to the Greensboro Massacre*, Vanderbilt University Press, 2003, p. 161

"not all like the bossy kind of men," Bermanzohn, *Through Survivors' Eyes*, p. 163

"Billed as 'Death to the Klan,'" Greensboro Truth and Reconciliation Commission, "Final Report, Executive Summary," 5-25-2006, via http://www.greensororrc.org/exec_summary.pdf

He was then shot in the neck, Elizabeth Wheaton, *Codename Greenkil: The 1979 Greensboro Killings*, University of Georgia Press, 2009, p. 141

Nazis and Klansmen claimed self-defense, Greensboro Truth and Reconciliation Commission, "Final Report, Executive Summary," 5-25-2006

"showed a stunning lack of curiosity," Greensboro Truth and Reconciliation Commission

Cauce described herself as "flattened," Gabriel Spitzer, "How the President of UW Was Shaped by Her Brother's Murder at the Hands of the Klan," KNKX, 5-26-2018

Her mentor at Yale, Hannelore Sudermann, "Ana Mari Cauce is an unprecedented UW president," *Columns* (UW alumni magazine), 12-1-2015

Gordon said Cauce was one of the best students, Hannelore Sudermann, "Ana Mari Cauce is an unprecedented UW president," *Columns* (UW alumni magazine), 12-1-2015

funded by the likes of the National Institute, Ana Mari Cauce, Curriculum vitae

"It was a humbling and painful experience," Julia Turner (host), "Women In Charge" podcast, *Slate.com*, 10-1-2018, via https://podtail.com/en/podcast/women-in-charge/ana-mari-cauce/

She was reminded of an old joke, Julia Turner (host), "Women In Charge" podcast, *Slate.com*, 10-1-2018

"So I will literally at times," Julia Turner (host), "Women In Charge" podcast, *Slate.com*

But Gordon, her mentor, framed the decision, Ana Mari Cauce interview with author, 3-1-2019

One colleague called her a "chairapist," Katherine Long, "Supporters of Cauce say look no further for UW's next leader," *The Seattle Times*, 9-27-2015

"What he really means is 'No,'" Katherine Long, "New provost sees UW glass half-full," *The Seattle Times*, 1-1-2012

students and regents line up for hugs, Katherine Long, "UW names provost as interim president," *The Seattle Times*, 2-13-2015

or were asked to leave, Steve Miletich, "UW regents pressured president to leave," *The Seattle Times*, 11-2-200

"made wild accusations," (footnote), Staff editorial, "ESSA's tactics hurt own cause," *The Daily*, 7-30-1997

"home means a lot to me," Katherine Long, "UW dean likely to be named next provost," *The Seattle Times*, 11-18-2011

"That, she said proudly, is a penguin bite," Katherine Long, "New provost sees UW glass half-full," *The Seattle Times*, 1-1-2012

She wrote it herself, Ana Mari Cauce email to author, 5-20-2019

disrupted by someone shouting "apes," Katherine Long, "Interim UW chief has project to combat racism," *The Seattle Times*, 4-17-2015

"The fact I was interim," Julia Turner (host), "Women In Charge" podcast, *Slate.com*, 10-1-2018

What's being "whitewashed," Ana Mari Cauce, "We the people: diversity, equity and difference at the UW," (text of speech), 4-16-2015

makings of a Molotov cocktail, Ana Mari Cauce, "We the people…" (text of speech), 4-16-2015

"Mack truck of persistence," Cauce, "We the people…" (text of speech)

"Now both my children are dead," Cauce, "We the people…" (text of speech)

She urged them to call out friends, Cauce, "We the people…" (text of speech)

had written a story, Katherine Long, "Supporters of Cauce say look no further for UW's next leader," *The Seattle Times*, 9-27-2015

She wrote on Facebook about, Katherine Long, "Supporters of Cauce say look no further…"

She wore sweatpants to the supermarket, Kim Chakanesta (host), "Women Shaking Up Universities," *BBC, The Conversation*, 2-1-2019, via https://www.bbc.co.uk/programmes/w3cswp2r

"Whether she's posing," Katherine Long, "Supporters of Cauce say look no further…"

"put her heart out there," Katherine Long email to author, 3-21-2019

"Their warts are known," Katherine Long, "Supporters of Cauce say look no further…"

"The further you rise," Julia Turner (host), "Women In Charge" podcast, *Slate.com*, 10-1-2018

"They're doing you no favors," Julia Turner (host), "Women In Charge," *Slate.com*

"On the one hand," interview with author 3-1-2019

As of November 2018, 43 percent of UW faculty (footnote), "2018-2019 Fact Sheet," *University of Washington Office of Minority Affairs & Diversity*, 10-12-2018

Women accounted for 33 percent of UW (footnote), "Fact Sheet 2018, Academic Personnel," *University of Washington, Office of the Vice Provost for Academic Personnel*, 10-31-2018

"I've overcome obstacles," interview with author 3-1-2019

described "rape culture" on campuses, Katherine Long, "UW, WSU brace for protests over Breitbart editor speech," *The Seattle Times*, 12-18-2016

He would later lose a book contract, Jeremy W. Peters, "Milo Yiannipoulos Resigns From Breitbart News After Pedophilia Comments," *The New York Times*, 2-21-2017

Thousands of people asked Cauce to ban, Katherine Long, "UW, WSU brace for protests over Breitbart editor speech," *The Seattle Times*, 12-18-2016

"babying students," Katherine Long, "UW, WSU brace for protests…"

"really signals," Katherine Long, "UW, WSU brace for protests…"

"A university should," Ana Mari Cauce, "On free expression, universities must light the way," *President's Blog*, 8-2-2016

"nazi scum and white power," Katherine Long, Lynn Thompson and Jessica Lee, "Shooting outside Breitbart editor's speech," *The Seattle Times*, 1-21-2017

124 UW and Seattle officers, Daniel Gilbert, "Milo Yiannopoulos at UW: A speech, a shooting and $75,000 in police overtime," *The Seattle Times*, 3-26-2017

Joshua Dukes, 34, Steve Miletich, "Couple plead not guilty to charges in shooting," *The Seattle Times*, 5-4-2017

Police had initially suspected, Steve Miletich "Police want charge," *The Seattle Times*, 4-13-2017

Glock handgun she had in a holster, Steve Miletich "Police want charge," 4-13-2017

A King County Superior Court judge declared a mistrial, Mike Carter, "Mistrial declared in trial of

couple accused of UW assault after jury can't reach verdict," *The Seattle Times*, 8-14-2019
Prosecutors dismissed the case, Mike Carter, "Prosecutors won't retry couple accused in shooting of antifa protester on UW campus during Milo Yiannopoulous event," *The Seattle Times*, 9-6-2019
called "complicit," Danny Westneat, "UW prez right to stand up for free speech," *The Seattle Times*, 2-1-2017
She held an impromptu, Katherine Long, cell-phone video, 1-30-2017
His talk to a UW audience, Danny Westneat, "UW prez right to stand up for free speech," *The Seattle Times*, 2-1-2017
"Here's a Cuban immigrant whose brother died," Danny Westneat, "UW prez right…"
"Certainly, I, you know, regret deeply," Ana Mari Cauce, interview with author, 3-1-2019
And she knew as president she had to work with, interview with author, 3-1-2019
"But you say 'yes,'" interview with author
About 30 percent of UW students, interview with author
"For me, it really is all about the work," interview with author
"But it really isn't about the work," interview with author

MARY-CLAIRE KING

"For her, science is personal," "Mary-Claire King," The Peter Gruber Foundation, 2004 https://gruber.yale.edu/genetics/mary-claire-king
"I fell in love with the logic," (caption) Evan Eichler (interviewer), "Conversations in Genetics: An Oral History of Our Intellectual Heritage in Genetics (with Mary-Claire King)," University of Washington, published 5-29-2016 https://www.youtube.com/watch?v=TiMv8L5sR-Y
wrote a pioneering textbook, (unbylined obituary) "Dr. Curt Stern, 79; influential teacher of human genetics," *The New York Times*, 10-31-1981
was enchanted, Mary-Claire King interview with author, 4-22-2019 ("I was really enchanted.")
She sat up front for lectures, Evan Eichler (interviewer), "Conversations in Genetics: An Oral History of Our Intellectual Heritage in Genetics (with Mary-Claire King)," 5-29-2016
deadliest year, U.S. National Archives, "Vietnam War U.S. Military Fatal Casualty Statistics," https://www.archives.gov/research/military/vietnam-war/casualty-statistics
"clean up the mess," Jeffrey Kahn, "Ronald Reagan launched political career using Berkeley campus as a target," *University of California Berkeley NewsCenter*, 6-8-2004
cracked down on dissident students, Donna Carol Voss, "Here's What Ronald Reagan Did When College Kids Went Ape at UC, Berkeley, *The Federalist*, 4-24-2017
"Who Owns California?" William M. Blair, "Nader Unit Finds Coast Land Abuse," *The New York Times*, 8-22-1971
That's for me, Evan Eichler (interviewer), "Conversations in Genetics (with Mary-Claire King)"
She came to think of Delores Huerta, King interview with author, 4-22-2019
Si se puede, Maria Godoy, "Delores Huerta: The Civil Rights Icon Who showed Farmworkers 'Si Se Puede,'" *National Public Radio*, 9-17-2017
"bag this graduate career and go do politics," Eichler interview, 5-29-2016
"like a tiger," Eichler interview, 5-29-2016
"somewhere between a family and a kibbutz," Eichler interview, 5-29-2016
would be righteous, interview with author, 4-22-2019
"I couldn't believe anything could be so much fun," (caption) Barack Obama, "Remarks by the

President at Ceremony Honoring the Recipients of the National Medal of Science," *The White House Office of the Press Secretary*, 5-19-2016

every "single American should be grateful," Barack Obama, "Remarks by the President at Ceremony Honoring the Recipients of the National Medal of Science," 5-19-2016

at a marathoner's pace, Paula Bock, "The Plan of All Plans," *The Seattle Times*, 5-31-1998

comparisons to Marie Curie, "Pioneers in Science: Mary-Claire King," World Science Festival (video), 8-12-2015 https://www.youtube.com/watch?v=4LXERmZkhmM

King even uncorked her own 12-minute excerpt, Mary-Claire King, "Who Can You Trust?" *The Moth*, 5-29-2014, accessed via https://themoth.org/stories/who-can-you-trust

"You miss 100 percent of the shots you don't take," (caption) ESPN.com, "55 Shades of Great: Random facts about Wayne Gretzky on his 55th birthday," 1-21-2016

"you bring your whole self into the lab," Eichler interview 5-29-2016

combining an activist's passion, "Mary-Claire King," The Peter Gruber Foundation, 2004

"Mary-Claire's scientific interest," Laurie McHale, "Putting the Puzzle Together," *Columns Magazine*, University of Washington, September 1996

"Like the Great One himself," Marc Tessier-Lavigne, "Award Presentation," *2014 Lasker-Koshland Special Achievement Award in Medical Science*, 12-14-2014

how vastly complicated recipes, or genes, Paula Bock, "The Plan of All Plans," *The Seattle Times*, 5-31-1998

The chairman of Carleton's math department, Laurie McHale, "Putting the Puzzle Together," *Columns Magazine*, University of Washington, September 1996

a retired labor relations manager, Lisa Yount, *An A to Z of Women in Science and Math*, Facts on File, New York, 2008, p. 154

He was often bedridden, Ushma S. Neill, "A conversation with Mary-Claire King," *Journal of Clinical Investigation*, 1-2-2019

How many hits does Cubs star, Ushma S. Neill, "A conversation with Mary-Claire King," *Journal of Clinical Investigation*, 1-2-2019

King grew up in Wilmette, (caption) Laurie McHale, "Putting the Puzzle Together," *Columns Magazine*, University of Washington, September 1996

In high school she had, Neill, "A conversation with Mary-Claire King," *JCI*, 1-2-2019

"totally clumsy," Eichler interview, 5-29-2016

Frustrated, she vented to Wilson, Thomas Bass, *Reinventing the Future: Conversations with the World's Leading Scientists,* Addison-Wesley, Boston, 1993, p. 221

There'd be no scientists, interview with author

compare the chemical properties, James Urton, "Appeal of 'genetic puzzles' leads to National Medal of Science for UW's Mary-Claire King," *University of Washington News*, 5-19-2016

King's friend and adviser, (caption) Robert Sanders, "Berkeley's Allan C. Wilson, the world authority on 'molecular evolution,' is dead at 56," *University of California Berkeley*, 7-22-1991

"I was in total despair," Thomas Bass, *Reinventing the Future: Conversations with the World's Leading Scientists,* Addison-Wesley, Boston, 1993, p. 221

"This is great," Bass, *Reinventing the Future*, p. 221

revealed that humans and chimps are 99 percent identical, Urton, "Appeal of 'genetic puzzles' leads to National Medal of Science for UW's Mary-Claire King," 5-19-2016

"almost genetic look-alikes," Michael Waldholz, *Curing Cancer: Solving One of the Great Medical Mysteries of Our Time*, Simon & Schuster, New York, 1997, p. 98

King and Wilson proposed that the differences, Marc Tessier-Lavigne, "Award Presentation," *2014 Lasker-Koshland Special Achievement Award in Medical Science*, 12-14-2014

than fossil records suggested, Jillian H. Hurst, "Pioneering geneticist Mary-Claire King receives the 2014 Lasker-Koshland Special Achievement Award in Medical Science," *The Journal of Clinical Investigation*, 10-1-2014

It was a bold theory, Ellen Elliott, "Women in Science: Mary-Claire King," *The Jackson Laboratory*, February 2017

swimming against the scientific tide, Michael Waldholz, *Curing Cancer: Solving One of the Great Medical Mysteries of Our Time*, p. 102

Two years passed before King's thesis became, interview with author

"all hell broke loose," Eichler interview

The U.S. Central Intelligence Agency had worked, History.com editors, "Allende dies in coup," *HISTORY*, 8-21-2018

air force jets fired rockets, "Allende dies in coup," *HISTORY*

bodies in the street, Eichler interview

"My mind and my soul," Eichler interview

"just a place to land," Eichler interview

"They were older," Jane Gitschier, "Evidence Is Evidence: An Interview with Mary-Claire King," *PLoS Genetics*, 9-16-2013

gave her a kind of freedom, Jane Gitschier, "Evidence Is Evidence," 9-16-2013

Broca didn't know why his family, Michael Waldholz, *Curing Cancer: Solving One of the Great Medical Mysteries of Our Time*, p. 105

Lane-Claypon reported evidence, Gitschier, "Evidence Is Evidence," 9-16-2013

President Nixon had declared, Neill, "A conversation with Mary-Claire King," 1-2-2019

wasn't a solid hypothesis, Gitschier, "Evidence Is Evidence"

Breast cancer was a common enough disease, Michael Waldholz, *Curing Cancer: Solving One of the Great Medical Mysteries of Our Time,* p. 104

cancer called Wilms' tumor, Michael Waldholz, *Curing Cancer,* p. 95

when she and Debbie were both 13, Bass, *Reinventing the Future* ("My best friend died of cancer when we both were thirteen."), p. 227

"I know for a fact," Michael Waldholz, *Curing Cancer,* p. 95

She heard about a large survey, Eichler interview

Men can get breast cancer, The American Cancer Society medical and editorial content team, "Breast Cancer Risk Factors You Cannot Change," *American Cancer Society*, 9-6-2017

questions added to the survey, Gitschier, "Evidence Is Evidence"

birth of her daughter Emily, Gitschier, "Evidence Is Evidence"

Affirmative Action was being ushered in, Gitschier, "Evidence Is Evidence"

"just got her teeth into it," Gitschier, "Evidence Is Evidence"

"because of all these new regulations," Gitschier, "Evidence Is Evidence"

"She is responsible for my career," Gitschier, "Evidence Is Evidence"

King took a sort of mini-sabbatical, Neill, "A conversation with Mary-Claire King," *JCI*, 1-2-2019

the military overthrew the government, Erin Blakemore, "30,000 People Were 'Disappeared' in Argentina's Dirty War. These Women Never Stopped Looking," *HISTORY*, 3-7-2019

"contrary to Western Christian civilization," Francisco Goldman, "Children of the Dirty War," *The New Yorker*, 3-12-2012

About 30 percent, Francisco Goldman, "Children of the Dirty War," *The New Yorker*, 3-12-2012

Calling them "las locas" or madwomen, (caption) Erin Blakemore, "30,000 People Were 'Disappeared' in Argentina's Dirty War...," *HISTORY*, 3-7-2019

kept alive until they'd given birth, Francisco Goldman, "Children of the Dirty War"

handed to orphanages, Erin Blakemore, *HISTORY*, 3-7-2019

clues from midwives and doctors, Thomas Bass, *Reinventing the Future,* p. 237-238

one even became a maid, Goldman, "Children of the Dirty War," 3-12-2012

collected 145 case records, Kat Arney (host), "Chimps, cancer genes and missing kids," *Genetics Unzipped, The Genetics Society podcast*, 3-14-2009

developed a blood test, Goldman, "Children of the Dirty War," 3-12-2012

In doing so, she was an innovator, Marc Tessier-Lavigne, "Award Presentation," 12-14-2014

He said she was perfectly suited, Neill, "A conversation with Mary-Claire King," *JCI*, 1-2-2019

"It seemed that as an American," Eichler interview

King was a consultant, Kat Arney (host), "Chimps, cancer genes and missing kids," *Genetics Unzipped, The Genetics Society podcast,* 3-14-2009

They needed samples from all four, Arney, "Chimps, cancer genes and missing kids," *Genetics Unzipped*

King and colleagues built a more powerful, Tessier-Lavigne, "Award Presentation," 12-14-2014

creating a kind of genetic family crest, Paula Bock, "The Plan of All Plans," *The Seattle Times,* 5-31-1998

With a sample from granny, Arney, "Chimps, cancer genes and missing kids"

first application of mitochondrial DNA, Arney, "Chimps, cancer genes and missing kids"

Logares was 23 months old, Vincent J. Schodolski, "Paula: an Innocent Victim of Argentina's 'Dirty War,' " *Chicago Tribune,* 9-29-1985

launch the United Nations forensic team, James Urton, "Appeal of 'genetic puzzles' leads to National Medal of Science for UW's Mary-Claire King," *University of Washington News,* 5-19-2016

At last count, 130 of the estimated, Abuelas de Plaza de Mayo, "Cases Resolved," accessed via https://www.abuelas.org.ar/caso/buscar?tipo=3, 9-10-2019

then buried and chaotically reburied, Francine du Plessix Gray, "Nicholas and Alexandra: the Sequels," *The New York Times,* 10-29-1995

but they claimed Czarina Alexandra, Toby Saul, "Death of a dynasty: How the Romanovs met their end," *National Geographic,* 7-20-2018

A pair of amateur sleuths, Toby Saul, "Death of a dynasty: How the Romanovs met their end"

"There's not going to be anything different," interview with author

genetics was proving to be the greatest puzzle, Thomas Bass, *Reinventing the Future,* p. 231

She had to collect a good number, Michael Waldholz, *Curing Cancer,* p. 106

inheriting the same stretch of DNA, Waldholz, *Curing Cancer,* p. 106

Other women with a family history contacted her, Waldholz, *Curing Cancer, p. 216*

that had aired on 127 network affiliates, Bill Dietrich, "Another Leading Researcher Joins UW," *The Seattle Times,* 2-23-1995

Can we, using the large number of families, Jane Gitschier, "Evidence Is Evidence: An Interview with Mary-Claire King," *PLoS Genetics,* 9-16-2013

King's analysis, published in 1988, Evelyn Strauss, "2014 Lasker-Koshland Special Achievement Award in Medical Science," The Lasker Foundation, 12-14-2014

with the help of young biochemist Jeff Hall, Waldholz, *Curing Cancer,* p. 215

now able to find "markers," Michael Waldholz, "Breast Cancer: A Common Inheritance?" *Wall Street Journal,* 1-5-1993

Still the quarry remained elusive, Waldholz, *Curing Cancer,* p. 88

In each of the families the cancer struck, Waldholz, *Curing Cancer,* p. 60

Other families did not fit the pattern, Newsweek Staff, "The Hunt for a Breast Cancer Gene," *Newsweek,* 12-5-1993

rolled them out across lab benches, Gitschier, "Evidence Is Evidence"

Let's look at this by age, Gitschier, "Evidence Is Evidence"

Chromosome 17 proved a strong predictor, Newsweek Staff, "The Hunt for a Breast Cancer Gene," *Newsweek,* 12-5-1993

"It was really clear that statistically," Eichler interview

she wasn't on the printed agenda, Waldholz, "Breast Cancer: A Common Inheritance?" *Wall Street Journal*

deeply skeptical of her work, Michael Waldholz, *Curing Cancer.* p. 43-44

While friends thought she remained, Waldhoz, *Curing Cancer,* p. 88

"terrier with a bone," Waldholz, *Curing Cancer,* p. 93-94

Earlier findings she had published, Waldholz, *Curing Cancer,* p. 46

she thought it was too risky, Waldholz, *Curing Cancer,* p. 218

"Show them," Waldholz, *Curing Cancer,* p. 44

Diplaying charts, graphs, Waldholz, *Curing Cancer,* p. 45

with a scary regularity, Waldholz, *Curing Cancer,* p. 45

some inborn biological error, Waldholz, *Curing Cancer,* p. 45

onto a premature path to cancer, Waldholz, *Curing Cancer,* p. 45

consistently altered in DNA of women, Waldholz, *Curing Cancer,* p. 46

"many times stronger than any other association," Waldholz, *Curing Cancer,* p. 46

Was it possible that her families, Neill, "A conversation with Mary Claire King," *JCI,* 1-2-2019

Henry Lynch, a doctor in Nebraska, Waldholz, *Curing Cancer,* p. 53

dismissed his evidence as anecdotal, Gina Kolata, "Dr. Henry Lynch, 91, Dies; Found Hereditary Link in Cancer," *The New York Times,* 6-13-2019

The next day he called his French colleagues, Waldholz, *Curing Cancer,* p. 54

he was coy with King, Waldholz, *Curing Cancer,* p. 55

"Those are mine," Eichler interview

"when I believed the result was real," Gitschier, "Evidence Is Evidence"

celebrated with both Lenoir and King over tea, Waldholz, *Curing Cancer,* p. 55

"Lenoir's talk was very convincing," Waldholz, *Curing Cancer,* p. 56

Both genes usually function like custodians, Laurie Garrett, "Prevention Is the Best Medicine," *Foreign Policy,* Winter 2019

about 5 percent of all breast cancers, The ACS medical and editorial content team, "Breast Cancer Risk Factors You Cannot Change," *American Cancer Society,* 9-6-2017

found the approximate neighborhood, Natalie Angier, "Fierce Competition Marked Fervid Race for Cancer Gene," *The New York Times,* 9-20-1994

"task akin to searching for a car key," Paula Bock, "The Plan of All Plans, *The Seattle Times,* 5-31-1998

Francis Collins, another superstar geneticist, (footnote), Waldholz, *Curing Cancer,* p. 60-61

how to craft diagnostic tests to look for, Natalie Angier, "Fierce Competition Marked Fervid Race For Cancer Gene," *The New York Times,* 9-20-1994

led a team of 44 colleagues, Natalie Angier, "Fierce Competition Marked Fervid Race for Cancer Gene," *The New York Times,* 9-20-1994

"was her reason for getting up," Angier, "Fierce Competition Marked Fervid Race for Cancer Gene"

"they had vastly more sophisticated equipment," Neill, "A conversation with Mary-Claire King," *JCI,* 1-2-2019

whether some mutations were associated more, Angier, "Fierce Competition Marked Fervid Race for Cancer Gene"

King wanted to get closer to surgeons, Eichler interview

King moved her lab north, Laurie McHale, "Putting the Puzzle Together," *Columns Magazine,* University of Washington, September 1996

brought a lifetime grant, Laurie McHale, "Putting the Puzzle Together"

"Athens of genetics," Paula Bock, "The Plan of All Plans," *The Seattle Times,* 5-31-1998

"I could've gone to many places," interview with author

captured the bustle, Paula Bock, "The Plan of All Plans," *The Seattle Times*

"It is replaced by the scientist's musical laughter," Bock, "The Plan of All Plans"

Calling King's movie character "bordering on icy," (caption) Stephen Holden, "On the Trail of a Gene That Kills," *The New York Times*, 5-1-2014

"we can do this together for the sake of science," Warren King, "Scientists work in harmony in din of Mideast," *The Seattle Times*, 4-24-2002

"It will be my words with perfect hair," (no byline), "A Seattle Geneticist Gets the Hollywood Treatment," *Seattle Magazine*, January 2013

***The Washington Post's* review,** Jen Chaney, " 'Decoding Annie Parker,' movie review," *The Washington Post*, 5-1-2014

get her mannerisms down pat, Emily Wax-Thibodeaux, "As Helen Hunt plays her in a move, the real Mary-Claire King still studies breast cancer," *The Washington Post*, 10-28-2013

afflicting about one in 500 American women, Dana-Farber Cancer Institute, "How Common Are BRCA Mutations?" March 2018, https://blog.dana-farber.org/insight/2018/03/brca-mutations-common/

whose mother, aunt and grandmother died, Rob Stein, "Angelina Jolie Pitt's Surgeries Will Reduce Cancer Risk, Doctors Say, *National Public Radio* (All Things Considered), 3-24-2015

1-in-12 women will have, Komen Perspectives, "An Update on Genetic Testing for Breast Cancer," *Susan G. Komen*, May 2016

"dropped from 87 percent to under 5 percent," (caption) Angelina Jolie, "My Medical Choice," *The New York Times*, 5-14-2013

"really good, very clear," Moira Macdonald, "New film puts UW breast-cancer researcher in spotlight," *The Seattle Times*, 6-2-2013

the "Angelina effect," Sharon Begley, "Were women foolish to follow Angelina Jolie into BRCA cancer gene testing?, *STAT*, 1-5-2017

cost at least $3,000, Sharon Begley, "Were women foolish to follow Angelina Jolie into BRCA cancer gene testing?, *STAT*, 1-5-2017

With her colleague Tomas Walsh, Ciara Curtin, "U. Washington's Targeted Gene Panel Pinpoints Breast Cancer Mutations in Quarter of Patients with Negative BRACAnalysis Test Results," *GenomeWeb*, 10-25-2013

the justices said genes, as products of nature, Justice Clarence Thomas (opinion of the court), "Association for Molecular Pathology vs. Myriad Genetics," *U.S. Supreme Court*, 6-13-2013

"quite possibly" may have won the race, interview with author

"as high as a flag," Neill, "A conversation with Mary-Claire King," *JCI*, 1-2-2019

potential therapies, Susan G. Komen, "Susan G. Komen Welcomes Five Leaders to New Research Advisory Roles," 4-14-2019, via https://ww5.komen.org/News/Komen-Welcomes-Five-Leaders.html

"To actually fix BRCA1," Dr. George W. Sledge, Jr., email to author, 7-15-2109

The UW is a "fabulous place," interview with author

after a "depressing" story, interview with author

"One of the great things," interview with author

Women account for a majority of her lab's, interview with author

"I had my own lab for 15 years," interview with author

"young men are very modern about this," interview with author

their child-bearing years coincide, Alice Park, "Lessons From the Woman Who Discovered the BRCA Cancer Gene," *TIME*, 6-2-2014

"Science is also a very demanding child," Alice Park, "Lessons From the Woman Who Discovered the BRCA Cancer Gene," *TIME*, 6-2-2014

"always going to be an impediment," interview with author

King once told *The New York Times*, Natalie Angier, "SCIENTIST AT WORK: Mary-Claire King," *The New York Times*, 4-27-1993

"They are to keep people happy," Alice Park, "Lessons From the Woman Who Discovered the BRCA Cancer Gene"

Asked in 2019 what she'd do, (footnote) Ushma S. Neill, "A conversation with Mary-Claire King," *Journal of Clinical Investigation*, 1-2-2019

Her UW lab continues to research breast and ovarian cancer, interview with author

She's collaborating on breast cancer, interview with author

she's gone to Israel almost every year since 1995, Judy Siegel-Iztkovich, "The Queen of DNA," *The Jerusalem Post*, 9-13-2014

she's part of a team, Breast Cancer Research Foundation, "Mary-Claire King, PhD, Full Research Summary," undated, accessed 6-25-2019 https://www.bcrf.org/researchers/mary-claire-king

created training programs for Palestinian nurses, Breast Cancer Research Foundation, "Mary-Claire King, PhD, Full Research Summary"

that Ashkenazi Jewish women face, Breast Cancer Research Foundation, "Mary-Claire King..."

In 2018, she received a $1 million, Dan David Prize, "Laureates 2018, Prof. Mary-Claire King," dandavid.org, 2-7-2018

"a salon for unrequited lefties," Mary-Claire King, "Leaders in Health Care Awards 2015," *Seattle Business Magazine*, 4-22-2015 via https://www.youtube.com/watch?v=La0QaDZJ-lY (2:25)

"Needless to say," she smiles, interview with author

At 80 she expects to still be in her lab, Eichler interview

Fawn Sharp

"expensive hoax," Trump tweet, 2013, quoted in "Donald Trump doesn't think much of climate change," Chris Cillizza, CNN Politics, https://www.cnn.com/2017/08/08/politics/trump-global-warming/index.html

"The glaciers that feed the rivers," "Quinault Indian Nation Plans for Village Relocation," U.S. Climate Resilience Toolkit, https://toolkit.climate.gov/case-studies/quinault-indian-nation-plans-village-relocation

"Native Americans continue to rank near bottom," "Broken Promises," U.S. Commission on Civil Rights, December 2018, https://www.usccr.gov/pubs/2018/12-20-Broken-Promises.pdf

"A Quiet Crisis," U.S. Commission on Civil Rights Report, July 2003, https://www.usccr.gov/pubs/na0703/na0204.pdf;

"a decidedly low degree of culture," *Traditions of the Quinault Indians*, p. 79, pp. 110-111

"If there are to be salmon here," *Traditions of the Quinault Indians*

"The productivity of their prey," quoted in "Blueback closure latest in Quinault climate change impacts," Angelo Bruscas, *The North Coast News*, 2-13-2019

"compared to the impact of fossil fuels," Fawn Sharp statement on blueback closure, 2-8-2019

"nearly gone as well," quoted in "Blueback closure latest in Quinault climate change impacts"

"Battle of Chow Chow Bridge," *Land of the Quinault*, pp. 204-206; *Slade Gorton*, pp. 120-121

"children's futures are at stake," DeLaCruz quoted in *The Seattle Times*, 9-26-1971

"For more than 50 years," *Portrait of Our Land*, p. 11

"our land has paid a terrible price," *Portrait of Our Land*, p. 29.

"almost beyond imagination," *Portrait of Our Land*, p. 37

Janet McCloud background, "Janet McCloud, 1934-2003: Indian activist put family first," *Seattle Post-Intelligencer,* 11-26-2003

"To terminate this relationship," Nixon on termination, *Indian Country Today*, Alysa Landry, 9-13-2016

Hannah Bowechop's work with linguist, "17 years with the Quinaults," Robert S. Johnson, *The Seattle Times*, 3-4-1973

Cosette Terry-itewaste's Ph.D. dissertation, https://repository.arizona.edu/bltstream/handle/10150/621357/azu_etd_14817_sip1_m.pdf?sequence=1&isAllowed=y

"The physical and spiritual discipline," quoted in "Emmett Oliver dies at 102," *Peninsula Daily News*, 3-9-2016

"When I was in eighth grade," quoted in "Guy McMinds Retires," *Northwest Treaty Tribes* news release, 10-12-2010

"Guy always understood," quoted in "Guy McMinds Retires"

Quinaults once whalers, *Indians of the Pacific Northwest,* pp. 178-179

"because of a high tide," *Indians of the Pacific Northwest*, p. 126

evidence of Klallam village tsunamis, "The oral history wasn't a myth," Tom Banse, KLCC, NPR, 5-8-2019, https://www.klcc.org/post/oral-history-wasnt-myth-tsunamis-hit-tribal-village-five-times-new-study-shows

"standing in knee-deep salt water," *Cascadia's Fault*, p. 125

"forest meadow into a salt marsh," *Cascadia's Fault*, p. 126

"had the same signature," quoted in *Cascadia's Fault*, p. 132

Hoquiam river "ate" the trees, "Hoquiam had a teen-age father," *The Daily World,* Aberdeen, Wash., 5-25-1990, C-1

"We breathe the same air," quoted in "Fawn Sharp wants Native voices to shake up politics," Manola Secaira, Crosscut, 11-5-2018, https://crosscut.com/2018/11/fawn-sharp-wants-native-voices-shake-politics

"We will hold these large corporations accountable," quoted in "Fawn Sharp has a message for big oil," Mark Trahant, *Indian Country Today*, 1-29-2019, https://newsmaven.io/indiancountrytoday/news/fawn-sharp-has-a-message-for-big-oil-time-s-up-HFQSuGTWQUW8kvtNdxvrfQ/

INDEX

THANK YOU

Ales Knettig
Alex McGregor
Amanda DeBard
Amber Raney
Amy Arnis
Amy Griffin
Amy Lin
Ana Mari Cauce
Angie Hogenson
Ann Murphy
Barbara Madsen
Barbara Reskin
Barbara Roberts
Becky Bogard
Ben Helle
Bill Murray
Bill Reader
Brandon Carlisle
C Louise Miller
Callie Birklid
Carla Santorno
Carolyn Dimmick
Charlie and Nancy
Wiggins
Chris and Michael
Gregoire
Chris Reykdal
Claudia Rowe
Colleen Overton
Cynthia Aden
Daughters of the
American Revolution
David Elliott
David Hansen
David Miller

Debbie Preston
Debbie Stewart
Debra Stephens
Douglas MacDonald
Elisa Law
Eric Johnson
Erin Aquino
Fawn Sharp
Frank Blethen
Frank MacDonald
Gail Girtz
Gary Moore
George Masten
George Sledge, Jr.
Gerry Alexander
Gonzaga University
Hans Zeiger
Heather Hirotaka
Heidi Hunt
Helen Knowles
Helen Remick
HistoryLink
Jennifer Belcher
Jennifer Kilmer
Jerika Ferguson
Jerri Honeyford
Jerry Price
Jim Bricker
Joanne Beswick
Joell Solan
John Brewer
John Conrad
John Hopkins
University School of
Medicine

Josh Garcia
Joshua Parker
Karen Blair
Karen Conway
Karen Fraser
Karen Johnson
Karin and Paul
Larson
Katherine Long
Kathryn Leonard
Kim Wyman
KING5
Kiran Boyal
Lanabeth Horgen
Laura Mott
League of Women
Voters of WA
Education Fund
LeAnn Neuleib
Lem Howell
Linea Laird
Lisa A. Oberg
Lori Drummond
Lori Henry
Lori Larson
Lynda Belt
Mari Clack
Marianne Nichols
Marieka Klawitter
Marjorie Kehoe
Mark Brown
Mark Neary
Mary Fairhurst
Mary Joan Hahn
Mary Pontarolo

We are grateful to the many individuals and organizations that lent expertise, artifacts, time and financial support to create this exhibit.

Mary-Claire King
Melissa Arnot Reid
Meredith Austin
Michael McCann
Michelle Akers
Mike Lindblom
Moonbeam Kupka
Museum of History
and Industry
Nita Rinehart
Northwest Indian
Fisheries Commission
Office of
Superintendent of
Public Instruction
Office of the
Secretary of State
Olympia Federal
Savings
Otter Tail County
Historical Society
Pat and Susan Dunn
Patricia Burgess
Patricia Mack
Patrick McDonald
Patsy O'Connell
Philip Kerrigan
Quinault Indian
Nation
RaeAnna Victor
Ralph Munro
Randy Hodgins
Regina Tollfeldt
Rodney Anderson
Rose Enos-Weedmark

Rotary Club of
Olympia
Ryan Parrish
Sally Paxton
Sam Hunt
Sam Reed
Sandi Doughton
Sandra Gray
Sandy Dunham
Sara Ludovissy
Sean Lanksbury
Shanna Stevenson
Sheri Nelson
Shirley Stirling
Slade Gorton
Stephanie Coontz
Steve Excell
Stevie Benge
Stuart Halsan
Sue Lean
Susan G. Komen
Foundation
Susan Muir
Suzanne Cofer
Suzy Lantz
T.J. Kelly
The Evergreen State
College Foundation
The George
Washington
University
The Seattle Times
Tom Quigg
Tom Robbins
Trish Millines Dziko

Trova Heffernan
University of
Washington
Vakil Smallen
Vicky Anderson
Victor Balta
Votes for Women
Centennial Grant
Program
Washington
Association of
County Auditors
Washington State
Association of
Counties
Washington State
Attorney General's
Office
Washington State
Heritage Center
Trust
Washington State
Historical Society
Washington State
Women's Commission
Wayne Ehlers
Wellesley College
Wenatchee Valley
Museum
William Jacobs
Women's University
Club Foundation

THANK YOU TO

WASHINGTON STATE
WOMEN'S COMMISSION

Daughters of the American Revolution

OUR SPONSORS:

UNIVERSITY *of*
WASHINGTON

GONZAGA
UNIVERSITY

LEAGUE OF WOMEN VOTERS®
OF WASHINGTON EDUCATION FUND

Empowering Voters. Defending Democracy.

WUC

FOUNDATION

Washington State
Association of Counties
The Voice of Washington Counties
www.wsac.org

*Olympia
Federal
Savings*

Legacy Washington is dedicated to preserving the history of Washington and its continuing story.
www.sos.wa.gov/legacy

Secretary of State
Kim Wyman